The Daughter's Dilemma

The
Daughter's Dilemma

Family Process and the
Nineteenth-Century
Domestic Novel

Paula Marantz Cohen

Ann Arbor

The University of Michigan Press

A CIP catalogue record for this book is available from the British Library.

Library of Congress Cataloging-in-Publication Data

Cohen, Paula Marantz, 1953–
     The daughter's dilemma : family process and the nineteenth-century
domestic novel / Paula Marantz Cohen.
       p.   cm.
     Includes bibliographical references and index.
     ISBN 0-472-10234-6 (alk. paper)
     1. English fiction—19th century—History and criticism.
     2. Domestic fiction, English—History and criticism. 3. Feminism
and literature—Great Britain—History—20th century. 4. Daughters
in literature. 5. Family in literature   I. Title.
     PR868.D65C64   1991
     823'.808'03520441—dc20   91-14574
                                                                                      CIP

British Library Cataloguing in Publication Data
Cohen, Paula Marantz
     The daughter's dilemma : family process and the
     nineteenth-century novel.
     1. English fiction
     I. Title.
     823.809355

     ISBN 0-472-10234-6

Distributed in the United Kingdom and Europe by
Manchester University Press, Oxford Road,
Manchester M13 9PL, UK

To Alan

Acknowledgments

Although there are too many influences on this book to name, there are three people whom I must acknowledge for their valuable comments on earlier versions of the manuscript: Annette Benert, who understands Henry James far better than I do; D. B. Jones, whose Confucian perspective has influenced my systems thinking; and Alan S. Penziner, who has kept me from falling too completely into the abyss of academic writing.

I also want to thank my parents, Ruth Marantz Cohen and Murray S. Cohen, and my sister, Rosetta Marantz Cohen, for their inimitable performance of that family "dance" of which this book is, in some sense, an elaboration. Finally, there are Sam and Kate, in whose dance I am implicated but who are fated to devise new steps.

An earlier version of chapter 3 appeared in *ELH* 54 (Fall 1987): 669–93; a part of chapter 5 in *CEA Critic* 46 (Fall 1985): 54–60; and parts of chapter 6 in *American Literary Realism, 1870–1910* 18 (Spring and Autumn 1985): 1–13.

This book was written with the support of a Drexel University Research Scholar Award.

Contents

Introduction

A Contemporary Clarissa

The case involves a young girl from a well-to-do family. The youngest of three children, she had always been praised by her parents for her docile temperament and for her eagerness to please. Well into her teens she had shown herself to be conscientious, self-effacing, and ladylike—the "perfect" daughter.

Around her sixteenth year, however, her world began to change. Her siblings began to tease her, her mother to pry and scold; her father became more remote. She had always been small and rather delicate in her appearance, but now she felt herself growing large and ungainly. Her clothes no longer fit. Her body seemed alien to her.

From the outset, she was confused by the attention of a boy at school. He was always sidling up to her in the hall and calling to her outside where he stood smoking with his group. When he began to telephone her at home, her mother expressed disapproval: he had the wrong background and a bad attitude, was not the kind of boy they wanted for her. Her father's client had a son they liked. Why wouldn't she go out with him, if only as a courtesy to them? Why had she become so stubborn, so unwilling to please?

The boy at school continued to hang around. She told him to leave her alone, but she didn't know how to be assertive. Besides, he made her feel more like the lovable little girl that she had ceased to be at home. She began to depend upon his flattery and mild harassment, and to encourage him in small ways. Finally, she began to go out with him on the sly. When her parents found out there were terrible scenes, but she stubbornly refused to listen. Her relationship with the boy, whom she was rather afraid of, became more intense. After several months of being coaxed and bullied, she slept with him. Then her mother found out; or she became disgusted with herself; or he dropped her. It's not clear what happened exactly, but the relationship ended. That's when she started to become concerned with losing weight. Getting control over her body—becoming thin, small, childlike again—became her overwhelming preoccupation. Her family didn't notice the change—it seemed so gradual, her mother said—until she had dropped to eighty pounds. Six months after she began her diet, she weighed sixty-five pounds.

Her parents have finally admitted her to the university hospital where she is now fed intravenously and is on a respirator. Too weak to undergo the intensive psychotherapy that is recommended, she is very sick, perhaps close to death. Her family is grief-stricken and keeps a constant vigil by her hospital bed.

Anorexia nervosa is an illness that first gained public attention some twenty years ago. It has since been estimated that 5 to 10 percent of female adolescents suffer from it, with some estimates for this group rising as high as 20 percent. At the onset of puberty, these girls become fixated on their body image and on the need to lose weight. They diet obsessively and, without medical intervention, can starve to death, convinced to the end that they are obese. Initially, the illness was interpreted psychoanalytically to reflect a fear on the part of the female adolescent of her developing sexuality. In recent years, however, therapists have begun to study the anorectic girl in the context of her family and to understand her as the visibly symptomatic member of a pathological system to which each family member contributes. It should be noted that most anorectic girls come from economically comfortable, intact nuclear families and, before the onset of the illness, have had the reputation for being model daughters.[1]

A seemingly exemplary young girl from a seemingly good family mercilessly starves herself to death. It is a compelling plot. And indeed, anorexia nervosa is an illness with a "plot" in two senses of the word. It is plotted in that it follows a clinically described course and tends to involve predictable variables in the sex, age, and family situation of those who suffer from it; and it has a plot behind it: a history bound up with the history of the family and with the history of domestic plot itself.

It is no coincidence that in writing the fictional case history above I have sought both to create a composite of contemporary clinical accounts of anorexia nervosa and to modernize the plot of the eighteenth-century epistolary novel and the first great domestic novel, Samuel Richardson's *Clarissa*. Clarissa, "an exemplar for her sex" as Richardson calls her, anticipates the anorectic girl described in so many medical case histories of the past twenty years. But there are limits to this comparison that I must point out at once. Although Richardson's Clarissa dies from apparent self-starvation in the context of a confused family, she is still the heroine of her story. Her behavior is shown to have meaning and value not only in respect to the other characters in the novel but also in respect to the novelistic tradition and the family ideal that will follow from her. In other words, Clarissa Harlowe describes a model of behavior that is functional for the novel and for the family over the course of the nineteenth century.[2] The contemporary Clarissa of my case history provides no such model but exemplifies rather the exhaustion of such a model. She has been assigned not to fictional immortality but to the dust-heap of clinical diagnosis. She has been reduced to the skin and bones of a medical case history.

The distance between Richardson's heroine and the contemporary anorectic girl is the space this book intends to illuminate. Such a statement of purpose suggests that I am writing a social history of the daughter's role in the family and, in some sense, I am. Yet it would be misleading to declare this as my book's primary intention. The book has as its starting point the study of novels in the nineteenth-century domestic tradition and looks to a variety of methodological tools to help trace patterns among characters in the novels and among the novels themselves. This is the activity of literary criticism. That said, I can now return to my earlier claim that the literature also serves as a tool of social criticism. For literary criticism and social criticism exist in a kind of symbiosis in this study: one feeds the other. The basis for this symbiosis lies in the ideological relationship that I see existing between the form of the family and the form of the novel.[3]

The relationship between the family and the novel can be clarified by a brief overview of their respective histories (to be discussed in more detail in chap. 1).[4] The family in Western society began conspicuously to change its structure from a porous, extended network of relations to a more restricted, "nuclear" unit of relations in the seventeenth and eighteenth centuries (although the origin of this change may well be traced to an earlier period). It achieved temporary stability as a relatively closed, affective system in the nineteenth century. The novel evolved in parallel fashion. It moved away from its seventeenth- and eighteenth-century origins in the loosely stitched accounts of picaresque adventure to become the intricate, psychologically resonant narrative form that I refer to as the domestic novel, which we associate with the genre's maturity in the nineteenth century. By the same token, both the family and the novel have, since the end of the nineteenth century, revealed difficulty in supporting their legacy of closure. Just as modern literature has progressively defined itself through either a dramatic disregard for nineteenth-century literary conventions or a parodic attachment to them, so the family, from the turn of the century to the present, has exhibited escalating tendencies in these two directions. Reactions against nuclearity are reflected in rising statistics on divorce and alternative life-style arrangements, while attempts to bolster nuclearity are evident in the high incidence of illnesses like anorexia nervosa that seem designed to maintain family closure at all costs.[5]

In both the nuclear family and the domestic novel we are dealing, then, with closed systems that achieved relative stability in the nineteenth century and are now experiencing visible strain and disruption. Of course, these systems, even during their heyday, were never more than relatively closed. Families must always interact to some degree with an external society; novels depend upon readers and are subject to individual values, tastes, and interpretive approaches. Yet the ideology of closure in the nineteenth century was a driving force in the development and elaboration of the form in which families and novels defined themselves. Families were seen as retreats from a hostile external world and, hence, the definition of sex roles, the requirements of etiquette, the rearing of children, and so forth, evolved to enforce that separation. Novels were expected to tie up loose ends, both structural and thematic, and so most novels tended to end with a well-deserved marriage or with a death that either glorified or appropriately degraded its subject. What this ideological dominance of closure in both nineteenth-century domestic novels and nuclear families suggests is that the novels not only have families as their subject-matter, but also operate like the families they represent: both are systems with boundaries seeking to maintain closure. It would follow that if we can study the interactive patterns that govern the novels, we may apply them to the families they represent and, through extrapolation, learn more about how our own families operate.

For this purpose, I am relying upon *family systems theory* as a principal methodology.[6] This is not intended to supplant other methodologies that have recently helped to illuminate cultural texts, on which I also draw extensively. Family systems theory, as I choose to use it, serves rather to "punctuate" (a favorite family systems term) many of the insights of deconstruction, feminist theory, and psychoanalysis, in new ways, and only occasionally to attempt to refute them. My rationale for this approach is that the family systems perspective is particularly suited, for reasons that should become clear, to a study of nineteenth-century domestic novels.

Although I shall explain the basic tenets of family systems theory more fully in chapter 1, it is important to stress here that the field is founded on a paradox. It recognizes that closed systems are ultimately pathogenic, and yet it tries to heal the pathologies of closed systems. This paradox springs from a fundamental premise of family systems thinking, namely that sick families are merely well families writ large—families trying too hard and exaggerating those very saving techniques that the nuclear family needs to define itself. Theorist-practitioners in the field operate according to this premise for the reason that as a culture we are still linked to a nineteenth-century ideology of closure even as that ideology is being revised.

Applying family systems theory to novels thus helps to bring our own ideological positioning into relief. It allows us to discern the interactive patterns that inform the novels—and families—of the last century while also making it possible to trace the transformation of these patterns into the present and to postulate the shape of the future.

Let me add, finally, that what can be learned from novels about how families operate can also provide us with a better understanding of individual identity as a product of family experience. What are the boundaries and limits of the self? How do our feelings and desires (conscious and unconscious) come about? What is it that defines us as masculine or feminine? How is the self redefined as the family experience changes? The answers to these questions derive from the ideology of closure that informed nineteenth-century family interaction and novel structure, even when the answers seek to oppose that ideology. In the end, my reading of novels from a systems perspective is a quest to understand my own relationship to experience and, more specifically, to understand why I have chosen to write, from this particular vantage point, this particular book.

* * *

Novels themselves have families and genealogies. They are parts of culturally established canons and literary traditions. For this reason, the novels that are included in a study that seeks to illuminate an ideological transformation should be representative of the canons and the tradition to which they have been assigned. Samuel Richardson and Henry James have been chosen as pivotal figures, bookends for the domestic novel tradition: *Clarissa,* I argue, initiates the tradition; *The Awkward Age,* I take (at least formalistically) to be its swan song. The novels of Jane Austen, Emily Brontë, and George Eliot that I will discuss are spaced so as to fill in the body of the tradition. (That the "body" of this study consists of women while the "bookends" are men is a point I reserve for discussion in the conclusion.)

This is to claim that the novels I have chosen are, in some sense, highly conventional, that they contain representative examples of structures, themes, and characterizations associated with the tradition of the domestic novel. Yet to rest here would be to see these novels as artifacts: simple reflectors of their ideological moment. Whether or not we can say there is such a thing as a simple reflector of ideology, this is certainly not the case for the novels I have chosen. While each occupies a respected place in its author's canon and in a larger, culturally established literary tradition, each also stands in some way at odds with the other novels in its "family." Each, in fact, has been labeled a "problem novel" at some point in its critical history. *Clarissa's* morbid conclusion so distressed Richardson's readers that they begged him to change it and provide the kind of happy ending that makes his two other novels so soothing to complacent readers. *Mansfield Park* is still dismissed by many readers for being dull and didactic and for having in sickly Fanny Price a protagonist totally unlike Austen's other heroines. *Wuthering Heights,* perhaps most of all, has been seen as aberrant, not in the author's canon (she had none), but in the literary tradition: a domestic novel that refuses to domesticate its violence, a realistic novel that often eschews realism and refuses to sentimentalize its main characters. *The Mill on the Floss,* generally seen as Eliot's most autobiographical work, has an ending that wrenches the novel in a sensational, unrealistic direction and that has long been cited as an expression of the author's immaturity. Finally, James's *The Awkward Age* has posed a problem to readers by denying us a Jamesian "central intelligence." The predominance of dialogue over explanatory narration in this novel makes it impossible for us to anchor ourselves in a sensibility; as a result, the conclusion becomes even more ambiguous than is usual in James.

The best analogy I can find for why these novels are especially useful in this study is taken, appropriately, from family systems theory. In dealing with a troubled family, the therapist will often choose to use "transforms"—exaggerated versions of the interactive patterns present in the family—in order to expose the destructive nature of these interactions *to* the family.[7] Likewise, the novels I have chosen to discuss help us to see interactive patterns more clearly. The problematic relation they bear to some group of literary conventions serves as the justification for my choices because the problems these novels pose are exaggerations of the very tendencies of the canons and the tradition from which they may appear to deviate. As such, they exist as both anticipatory symptoms of a system that will ultimately prove unworkable, and adaptive agents of a new way of being. The capacity of certain works of literature to push the boundaries of convention to the edge of deviance and lay bare their culture's ideological limitations and potentialities is perhaps the basis for a functional theory of literary value.

I must add a final comment on certain assumptions that inform this book. I have already suggested that both despite and because of their deviant tendencies I find the novels in this study ideologically representative of their age. The same can be said for their authors. Uniquely creative and personally idiosyncratic though they were, these novelists were also produced by their times. Even Henry James, who grasps a revised ideological configuration amazingly early, records only what the circumstances of his life in culture allow him to see. This is in no way a criticism of my subjects, for I understand ideology not in some normative way but as the prevailing idea of our lives that the structures of our lives seek continually to support and elaborate, ultimately bringing about a transformation of the ideology in the process. Thus, I oppose Marxist critic Terry Eagleton's approach, for example, which understands reality and ideology as distinct, and privileges critics as being able to gain access to the "real" through its "absences" in fictional texts.[8] All critiques of ideology come from an ideological position—Eagleton's and my own included. I likewise take issue with many feminist critics who read female authors as covertly struggling against a prevailing ideology that seeks to crush them. Part of the argument of this book is that by passing through the ideology of the nuclear family women acquired the kind of subjectivity that is now finding expression in feminist politics and criticism. I tend to agree with the literary critic who has noted that "the fault of much of our criticism of nineteenth-century literature is to mistake art for rebellion."[9] In my terms, art is ideology given such unique and powerful expression as to make visible its transformative potential.

If the perspective of this book appears deterministic, it is so in the sense that I am skeptical of attempts to get out of ideology and into "reality." It is not deterministic, however, if we expand the frame of reference beyond the individual will. A systems analysis, when it involves itself with human beings (and novels, for all that they are not alive, derive from human minds and depend for their effectiveness on human feelings), reveals that the future forms of a given system are ultimately unpredictable and open to creative input, and that feedback from even seemingly stereotypical interactions can have new and unforeseen effects.

CHAPTER 1

The Family and the Novel: The Evolution of Closed Form

The nuclear family—the unit of parents and children living under one roof, bound together by strong emotional ties and relatively detached from the surrounding community and from other blood relations—apparently had its birth in Western Europe some time between the fifteenth and eighteenth centuries. The traditional view, elaborated by mid-twentieth-century sociologists such as Talcott Parsons, associated the development of the nuclear family with the emergence of an industrial economy and the rise of a middle class in the seventeenth century.[1] This view has been variously challenged by recent historians. Philippe Ariès is among the first and most notable to argue for a more gradual change in familial relations dating from the fifteenth century—although he continues to associate the new family form with a nascent middle class.[2] Randolph Trumbach and Lawrence Stone have also located the origins of the nuclear family in a preindustrial era, but they argue that the change emerged out of the aristocratic classes from about 1550. This was the result, they say, of a political complacency in that class that allowed it temporarily to disregard patrilineal norms in favor of egalitarian, relational ones.[3] Finally, Edward Shorter in his more popular history of the family has offered a variation on the traditional linkage of industrialization with the nuclear family. He locates the origin of family change in the lower rather than the middle class, maintaining that the new family emerged in the eighteenth century "as a subculture of the oppressed, as a new code of behavior binding together those lower-class people who were torn from their traditional environment into the vortex of the market economy."[4]

Despite disagreement concerning when and with whom the nuclear family was initiated, all of these historians associate it with an ideology that had managed to impress itself upon all social classes by the nineteenth century. This is not to say that nineteenth-century families did not possess characteristics of the nonnuclear or "extended" family. As novel readers know (and as shall be discussed in chap. 5), Victorians often maintained close ties to aunts, uncles, and cousins. Still, these relationships seemed to reflect vestiges of an older family model that, important though they may have been for the novels' plots (one thinks, for example, of the functional value of such relations in Dickens), were nonetheless depicted as being different from the intensely affective ties between parents and children. The ideology of the nuclear family, in short, dominated the nineteenth century, even though families might not always have strictly conformed to the nuclear model in practice.[5]

This ideological dominance of the nuclear family in the nineteenth century is what best accounts for its reputation as a middle-class institution. For whether or not the middle class was the site of origin, it was the great ideological supporter and promoter of the nuclear family. Thus, when I speak of the bourgeois nuclear family and use novels by middle-class authors about middle-class family life to illuminate family experience, my emphasis falls on the most developed expressions of an ideology. Although I am dealing with details of daily life that are drawn from only one part of a diverse social fabric, I operate under the assumption that the structure and dynamics that support the nuclear family in its middle-class manifestation are not fundamentally different from those of nuclear families elsewhere— that the ideology of closure entails a set of interactions that shows a certain uniformity across time and across social class. Indeed, the swelling of the middle class in modern times—or at least the tendency that has been documented in Western society of people to designate themselves as middle-class—may have more to do with the pervasiveness of this family ideology of closure than with any measurable relation these people have to some economic norm.

Three of the novelists in this study are English novelists of the nineteenth century. The other two are Samuel Richardson, who, writing in the eighteenth century, initiated the tradition of the domestic novel within which the other novels fall; and Henry James, American-born, who nonetheless wrote his most innovative work after having moved to England. Nineteenth-century England represents the apotheosis of the family ideal with which I am concerned.[6] In England, where industrialization and other modernizing trends appeared early and made steady progress and where the middle class showed an unparalleled success in the maintenance and elaboration of its institutions, the nuclear family established itself with special definiteness and tenacity. Both Lawrence Stone and Jeffrey Weeks have noted that Victorian England was a unique moment in the history of the family, when the decline in mortality rates had not yet been offset by rising divorce rates. As Weeks puts it: "it was only in the nineteenth century when all the loopholes had been stopped up that marriage became in fact what it had always been in theory, indissoluble. The Victorian family was the first family form in history which was both long-lasting and intimate."[7] Add to this the promotional assistance provided by a female monarch, herself the embodiment of domestic values, whose reign spanned most of the century, and we can see why the nuclear family acquired the status of a divine and immutable institution. It is no wonder that, even now, despite a wealth of qualifying historical evidence, we still tend to think of nineteenth-century England as the site of an ideal model of family life and to still shape our expectations of family on what we imagine that model to have been like.[8]

A tendency today is to blame insidious social forces for eroding the family ideal that we associate with this earlier age. Christopher Lasch, in his angry denunciation of the way social interference is destroying the nuclear family, is perhaps the most eloquent spokesman for this point of view.[9] I do not disagree with Lasch that society-licensed "experts" have become incorporated into the family experience, gradually changing the institution from a closed, privatized space into an annex of the social sphere. But I will argue that what Lasch sees as a disaster produced by society is more a case of the family seducing society into its embrace than of society meddling in a precinct in which it does not belong. The nuclear family has, since the end of the nineteenth century, increasingly required social interference to keep it going, to prop it up. While I agree with Lasch that this social interference is destroying the very institution that it was developed to support, I see this as a logical outcome given the laws that govern the nuclear family. The maintenance of the family in a conventionalized nuclear form has simply come to require an emotional and physical investment on the part of its members and on the part of external society that cannot be sustained without great strain—an investment that leaves little energy available for anything else (as the case of the anorectic daughter graphically demonstrates). Instead of lamenting the loss, we ought to regard the "death" of the nuclear family not as a death but as a passage to something new, to some alternative configuration for social order that is struggling to find its own, albeit temporary, stability and equilibrium.

When we turn to the novels, we can use these observations about the history of the nuclear family to better understand the ideological history that informs the genre. By drawing on the tools of family systems theory, it is possible to expose the structure and dynamics that the novels share with the families of the same period. Indeed, as the five novels I have chosen to discuss span the century, they trace a trajectory that I conceive to be at work in the family: of temporary stability among relationships within a closed system undergoing elaboration and finally giving way to instability, breakdown, and revision.

Before turning to an examination of the novels, however, it is necessary to provide some background on the systems perspective that informs this book and on the methodology of family systems theory in particular.

* * *

General systems theory was pioneered by Ludwig von Bertalanffy in the 1940s, growing out of his study of biological organisms. The theory is concerned with tracing the interconnectedness—what has since been termed by Gregory Bateson the "ecology"—of life processes. It conceives of life as a series of hierarchically arranged systems that have some degree of independence but are also mutually dependent. Each system has a boundary and a basic structure that defines it at the same time that it also has a dynamic by which it attempts to accommodate itself and respond appropriately to its environment. In its attempt to maintain its equilibrium, therefore, a living system is never static; it is continually interactive within itself and with its environment. This interaction produces continual *feedback*—the energy or affect produced from a living exchange—and this feedback acts on the system in turn, requiring assimilation and sometimes forcing change in the basic structure of the system.[10]

Family systems theory applies the epistemology of general systems theory to the organism of the family. This has important implications for the study of mental illness. According to the traditional, psychodynamic view, the symptomatic individual could be studied in a vacuum. In the family systems model, by contrast, individual symptoms are seen in the context of family interaction and hence as the function of that interaction: "In the systems model, the locus of pathology is the individual in context. The dysfunctional sequences that link individual and context, regulating the utilization of the symptoms by the system, are particularly significant."[11] According to this perspective, the boundaries of the self in the context of the family are brought into question. Mental illness in an individual family member is understood as belonging to the family as a whole whose destructive patterns of interaction help to produce and maintain it. Individual therapy can only have short-term or cosmetic effects according to this view; only through family therapy can destructive patterns be recognized and changed and the patient's symptoms cured and not simply replaced by new symptoms or transferred to other family members.

The willingness of many psychiatrists and psychoanalysts in the 1950s to use systems thinking in developing new treatments for mental illness is significant in telling us something about the state of family ideology during this period. In the aftermath of the social dislocation and existential horror produced by the Second World War, Western society was more likely to act defensively to preserve a family ideal of the last century that now seemed threatened at its core. The turn to more rigidly defined familial roles and to prescriptive formulas for marital behavior and child-rearing reflects this defensive attitude. Psychoanalysis, which essentially saw the individual as an isolated entity and focused on unconscious drives and traumas of childhood, seemed to offer little in the way of help for the family as an institution. One alternative lay in the field of ego psychology. As propounded most successfully by Erik Erikson, this was a spin-off of Freudian theory that stressed real-world adjustment rather than instincts and drives, and which coded the jolts and dislocations of life in the family into appropriate life-cycle behavior.[12] Another alternative took the form of family therapy. At first a modest attempt to involve the patient's family in the treatment program, this approach soon gave way to a new orientation in which the focus for therapeutic intervention became the "family system" rather than the individual— an orientation that promised to be the most direct and practical means of bolstering the institution of the modern family.

Probably the most influential mind in the development of family systems theory was Gregory Bateson, a scientifically trained anthropologist who, in a handful of papers, outlined the basic theoretical issues that family therapists have been elaborating ever since.[13] Yet significantly, Bateson did not occupy himself with families for very long. This was, I think, both a function of his temperament and of a growing suspicion that the nuclear family was incompatible with the epistemology of systems thinking—that the epistemology must ultimately lead away from the notion of "fixing" nuclear families.

Originally, however, the limited contexts within which Bateson's research was framed made it seem a panacea for the ailing family. At the Veterans Hospital in Palo Alto in the mid-1950s, he had assembled a cross-disciplinary group of scholars and practitioners and set them to work on the subject of schizophrenia. Despite a vague initial objective, this research resulted in a ground-breaking paper that would initiate an entirely new direction for investigation and treatment in the family therapy field. Entitled "Toward a Theory of Schizophrenia" (1956), the paper argued that families with a schizophrenic member show an unusually high incidence of certain kinds of communication patterns called *double binds*.[14] A double bind, Bateson and his colleagues explained, is the impasse produced when a message says one thing on a literal level but contradicts itself at another logical level (a mother's demand for affection, for example, may be contradicted by the stiffening of her body when her child touches her). The group argued that the victim of chronic double binding will in time cease to differentiate between logical levels of message. To such an individual, a simple question like "What can I do for you?" becomes a source of interpretive confusion: is this a veiled threat, a friendly offer, or a sexual proposition? The Bateson group concluded that such failure to distinguish between logical types of message is one of the hallmarks of the schizophrenic. What must be explored, they insisted, was not some mechanism in the individual that might be responsible for the inappropriate reaction (the route that psychoanalysis had taken without success) but the communicational context within which the individual's seemingly aberrant behavior became appropriate behavior. When the perspective shifted from the individual to the individual in the context of the family interaction (usually, in Bateson's cases, in the context of interaction with the mother) many of the schizophrenic's symptoms—hallucination, catatonia, unpredictable affect—could be construed as *solutions* the patient had found to deal with the stress and the erosion of identity produced by continual double binding.

Bateson's paper reflects a systems orientation insofar as it shifts the focus of concern away from the individual to the individual in the context of an interaction. But it also reflects a trend that already dominated the medical literature of the 1940s and 1950s. By shifting the focus to the mother-child interaction it implicitly shifts the blame for mental illness from the patient to the patient's mother. This tendency to blame the mother occurs repeatedly in the work of psychologists, anthropologists, and social theorists of the period.[15]

Over the course of the next decade, the "blame-the-mother" tendency was gradually discarded and replaced with the concept that the family as a whole was engaged in a destructive dynamic. (Indeed, the notion of "blame," with its implication that culpability can be localized and is the result of a singular behavior pattern, is now considered to be incompatible with the epistemology of the field.[16]) More recent therapeutic trends attempt treatment with the extended family and with coworkers and friends. Yet the process that has gradually filled what has at each point appeared to be a gap or blind spot in the systems model verifies my conviction that there is an ideologically determined limit to what one can perceive at any given historical moment, and that it is only when a new ideology and supporting structural configuration are emerging that comprehensive cultural criticism of the past can be carried out. Henry James, owing to the circumstances of his life and his unusual sensitivity as an artist to emerging social trends, saw around the ideology of the nuclear family in the 1890s. But the experts (and only a small minority of them at that) did not begin to understand that the nuclear family was an institution undergoing radical revision until the 1960s, with the antipsychiatry movement.[17]

In "Toward a Theory of Schizophrenia" and in his signature work published fifteen years later, "A Cybernetics of Self: A Theory of Alcoholism," Bateson essentially outlined a philosophy of systems thinking whose full implications remained hidden even to himself and which, as I have noted, theorists and practitioners have been fleshing out ever since.[18] In its willingness to cross boundaries between disciplines and repunctuate events, the philosophy has progressively functioned as a critique of the methodology of family therapy. In particular, Bateson's open-systems premise that the "observer always participates in what he observes" has become an increasingly problematic insight for therapists struggling to situate themselves in relation to the families they treat.[19]

If Bateson's philosophy has called into question conventional therapeutic method, it has also more disturbingly emerged as a critique of therapeutic content. We need only apply Bateson's "ecology of mind" to the concept of family propounded by John Ruskin, an intellectual spokesman of the last century, to see how the theory now functions to undermine the ideology that it had originally sought to support and strengthen. The family, according to Ruskin, is

> the place of Peace; the shelter, not only from injury, but from all terror, doubt, and division. In so far as it is not this, it is not home; so far as the anxieties of the outer life penetrate into it, and the inconsistently minded, unknown, unloved or hostile society of the outer world is allowed by either husband or wife to cross the threshold, it ceases to be a home; it is then only a part of the outer world which you have roofed over and lighted fire in.[20]

The fact that Ruskin remained intensely close to his parents throughout his life, living with them or having them close by until their deaths, and that his marriage was a short-lived catastrophe that made him only more devoted to his parents, suggests that the family idyll he describes is an idyll of childhood, a family of origin sanctified into an everlasting, ideal home.[21] This is in keeping with the logic of the nuclear family, which, if consistently enforced, would never release its members. From Bateson's ecological, systems viewpoint this is surely not a healthy context for growth. Yet significantly Ruskin's words still have the power to move us and describe a family ideal that conservative social critics such as Lasch nostalgically invoke. It is also worth noting that Ruskin's concept of the family, which was echoed throughout so much of the literature of the nineteenth century, envisions the closed system of family as a source of social and individual well-being, as a site not of sickness but of health. Indeed, if it did not provide some of the solace and support that it promised—if it were not, in short, functional for its time—it could hardly have held sway as it did. Even today, we see that individuals may resist medical attention and cling to their symptoms as a means of keeping an otherwise disintegrating family intact. The benefits they gain from maintaining family closure seem to outweigh the suffering and debilitation they pay for them.

Nathan Ackerman, one of the pioneers of family therapy, has asserted that "the family is called upon to make up to its individual members in affection and closeness for the anxiety and distress that is the result of failure to find a safe place in the wider world."[22] His words continue to echo Ruskin's, but they also anticipate the difficulties involved in applying systems thinking to the nuclear family. For while he describes us as still harboring the expectation that the family will operate as a closed system, he implies that the expectation is an unrealistic one—that the family cannot make up to its members for pain suffered in the larger world and to expect that it can may make things worse.

The paradox of what it means to maintain a stable, relatively closed family in a systems context emerges if we consider the concept of family *homeostasis*. Don D. Jackson, who introduced the concept in the 1950s, likened it to the climate control produced by a thermostat in a heating system. Families, he said, are "rule-governed systems," and "norms (desired behavior) are delimited and enforced" to produce homeostasis.[23] Jackson's concept reflects a view of the family in which communication with the "outside" occurs only in a highly controlled fashion designed to maintain closure. Yet increasingly, clinical studies seem to reveal that sick families suffer from what looks like over-developed homeostatic behavior. It is the psychosomatic and schizophrenic families that seal themselves off most persistently to external reality and develop finely calibrated homeostatic mechanisms by means of their members' symptoms. Thus, one source in the field can analyze schizophrenia in terms of its homeostatic properties as "a by-product of a long series of compromises the system has made, compromises that stabilized the whole at the expense of some of its parts."[24] By the same token, however, theorists maintain that when the family opens itself up to social penetration and makes no attempt at homeostasis, its members are left without a context for forging a self as we know it. In other words, with the closed family as the norm, the open family cannot produce acceptably conditioned individuals: emotional "cutoff" becomes as much a form of pathology as emotional "enmeshment," although one may be a direct reaction against the other.[25] One team of theorists has stated the problem bluntly: "the achievement of autonomy is dynamically antithetical to loyalty to the family of origin."[26] This kind of paradox leads to the qualifications that now clutter the theory concerning the acceptable limits and direction of change. Thus, Jackson's original concept of homeostasis has since been elaborated into two opposing concepts: *morphostasis,* an attempt to keep the family equilibrated through keeping it the same, and *morphogenesis,* an attempt to keep the family equilibrated through controlled structural change.[27]

Such attempts to adjust the definition of what constitutes healthy family function seem to me to invite an examination of the family in the context of its history. How was the nuclear family structured at its origin and are certain kinds of dysfunctional behavior patterns a logical by-product of this family form? The question has tended to be left unanswered by family systems theorists, who are caught at the crossroads of ideology. At once linked, if only by virtue of their vocation as family therapists, to a traditional ideology of the family, they are, at the same time, conditioned to a new ideological orientation through the epistemology of systems thinking.[28]

This, then, may explain why no consistent attempt has been made to understand the dysfunctional behavior of families in the present through an exploration of the structure and homeostatic mechanisms of families in the eighteenth and nineteenth centuries. Yet correspondences appear increasingly evident. Family theorist Murray Bowen's concept of the *triangle,* for example, is particularly illuminating in a historical context. "A two-person system may be stable as long as it is calm [Bowen explains in his analysis of the way alliances tend to work in families], but when anxiety increases, it immediately involves the most vulnerable other person to become a triangle."[29] In other words, a conflict between a husband and wife may be camouflaged through their mutual concern for their sick or delinquent child. If we place Bowen's remarks beside Edward Shorter's observation in *The Making of the Modern Family* that the new "companionate marriages" that ushered in the nuclear family (a phenomenon that Shorter locates in the eighteenth century) were founded upon a tenuous tie of romantic love and that "if true love is the only cement holding the couple together, the family will dissolve once it's gone,"[30] it becomes clear that the stabilization of the nuclear family, once romantic love had dissipated, could be effected by means of the couple's triangulation of their child. This, I believe, *was* one of the stabilizing strategies for the family in the nineteenth century. Only as the pathological effects of this chronic triangulation began to surface in the culture, threatening the functioning of the family as an institution, did other "regulators" in the social community (social workers, psychiatrists, policemen— Lasch's interfering experts) need to be brought in ("triangled") in an effort to reestablish family equilibrium. This supports Bowen's further observation that "when tension in the triangle is too great for the threesome, it involves others to become a series of interlocking triangles." The welfare state becomes at once a by-product of and a contributor to this systems evolution.[31] Conversely, in those cases today in which social influence is severely curtailed in an effort to preserve homeostasis within the triangle of the nuclear family, the result is likely to be psychosomatic illness in the child (stereotypically, as I shall argue, in the daughter). Illness, in other words, struggles to perform the regulating function and keep the family together.

Similar conclusions can be reached if we consider many of the mental disorders prevalent in society today as the result of progressively dysfunctional patterns of interaction within the nuclear family over many generations. Again, Bowen's remarks are suggestive. He maintains that "the emotional forces that drive these dysfunctions have their roots four, six, eight, maybe ten generations back in the family."[32] Going back that far brings us to a period in which the shift to nuclear structure for the family in Western society is taking place. If we return to Weeks's observation that the Victorian period was the period of longest duration for the middle-class nuclear family, Bowen's multigenerational model for mental illness assumes a historical significance. Weeks's observation highlights the fact that the Victorian period spanned the adult life of one generation—that of its queen—and that this generation institutionalized an ideology of family suited to its needs. The ideology also produced a family structure and dynamics uniquely suited to conditioning children in the image of their parents. It was this generation, then, that initiated a model for thought and behavior that would demand increasingly elaborate forms of accommodation and would inspire increasing ambivalence in future generations.

The initial results of this (de)formative process are evident in that first post-Victorian generation who looked back at their eminent parents with what has too simply been described as contempt. The case of Samuel Butler seems, in many ways, paradigmatic. A study of Butler's private correspondence reveals that he struggled as much to appease his father and maintain ties to his family of origin throughout his lifetime as he struggled to sever them; we learn as well that his attitude toward a prodigal younger brother was rigidly authoritarian and intolerant in the extreme.[33] The same tendencies are discernible in his novel, *The Way of All Flesh*. On the surface, it appears to be a vitriolic attack on the nuclear family. But a more profound analysis of the book's structure and point of view reveals that the attack masks other, opposing attitudes. Most revealing is the strange position of the narrator, Overton, a bachelor who is at once a member of the parents' generation and a sympathizer with the son's. The singular detachment of the narrator from family relationships of his own in the present (although they are fondly alluded to in the past), combined with his voyeuristic involvement in a younger man's family trauma, suggests that the novel is as much a struggle on the part of the adult to come to terms with the loss of the family of childhood as it is a critique of that family. One might even argue that where Overton is denying the possibility of creating a healthy nuclear family through his attack on Theobold Pontifex (a surrogate for himself had he chosen to become a husband and father) he is doing so out of his attachment to a childhood family that he cannot hope to detach himself from or see duplicated. In this, he resembles Ruskin, whose loyalty to his family of origin seemed to have been incompatible with the creation of a family of his own. Butler's case also appears consistent with the view put forward by the psychoanalytically oriented historians Fred Weinstein and Gerald M. Platt: that rebellion against authority is always a matter of what history has made available to rational manipulation. Weinstein and Platt argue that an object associated with what is clearly inimical may continue to remain uncriticized because our continued emotional attachment to this object makes its rational critique impossible.[34] I would explain what happens in somewhat different terms—that there remains a lag-time between our willingness to intellectually critique an object and our ability to become emotionally detached from it, so that what begins as a rational analysis will be transformed into a sentimental evocation of the past if the subject-matter is connected with patterns from our earliest experience and, hence, with the formation of our identity. (This argument will be developed further in chapter 5, on George Eliot's life and work.)

Can we postulate something about the organization of the nuclear family, which found its most visible expression during the Victorian period and has been the source of an intense loyalty and an equally intense rebellion ever since? What family pattern is capable of triggering the kinds of mental illness on the one hand and the creative forms of human relationship on the other that exist in our society today?

One obvious answer resides in the conventional complementarity of male and female sex roles as fitted to the structure of the nuclear family. Embedded in the notion of role complementarity within a relatively closed system is the notion of hierarchy. A system that aspires to closure must be governed; its boundaries must be maintained and, hence, it must rely upon one who defines structure and one who submits to it. This basic inequality was, of course, an accepted part of the nineteenth-century ideology of "separate spheres," which dictated that the woman was the emotional helpmate of the man (in Ruskin's words: "her function is praise"[35]) as well as his legal subordinate (in the words of Blackstone's *Commentaries,* husband and wife are "one person"—the husband—with "the very being or legal existence of the woman . . . suspended during the marriage"[36]). To be sure, the asymmetry of sexual roles does not originate with the nuclear family and was probably present much earlier in civilization, as Claude Lévi-Strauss's work on elementary kinship structure suggests; however, hierarchical complementarity of the kind engendered by the relatively closed system of the nuclear family had to give rise to its own particular dynamics.[37]

Complementarity, as Bateson points out, is a structural arrangement vulnerable to *escalating positive feedback*—the behavior pattern proper to a system lacking appropriate controls or brakes. Under these conditions, the basic oppositions that keep the system originally in balance are exaggerated on an escalating basis to the point that the powerful member destroys the subordinate member and the system as a whole is destroyed in the process.[38] A systems analysis of the nuclear family suggests that husband-wife complementarity as embodied in the companionate marriage would not function as the structural core of the family for long. Such complementarity, though initially checked by the counter-conventions of romantic love, would, if that love dissipated, quickly harden into conventional role-playing and escalate to the point where the system became unviable. (It is just such conventionalized, nonromanticized complementarity that fuels pornographic literature and gives it its escalating, sadomasochistic quality.[39]) Since a stable complementarity is one in which the complementary elements also contain built-in checks that short-circuit or de-escalate interactions when they surpass a certain level of intensity, the nuclear family needed to incorporate such checks early on.

As I have already noted in my discussion of triangulation, the couple did indeed have the means of instituting such checks through the strategic use of its children. In other words, the problem of escalating complementarity facing the couple who had originally married "for love" could be solved by involving the child in the dynamic relationship of the couple. This would produce an alternative configuration (a triangle) able to contain and redistribute forces that would otherwise rupture the family. But this triangle of parents and child was, I contend, a stop-gap measure for the nuclear family, a temporary arrangement principally valuable in producing a new, more stable dyadic relationship consisting not of husband and wife but of father and daughter. For it is the daughter, after all, who physically, emotionally, and intellectually embodies the nineteenth-century ideal of femininity:

> Much more successfully than her mother, a young girl could represent the quintessential angel in the house. Unlike an adult woman, a girl could be perceived as a wholly unambiguous model of feminine dependence, childlike simplicity and sexual purity. While it might be believed that an adult woman should retain a childlike simplicity, clearly a real child could be conceived of as more childlike than could an adult woman.[40]

It is my contention that this cross-sexual, cross-generational relationship of father and daughter functioned as the core of the nuclear family because, unlike the husband-wife relationship, where complementarity was purely a matter of convention (aided by the imaginative projection produced by romantic love), the father-daughter relationship was based on a more enduring and profound structural complementarity. That is, the basic hierarchy of sexual roles was preserved, and yet the daughter, bred from infancy to complement the father, also tended, through her interaction, to mold the father to her, creating something akin to the functional complementarity of parts in biological organisms.[41] It is this initial structural complementarity, arising out of the ideology of the nuclear family, that accounts for the absence or thematic inconsequence of the mother in nineteenth-century literature.[42] At the same time, it is this father-daughter complementarity that, I shall argue, will carve out a space in which the mother, originally absent from the ideological nexus of the family, can eventually be ascribed a role as the child's "primal" influence.[43]

Ultimately, of course, the complementarity of father and daughter would have to produce its own varieties of disequilibrium. For the relationship carried with it the potential for a future power reversal as the daughter's privileged tie to her father made her implicitly more powerful than her male peers, husband and brother. This privileging of the daughter as it has found expression in culture dating from the mid–nineteenth century has inspired various reactions. It has been denigrated as "feminization" (a term that implies a trivializing and emasculating of presumably more serious and worthy patriarchal institutions) and, in a reverse sort of essentialist treatment, it has been extolled as the "return of the repressed" both for the individual and for the culture.[44] Regardless of how this daughterly power has been interpreted, however, it clearly continues to emerge as a force to be reckoned with. Indeed, one of the conclusions of this book is that the progressive realization of the daughter's power—a by-product of her role in relation to her father in the nuclear family as it gets translated into a more general human, interpretive power—is destined to be the shaping force behind social organization as the nuclear family breaks down.

Yet it also must be noted that this female power has emerged only fitfully and not until relatively late in the evolution of the nuclear family. Instead, the socially institutionalized by-product of the father-daughter dynamic that became attached to an ideal of femininity in the nineteenth century was the arrested development of the daughter. Since the daughter's role in relation to the father in the nuclear family was a stabilizing function in a spatial frame (it brought the system into equilibrium), it was destabilizing in a temporal frame (it made structurally problematic the daughter's entry into other relationships). That is, it made it difficult for her to leave home. A basic tenet of psychoanalytic theory—that the daughter's difficulty in separating from her family of origin is connected to her sexual identity—both supports my conclusion and ignores the context in which it is reached. Even contemporary psychoanalytic theorists who have taken into account aspects of social conditioning and family role structure have failed to acknowledge the sense in which a daughter's tie to her father's house might be functional for the stability of the family as a whole.[45]

The illness of anorexia nervosa, so prevalent among adolescent girls in intact nuclear families today, seems especially suited to cast light on the stabilizing role performed by the daughter in the nuclear family. Family systems theorists have claimed the illness of anorexia as a family disease, postulating an "anorexia syndrome" that pertains to the psychodynamics of the family as a whole. They contend that the sick daughter carries the symptoms for the family, which is generally fraught with multiple covert tensions. The anorectic localizes what would otherwise be a family trauma in the form of her symptoms, and the family, in turn, unites "in a concern for and protection of the child, thereby rewarding the symptoms."[46] Concern for the sick daughter thus allows the family to avoid dealing with conflict among its members and with its external environment. The daughter is logically the most prone to occupy the symptomatic role since she is stereotypically conditioned, by reason of age and sex, to be most accommodating to others' needs. As already suggested, she is specifically conditioned to the needs of the father, the individual who, by choosing his wife, is responsible for bringing the family into being in the first place.[47]

If we look for the beginning of what today appears to be an epidemic of anorexia among middle-class girls, we must turn to the end of the nineteenth century, when documented cases of the illness began to appear, and when hysteria was the more prevalent "female" illness. Both of these illnesses—hysteria from 1840–90; anorexia more commonly and progressively seen in this century—seem to be attempts at homeostasis for the family system. Indeed, the other side of the family idyll of the nineteenth-century was the high incidence of female illness, a phenomenon feminist historians have extensively documented.[48] Nonetheless, there appears to be a difference between nineteenth-century female illnesses and twentieth-century ones. We can understand the illnesses that women suffered during the nineteenth century as short-term stabilizers for the family system. Although they can be read as signals that the family will eventually need to undergo structural revision, they serve to delay rather than to hasten that end. Women of the last century from all levels of society appeared to suffer from hysteria, anorexia, and the catch-all psychosomatic condition, neurasthenia, at any point in their lives when they found themselves frustrated in their roles and in need of an outlet that would renew or enhance their function within the family system.[49] The current outbreak of anorexia is different from these earlier illnesses insofar as it seems programmed to emerge at a particular moment in a girl's life, carries predictable symptoms, and occurs, predominantly, among middle-class, "model" nuclear families. In its mechanistic appearance it not only betrays itself easily (where nineteenth-century anorexia was as often confused with other illnesses), it also betrays the logic upon which the nuclear family is based, a logic that the previous female illnesses had disguised through displacements of various kinds. In other words, it helps us to see how the daughter's role in the nuclear family, internalized through multigenerational transmission, has become increasingly inadequate to its original function of focusing a family dynamic to produce temporary family equilibrium and closure.

* * *

It is only a short step from what I have written concerning the regulatory role of psychosomatic daughters who, through their symptoms, help to establish equilibrium and closure for their families to the role of heroines in nineteenth-century domestic novels. The novels with which I am concerned deal explicitly with problems of family stability and have young women as their central characters. These heroines serve a double regulating function: within the family systems depicted in the novels, they balance the values and behavioral tendencies of other family members; within the fictional systems that *are* the novels, they are the characters most suited to the enactment of balance and closure that the genre favors. Insofar as the evolution of the novel is connected with the evolution of the nuclear family, an examination of the thematic and structural role of the heroine can help us to confirm and expand upon what has been postulated about the role of the daughter in the nuclear family.

It is a convention of the genre, for one thing, that heroines are daughters and only potentially or fleetingly wives or mothers. By locating this convention in a family systems context, we can reconsider the significance of the courtship plot that is central to almost all nineteenth-century domestic novels. For now it seems to function less as a transition for the heroine—a means by which she can cross over to something new—than as a source of deferral of that most disruptive event in the life of the nuclear family: the event of leaving home. Joseph Boone has associated the delay that courtship provides with an erotics of delayed gratification.[50] I would suggest that the novels enact an erotics not of delayed gratification but simply of delay. The plot creates the illusion of a passage to a new life when it really prolongs and elaborates the heroine's life in her family of origin; it defers her new life and attempts in the process to incorporate it into the old. This is the strategy in many of Dickens's novels: the suitor is incorporated into his future wife's family when he is still a boy as in *David Copperfield*—or the daughter is incorporated into a surrogate family containing her future husband, as in *Martin Chuzzlewit* and *Little Dorritt*. In each of these cases, the romantic relationship that develops has already been coded as a familial one. In effect, the plot has the sister-heroine remain at home and the brother-hero follow a circuitous route into the world and back to this original object of affection. In other Dickens novels, the courtship and marriage plot are used as devices to bring the original family more closely together: in both *Hard Times* and *Dombey and Son,* the daughter's marriage is simply the means by which she can arrive at an improved relationship with her father.

Dickens's heroines are generally frail if not outright ailing creatures, as if their author recognized that the strain of their role in the family must tell on their physical frames. The poor health of many nineteenth-century heroines is also explicable in this way. What makes female protagonists like Austen's Marianne Dashwood, Fanny Price, and Anne Elliott; Charlotte Brontë's Jane Eyre, Caroline

Helstone, and Lucy Snow; Gaskell's Molly Gibson and Mary Barton; Collins's Laura Fairlie; and Thackeray's Amelia Sedley symptomatic is also what makes them heroines. Their symptoms function as homeostatic mechanisms, helping to maintain a precarious equilibrium within families that have been made subject to serious loss or disruption.

Even when the heroine appears to leave her family for marriage and a new life, the family seems to lie behind the choice of suitor. In her study of what she calls "the two-suitor convention" in the English novel, Jean Kennard has noted that domestic fiction tends to place the heroine between two men, both seeking her hand; her deliberation on the attributes of these two suitors and her eventual "right" choice of a partner constitute the novel's action.[51] What Kennard does not note is that the good suitor is generally a positive or improved aspect of the heroine's family of origin; the bad, a negative aspect of that family or of the family as it undergoes disruption or merges with a corrupt society "outside" (we may recall Ruskin's definition of a bad family as "only a part of the outer world"). Thus, the courtship becomes a negotiation toward a restored or reconstituted form of the heroine's family of origin: she enacts through her union with the good suitor and her dismissal of the bad suitor a symbolic closure of her original family that may not have existed before or that had been lost to her. This is the case in *Clarissa*, where the Harlowes' support of the wealthy but philistine Solmes as their daughter's suitor reflects their unrealized potential as a nuclear family. The good suitor in this novel is none other than God (Clarissa's ritualistic preparation for her union with her heavenly father makes explicit the link between the good suitor and the family in this novel). The daughter's symbolic union with God improves the family if only by creating a new coherence and closure for the family in guilt. (How the novel does this is the subject of the next chapter.)

A less symbolic version of this pattern can be said to operate in *Pride and Prejudice*, where Mrs. Bennet's support for Mr. Collins as a suitor to Elizabeth reflects the family's failure to promote proper values and to act as a domestic refuge for its members. This failure is exemplified in Mr. Bennet's detachment from the family and continual retreat to a surrogate refuge—his library. In observing Darcy's relation to his sister, Elizabeth is positively affected, it can be argued, because the relationship suggests an idealized version of her relationship with her father. She will realize this ideal only after her marriage when she gains access to the closed, domestic space of Pemberley where she can entertain her father freely and his best qualities can flourish.

George Eliot, writing later in the century and more skeptical of a family ideal, has her heroines' destinies take a more pragmatic turn and involve a lowering of expectations, but her concern is still with the symbolic reconstitution of a family of origin. In *Middlemarch,* Dorothea Brook marries the first time imagining that she has found that embodiment of paternal perfection which her uncle has failed to be for her (she consciously desires to play Milton's daughter to Casaubon). Her second marriage becomes a corrective to that ideal, a turn back to a "real" father-substitute: the marriage to Ladislaw serves as a form of reassessment and vindication of Dorothea's earlier life with her uncle. In *Daniel Deronda,* too, the drive is toward the retrieval and acceptance of a family of origin. This is true in a spiritual sense for Deronda who must discover and accept his heritage and his people; it is also true, in a more personal, psychological sense, for Gwendolen Harleth. We learn early on that as a child she had experienced two levels of paternal deprivation: first, she had suffered the literal death of her father in infancy; then, the repression produced by being unable to speak of him. The repression of the paternal idea—a second level of loss—is owing to the fact that once, as a young child, she had innocently asked her mother why she had married their irresponsible stepfather, and her mother's shamed reaction had made her not wish to raise the subject of her dead father again. This scrap of psychological history helps explain Gwendolen's later position between two men: the nurturing but ultimately out-of-reach Deronda and the cold, repressive Grandcourt. The triumph of Deronda's influence can thus be read (in keeping with the two-suitor convention discussed earlier) as Gwendolen's recuperation of the paternal idea that she had been forced to repress.

In each of these cases, the family of origin functions as the structural directive behind the heroine's destiny. Encounters that may seem to lead away from her life at home actually lead back—are elaborations or complications of earlier childhood interactions. Evelina Anville in Fanny Burney's *Evelina,* Caroline Helstone in Charlotte Brontë's *Shirley,* and Esther Lyon in Eliot's *Felix Holt* exist initially in simplified relations to fathers or father-figures and then have that relationship disrupted through the introduction of new knowledge concerning their family of origin. The assimilation of this knowledge is then closely connected with the heroine's union with the hero. It is the daughter's integration of herself into an original family system that has long been lost to her that informs and stands behind her integration into her new life as a married woman.

Insofar as the novel's thematic drive to establish a closed family system is connected with its formal drive to closure, this puts a special strain on the heroine when her ties to an original family are represented as damaged or severed. She must not only find a surrogate family in which to insert herself, she must also revise the interactive patterns in this new family so that she will have a role to play. In Maria Edgeworth's *Belinda*, Belinda Portman, a provincial orphan, is transplanted by her aunt to a frivolous urban environment with the apparent goal of locating her a husband. But though the achievement of this goal is certainly a by-product of the novel's action, the principal drama revolves around the psychological demands that face Belinda as she observes and helps to reverse the deterioration of the Delacour family with whom she has been sent to stay. In *Mansfield Park*, Fanny Price's role among the Bertrams, her adoptive family, involves a gradual, often painful insertion of herself into the dynamic of that surrogate family (a process that will be analyzed in chapter 3). Molly Gibson in Elizabeth Gaskell's *Wives and Daughters* exists originally in an idyllic relation to her widowed father until her father's remarriage creates a new, more complex family system that places new demands on her daughterly role.

Charlotte Brontë's heroines, Jane Eyre and Lucy Snow, are also emotionally strained by the familial roles they are expected to play. Both are locked into childhood families in which they do not have a legitimate place. And yet, as is the case with Fanny Price, their dogged ability to play the outsider role that the family assigns to them makes them the heroines they are. Thus, Jane Eyre never really disentangles herself from the Reeds, for whom at the outset she served as the focus for aggression. Although that family recedes from our notice early in the novel, the dynamic of life at the Reeds' repeats itself again and again for Jane—at Lowood School, with Rochester, and with St. John Rivers. In each case, as in her original situation at the Reeds', she is scapegoated and responds with passive resistance—the sign of her character and the source of her ultimate triumph.

It is noteworthy that in charting Jane Eyre's destiny Brontë introduces two explicitly pathological forms of female regulatory behavior in two other female characters in the novel: the anorectic Helen Burns and the hysteric Bertha Mason (the connection between anorexia and hysteria will be discussed in chapter 4 in connection with Catherine Earnshaw's symptoms in *Wuthering Heights*). Similar extremes appear in Harriet Beecher Stowe's novel *Uncle Tom's Cabin,* where the anorectic little Eva contrasts the hysterical Cassy. Unlike Brontë, however, Stowe makes the extreme characters her heroines. Eva and Cassy function in different sections of the novel and in relation to different men as examples of the kind of female regulation necessary to provide some meager stability for the family, faced with a great moral threat. Slavery looms in this novel both as a literal threat to black families and as a figurative threat to the nation-family. As an American faced with the reality of people buying and selling other people and with a country divided and on the brink of war, Stowe logically chooses to omit the kind of moderate bridge character that Charlotte Brontë supplies with Jane Eyre.

In each of the novels I shall discuss in this book (*Clarissa, Mansfield Park, Wuthering Heights, The Mill on the Floss,* and *The Awkward Age*), the heroine can be understood best as a regulating daughter. Her virtues, from a systems perspective, are metaphorically and often literally symptoms by which a disequilibrated family can, at least temporarily, correct or revise itself. Clarissa, whom I term the original anorectic daughter, has her symptoms sanctified and enshrined at the center of family life. Her story provides an archetypal model for the making of a family ideal that will inform the domestic novels of the next century. Fanny Price in *Mansfield Park* can be called Clarissa's literary daughter: she has her symptoms controlled in the service of the family. Through the gradual insertion of Fanny into the Bertram family system, the novel fashions a vision of family life in perfect equilibrium. *Wuthering Heights* elaborates the interactive dynamic that *Mansfield Park* had presented in a simplified, ideal form. Although, in the process, it lays bare structural problems arising from an ideology of closure, the novel finds a means of patching these over and rehabilitating the family in the end. The story of Maggie Tulliver in *The Mill on the Floss* also exposes the increasing difficulty with which, over the course of the century, the daughter performs her regulating role in the family. Yet Eliot, like Brontë, continues to emotionally support the ideology of the nuclear family even as she critiques it. Finally, James's *The Awkward Age* breaks free of the pattern. In James's novel, the family has ceased to function as a closed system with a single father-daughter dynamic at its core. Now, the daughter of the previous generation need not relinquish her role, and the family (if we can call it that any longer) must negotiate a new equilibrium that incorporates two daughters—that indeed can accommodate any number of regulating "daughters." As genealogical and emotional concerns are made subject to purely relational ones, age and even sex no longer need to serve as defining characteristics. James can be said to anticipate the breakdown of the nuclear family and to postulate a revision of the family into new, mobile patterns of relationship.

* * *

My interest in the systems properties of families depicted in nineteenth-century novels opposes a number of literary studies that see the nineteenth-century novel as concerned primarily with reproduction—with what one critic calls "the genealogical imperative."[52] For what concern there is for the problems of family survival in these novels seems to me to be outweighed by the far greater concern for "relationships" in both life and art during this period. Ultimately, I would argue, genealogical issues exist only as traces in the novels and in the lives of their authors, subsumed within concerns that are first emotional in nature, and finally discursive and interpretive. This is to extend Michel Foucault's thesis that a proliferating relational function (what he calls "deployment of sexuality") that began to occur in the seventeenth century was checked through the continued operation of a genealogical imperative (or "deployment of alliance"), specifically by means of the incest taboo.[53] It is to argue that by the end of the nineteenth century the ordering function of blood ties was no longer necessary, for the emotional investment supplied through the nuclear family had engendered its own means of ordering experience. Thus, thematically, the novels, like the nuclear families of their age, show relationships within the system taking priority over the safeguarding of title and property for posterity. Even where novelists of the period dealt with families over generations, what seems to matter in reproducing these families—even in such richly materialistic worlds as that of Trollope or, later, Galsworthy—is the context of interaction and not the bloodline or the property. Such novels are concerned with the family as it is faced with a new set of cultural variables while struggling to maintain its unconscious loyalties to the patterns of an earlier age. In such mid-century potboilers as Mary Brandon's *Lady Audley's Secret,* this seems to be quite explicitly the point: it is not patrimony but family pattern that is bequeathed. The secrets of these novels—which include bigamy, incest, murder, insanity—are secrets of family interaction, patterns that are latent in the daily lives of their heroines. In short, the plots of these novels are best understood in terms of evolving systems of relationship rather than historically determined events. They favor what, for shorthand, I will refer to as a spatial (as opposed to a temporal) order.

Structurally, the novels of the nineteenth-century reflect this same eclipse of the temporal by the spatial. George Eliot's "baggy monsters" are examples of structural spatialization, as are Dickens's multi-plot novels. But even nineteenth-century novels that seem to keep to a singular plot line are spatialized through a complex of vignettes and narrative frames that act on and resonate with each other: the psychological collage effect in *Villette,* for example; the ironic authorial interjections in the work of Thackeray and Trollope; the narrative framing devices in novels like *Wuthering Heights, Frankenstein, The Turn of the Screw,* and *Heart of Darkness.* The impulse behind these novels seems to be less focused on a narrative trajectory than on the guiding of even the most unwieldy experience into systems of thought or relationship that make them meaningful as models, parables, "transforms" for readers.

In noting these tendencies in nineteenth-century novels, Peter Garrett has argued for their dialogic nature, for reciprocity between linear, plotted, temporal aspects of narrative and spatial ones.[54] I would simply argue that a relative priority is increasingly given to spatial aspects over temporal ones, as a reflection of the ideology of closure that the novel, like the family of the period, supported. Peter Brooks has explained the mechanism of narrative as a transformation of metonymy into metaphor.[55] I would say that metonymy becomes metaphor with a vengeance in nineteenth-century novels, for in these novels the drive to closure is connected to a notion of realism that sees meaning as unified, coherent, absolute—that conceives, in short, of some representable reality "out there." This means that while a linear plot may be the means of arriving at a "proper" conclusion, this conclusion is continually prefigured; the plot continually resonates back on itself. Brooks, significantly, makes his points about narrative by drawing upon Freud, the great apostle of the nuclear family and the scientific exponent of representational realism. In fact, Brooks's theory is itself the product of a nineteenth-century ideology of closure. It is not a universal description of the way narrative operates but a particular description of the way nineteenth-century narrative operates. Admittedly, the lingering legacy of that period may cause us, like Brooks, still to read everything that way, but surely literary antecedents to the nineteenth-century novel did not produce in their readers the effects Brooks describes. Indeed, even immediate precursors of nineteenth-century narrative—the picaresque novel, for example—seem stubbornly devoid of such effects. By the same token, most modern and postmodern literature seems determined to avoid being experienced as closed form, seeking a setting loose of metonymic effects rather than a roping in and collapsing of these effects.[56]

The eclipse of the temporal by the spatial in the nineteenth-century novel can also be formulated in Darwinian and Lamarckian terms. While Darwin viewed evolution as a matter of luck (the strongest survive), Lamarck substituted the notion of cunning (those who adapt to the environment survive).[57] In the nineteenth-century domestic novel, it is adaptability, not simple survival that is at issue. This is the role that falls to the heroine, and her context for adaptation is the family.

Yet a corollary also reveals itself increasingly in the novels of the century, namely that certain limited forms of adaptation can lead to the death of the adaptive element when the system of which it is a part has failed to properly adapt to *its* environment. By the end of the century, in Henry James's novels, we see family systems running down or becoming inoperable and heroines desperately trying to keep them going. Maggie Verver in *The Golden Bowl* is a brilliant example of Lamarckian cunning, which seems nonetheless like wasted effort given the inhumanly exclusive and brittle system that the institution of marriage has become. This, I believe, is precisely the perspective we need to understand the ingenious but ultimately pointless efforts of the modern-day anorectic daughter for whom adaptation to a failed system can be a literal death sentence.

But this conclusion too is incomplete. After all, it is the anorectic daughter who, as a result of her aggravated symptoms, can help to expose the family system to itself and effect a disinvestment in destructive relational patterns. In a similar sense, James's heroines are often the creative facilitators of new configurations as well as the pathetic adapters to old. They anticipate the fiction and real lives of modern and postmodern female writers such as Virginia Woolf, Kate Chopin, Doris Lessing, Sylvia Plath, Margaret Atwood, and Margaret Drabble.[58] For these female protagonists, both real and fictional (the line between the two becomes suggestively blurred at this point), madness can be understood both as the extreme effort to regulate a disintegrating family and as the "voyage out" of a confining space and role into new and uncharted relational configurations. If the daughter is the doomed regulator of a doomed family system, she is also the character most formed to be adaptive as a new context for experience emerges.

CHAPTER 2

Clarissa: **Origin**

Clarissa is the youngest child of the Harlowe family: "from her in-fancy a matchless young creature . . . admired by all who knew her, as a very extraordinary child."[1] So exemplary has she shown herself that her grandfather deviated from patrilineal custom and left her his estate in his will. But this angelic daughter will suffer a mythic ordeal in the course of the novel. Courted by the aristocratic rake Lovelace, her brother's enemy, and forced by her family to suffer the advances of the "squat," "very illiterate" but *"Rich* Solmes," she is driven to desperation. Through an elaborate stratagem that exploits her fear, Lovelace prevails upon her to run away with him. He pre-tends to settle her in a reputable house that in reality covers for a brothel, and he attempts to seduce her. Suspecting his designs, Clarissa at last manages to escape, only to have Lovelace trick her back to the house and rape her. Escaping again, she finds her own lodgings, where, growing rapidly weaker and more wasted, she now occupies herself in an elaborate preparation for death. When she finally dies, her family and Lovelace are overwhelmed with remorse. Lovelace is killed in a duel with her cousin—expiring in the agonized consciousness of his crime—while the Harlowes spend what remains of their lives suffering pangs of guilt and singing the praises of their daughter.

This, in brief, is the plot of the eighteenth-century epistolary novel that describes the family ideology—and outlines the dynamic neces-sary to support it—that would dominate the nineteenth century in fiction and in life.

Despite her physical separation from her family early in the novel, Clarissa, Richardson tells us in the Preface, is "inseparably connected" (1: xiv) with her family. Our tendency as post-Freudians is to assume that Clarissa is psychologically dependent upon her family. But I think we need to approach the statement differently if we are to understand the historical importance of this novel. Clarissa's dependence on her family at the outset is a matter not of psychic structure but of role structure. It is a horizontal, a flat dependence—the dependence that some part has to some whole. In the course of the story, however, this horizontal dependence will be transformed into vertical dependence—depth will be created from surface; psychology kneaded into role.

The shift from surface to depth is related to a shift in the ideology and structure of the family occurring at the time Richardson was writing. This shift was from an ideology of openness as it corresponded to a system organized through kinship ties to an ideology of closure as it corresponded to a system organized through emotional investment. The use of these terms—"open" and "closed," "kinship" and "emotional investment"—in counterpoint to each other finds justification in anthropological and historical studies of the family. In *The Elementary Structures of Kinship*, Lévi-Strauss attributes the transition from nature to culture to the operation of the incest taboo: with the initiation of an incest prohibition that stipulated that women not be kept by their fathers and brothers but be given up for exchange by them, a pattern was superimposed upon the randomness of nature. This pattern, produced by the exchange of women across families, was, according to this theory, the fundamental ordering process by which civilization came into being. Kinship thus developed as an increasingly intricate and expanding (open) system of blood ties based on the exchange of women across families.

To relate this model of elementary kinship structure to the historical moment of mid–eighteenth-century England we need to draw on the work of recent historians of the family, particularly that of Lawrence Stone, who has shown a special sensitivity to the structural changes that have occurred in the English family since the Middle Ages. According to Stone, the predominant form of family organization until the seventeenth century was the *open lineage family*. This type of family was characterized by weak boundaries between and among the nuclear core (i.e., parents and children), more remote (or extended) relations, and the wider definitions of social space. This family model was essentially patrilineal in form whenever land, however meager, was at issue, and the family's interests were sustained through its stipulation of acceptable marriage alliances as well as through primogeniture and entail. The marriage of the heir, accord-

ing to Stone, "was the most important strategic decision of a generation, and it was made by the father and the family council of elders,
negotiating directly with equivalent representatives of the family of
the bride."[2] As we examine the open lineage family and its
specifically patrilineal articulation, we can see that it shares the patriarchal premise that Lévi-Strauss attributes to elementary kinship
structure: "The total relationship of exchange which constitutes marriage is not established between a man and a woman, where each
owes and receives something, but between two groups of men, and
the woman figures only as one of the objects in the exchange, not as
one of the partners between whom the exchange takes place."[3] An
open lineage, patrilineal family model assumes the exchange of
women as a means of supporting or, in the case of the middle classes,
improving the male line. Patrilineage is thus an elaboration of the
premise of elementary kinship structure (matrilineage would be an
alternative elaboration—it would merely be the wife's male relatives
rather than the husband's male relatives who would inherit property,
title, position, and so forth). In short, patrilineage is the visible form
that elementary kinship structure has taken in Western culture in
organizing the family ideal over time.[4]

However, in the sixteenth century, according to Stone, the open
lineage system began to undergo transformation into what he has
termed the *restricted patriarchal nuclear family*. Now, the network of
kinship began to recede, the family became more circumscribed as
the unit of parents and children, and the father, who in the open
lineage system served as the emblem of the patrilineal line, now became a force of authority in the household. It is this restricted patriarchal nuclear family that Stone posits as preceding the more ideologically closed but more role-flexible and egalitarian *domesticated nuclear
family* that began to emerge in the eighteenth century, which he
equates with the modern family. Thus, Stone's three family models—
open lineage, restricted patriarchal nuclear, and closed domesticated
nuclear—are attempts to trace systematically an evolution that other
historians have described more loosely. What makes Stone's categories so suggestive to the systems thinker is the way they sketch the
evolution with some precision yet leave unexplained the internal dynamics by which the evolving structures can be understood to relate
to each other. Stone notes, for example, that although the evolving
nuclear family briefly served as the reinforcement for patriarchal

privilege, it eventually reversed this trend and shifted to a more egalitarian family model.[5] Although he invokes a number of external influences to explain this (arguing, most notably, that the breakup within the state of competing foci of power helped to temporarily centralize patriarchal authority in the home), his explanations do not provide us with the systems knowledge we need to understand why the shift from open lineage to nuclear structure is a turning point in cultural organization and not simply an offshoot or variation of exchange, as Lévi-Strauss's structuralist model would have it. Through what process, in short, did patrilineage, the Western form of an open lineage family model, become assimilated to an ideology of closure so that it was ultimately eclipsed by it? Indeed, by answering this question we can reconcile the arguments of historians such as Alan Macfarlane and Peter Laslett, who maintain that the nuclear family always existed, i.e., that families were always relatively small and did not include extended kin in their living arrangements. According to the systems perspective I propose, what made a family a domesticated nuclear family as opposed to a traditional, open lineage or extended family was not the physical make-up of the household (the number or kind of blood relations). It was instead the quality of affect that characterized the arrangement and, more specifically, the binding dynamic that brought that affect into being by conditioning members to an idea of family closure and solidarity.[6]

Family systems theorists have noted that in the life cycle of individual families there can exist points at which the family as a system tending toward disequilibrium is either adjusted back to a given, relatively stable configuration or transforms itself—leaps to a new level of organization and acquires a new structure.[7] Unfortunately, such thinking has only focused on particular cases of family function in contemporary culture and has lacked a larger historical awareness. Yet the notion of a leap in structuration is ultimately necessary to explain the shift from open lineage to nuclear structure that occurred in the history of the family. To understand the nature of this leap, we must build on Lévi-Strauss's original ideas concerning the operation of the incest taboo.

The incest taboo, says Lévi-Strauss, is a first-order change from nature to culture: "It sparks the formation of a new and more complex type of structure and is superimposed upon the simpler structures of physical life through integration.... It brings about and is in itself the advent of a new order."[8] This, then, can be viewed as an *initiating* leap in structuration. (Although I do not want to assert a belief in an essential origin, I find Lévi-Strauss's model explanatory as an initiating model for patriarchy.[9]) If the exchange of women is understood as the first leap in structuration, the nuclear family is the next such leap. It is a *second-order* change, superimposing upon the first-order structure that Lévi-Strauss describes a second order of complexity through integration. For while the idea of family closure can be said to have evolved as the long-term by-product of life in an open lineage system, the rules governing the superimposed closed structure are liable to be different from, even ultimately oppositional to, those governing the elementary open structure from which they spring.

Richardson's novel describes the superimposition of this ideology of family closure upon an open-lineage past. This involves the gradual replacement of a system of organization based on alliance through blood over time by a system of organization based on emotional ties to family members in the present. By examining *Clarissa* in light of the history of the family, we can arrive at a better understanding of the family structure and of the individual psychic structure needed to support the ideology as it would continue to define and elaborate itself over the course of the next century.

* * *

Most critics have recognized Richardson's place at the origin of something. He has been called the original novelist of the emerging industrial middle class, of the bourgeois nuclear family, and of the domestic heroine—the "angel in the house"—in her association with leisure, moral purity, and death. In 1936, Joseph Wood Krutch distilled what has been the prevailing view ever since when he asserted that Richardson wrote "in the interests of virtue—as virtue is conceived by the tradesman."[10] But such assessments of Richardson as the prototypical "new man" of his age miss the transformational quality of Richardson's life and work.

We know little of Richardson's early life, only that he was born into a family of moderate means, that his father was a joiner or cabinet-maker, and that he was apprenticed at seventeen to a printer.[11] That the novelist left so little to posterity concerning his childhood and early youth is noteworthy. Richardson was not a particularly reserved or secretive man, and the few details he gives us concerning his family of origin appear less the result of reticence than of an absence of any special association or affect associated with those years. This is in striking contrast to the intensity of feeling and the concern for detail that infuse his novels in their treatment of family life.

A clue to why Richardson's early associations were so few and shallow may be found in the fact that he was apprenticed. The practice of apprenticing youth to a trade, still common in the sixteenth and seventeenth centuries, is an example of the kind of mobile, non-insulated behavior associated with the open lineage family. It was a practice that seems both to reflect the absence and to prevent the development of any strong emotional investment among family members. It is worth noting that Richardson's father had not originally intended to apprentice his son; he had marked him for the clergy, but financial reverses had made this route impossible. While a clerical vocation would immediately have introduced Richardson to a situation associated with a higher class and a different affective atmosphere than the one in which he had grown up, the apprenticeship continued his association, at least temporarily, with the social class and the family model into which he was born. Thus, Richardson's eventual rise to a position of middle-class security and respectability and his initiation into a different style of family life must be seen as a lengthier, more complex process than it would have been had he taken orders. The manner in which he achieved such a rise and such an initiation—his particular exploitation of the printing trade to effect this transformation—makes his family experience seem a kind of paradigm for the ideological transformation of the English family during this period.

To grasp the full significance of Richardson's self-transformation, we need first to examine the practice of apprenticeship in relation to the laws of elementary kinship already discussed. Lawrence Stone dates the practice from the Middle Ages but admits to not knowing the reason for this "mass exchange of adolescent children."[12] But a reason can be found if apprenticeship is viewed as a lower-class equivalent of the aristocratic arranged marriage, which was performed to protect or improve a male line and which also, as already explained, was an elaboration of the more basic ordering process inherent in elementary kinship structure. In this context, young men who were apprenticed to a trade can be understood as lacking the resources of higher-class men and requiring a way station where they could gain the position, expertise, and financial security necessary to enter into the exchange process with the fathers or brothers of appropriate women. Richardson appears to have profited by his apprenticeship in precisely this way. After learning the trade of the printer, he married the daughter of his employer. She died after bearing him six children (none of whom survived), but he speedily replaced her, marrying this time the sister of a successful bookseller. Both marriages were the direct by-products of his position in the trade to which he had been apprenticed (his second marriage was a socially better marriage than his first, reflecting his "rise"). The rapidity with which the move from first to second wife was made conforms to the elementary kinship model of family in which women are interchangeable (valuable in their relationships to men and not in themselves), and it also appears to reflect that low affect in relationship that historians have associated with the open lineage family.

In the course of his second marriage, however, Richardson's success in business began to work a change in the shape of both his career and his family life. His prosperity brought with it a reputation among booksellers that made him valuable to them, as he put it, in "writing Indexes, Prefaces, and sometimes, to their minor authors, *honest* Dedications; abstracting, abridging, compiling, and giving my Opinion of Pieces offered them."[13] He was also encouraged to write a number of advice pamphlets culminating in a guide to familiar letter-writing. It was this last that served as the impetus for his entry into fiction late in life (he wrote his first novel, *Pamela,* at 51). It should be noted that up until the end of the seventeenth century, printers, publishers, and booksellers were not clearly differentiated. Although by Richardson's time the printer had become subordinate to the bookseller, who still acted largely as publisher, close links continued to exist among all these functions. This meant that as a printer Richardson was a specialized tradesman while still part of a profession in which all aspects of book production overlapped. His ties to booksellers through his brother-in-law reinforced this connectedness. At the same time, he was operating in an atmosphere that had become more cognizant of the rights and prestige associated with authorship. The need to shape and improve public taste, to protect copyright ownership, and to court writers of established reputation and nurture new ones began to become part of the concerns of publication as the private patronage of authors declined.[14] Within such a climate one can understand why Richardson might have been inspired to combine his business sense and his literary interests and to take advantage of his links to all aspects of the publishing trade by trying his hand at writing a popular novel.

Richardson's prosperity and his entry into literature combined, in turn, to support a style of family life that differed substantially from anything he could have known from his childhood. His second wife bore him six children, four of whom, all daughters, survived. In a traditional patrilineal society, to have only daughters would have been problematic to say the least. But Richardson's family existed in a period when the priorities associated with family life were changing. His wife and daughters came to embody a new idea of family that Richardson's growing income made possible and that his novels would help to promote. Rarely leaving home, they existed as the fixtures of his hearth and as the guaranteed audience for his fiction. And with his wife and daughters ministering to him at home, Richardson could the more easily proceed to assimilate his readers, the vast majority of whom were female, to this domestic idea. With a few exceptions, his most valued readers were the age of his daughters, and their relation to him, though focused on literature, was daughterly.[15] These women helped to reinforce the idea of insular domesticity made popular by his novels, writing him for counsel and explanations concerning his work and flattering his moral character. His literary relationships also incorporated the dynamic that his novels would help to promote as proper to family harmony. The conventions of male power and female subordination were an assumed part of these relationships, but they were enforced with subtlety and a certain flexibility. Richardson certainly embodied authority to his female correspondents, but it was an authority willing to explain itself and take into account their reactions. His correspondents, for their part, were not mere sheep or silly sycophants. They were ladies with eloquence and ideas who appreciated the condescension of their literary master. As shall be seen, this dynamic of patriarchal severity checked by emotional empathy, of daughterly devotion vitalized by imagination, is precisely the dynamic that would allow the family to function, at least temporarily, as a relatively closed system over the course of the next century. *Clarissa* would provide the blueprint for this dynamic in literature.

* * *

A number of critics have maintained that Richardson articulated in his novels two assumptions that existed in opposition to each other in the culture of the period: that children need to obey their parents and that parents need to treat their children as autonomous beings. The coexistence of these two assumptions, it is argued, reflects a culture divided between its allegiance to past forms and its inclination toward new democratic philosophies—a cultural division that has been associated with the famous debate between John Locke and John Filmer (in which the former advocated personal autonomy, the latter, the sacredness of authority).[16] But understanding Richardson as merely articulating a contradiction in culture is incomplete. As in his life, where he appears to have transformed one form of family organization into another, his work must be said to describe a process by which old ideas were assimilated to a new cultural configuration— where the seeming contradiction between parental authority and filial rights was reconciled.

In this, Richardson really approximates John Locke's position. Locke has been too simply understood as an advocate for individual freedom against authority, as though the terms of his debate with Filmer were really a matter of opposites. As Jay Fliegelman has argued, a more careful analysis of Locke's position shows him advocating parental guidance in place of parental tyranny, a guidance that essentially is a form of conditioning in parentally prescibed behavior.[17] In other words, if the child internalizes the law of the parents— developing a superego, as it were—then strict parental control is no longer necessary; the child's "internal governor" now replaces external authority. For such an upbringing to be possible, however, the structure of the family has to allow for such intensive conditioning—it has to be conducive to the internalizing process. The interactive dynamic by which the nuclear family stabilized itself and the internal dynamic by which the individual became formed as a psychological self are thus inseparable and mutually supporting. In *Clarissa*, Richardson conceived a novel that represents the process through which both the new family and the new self produced each other. In conceiving such a novel, he also initiated the genre of domestic novel that would depend upon this dynamic for its stability.

Clarissa is a novel of letters, and letters, when we think solely of the form, suggest an open system of exchange in their patterns of sending and receiving, acting and reacting. Edward Shorter, in depicting the open lineage family as "pierced full of holes, permitting people from outside to flow freely through the household, observing and monitoring,"[18] describes a manner of life to which epistolary correspondence would appear to be connected. Certainly, in the sixteenth century and before, letters, like families, were rarely private. They served the predominantly public function of relaying political and commercial information. In the seventeenth century, however, the "familiar letter," in which details of domestic life were transmitted to relatives and friends, became an established form of expression. Indeed, the form became popular enough to warrant the booksellers of Richardson's day to encourage him to write a guide to familiar letter-writing (*Familiar Letters* was published in 1741, the year after *Pamela*, though begun before and the impetus for the novel). This project, by its very nature, emphasized the fact that letters had a new, or at least expanded, role to play in the social system. No longer purely informational, letters now served an affective role as well.[19]

The role of the familiar letter in eighteenth-century English society thus carries with it a number of contradictions. One could argue that its association with women, who were the principal utilizers of the form, and its rapid conventionalization (evidenced by the market for "model" letters like those provided by Richardson's *Familiar Letters*) continued to tie it to a traditional family model: the conventionalized letters circulated *by* women being metonymic of the conventionalized circulation *of* women in society through marriage alliances. At the same time, the very notion of the "familiar," while it might lend itself to conformity and conventionality, also carries associations of privacy and secrecy. Thus, while the familiar letter represents a system of exchange, it also defines a space of domesticity—of privacy—both for the one who writes and for the one who reads and responds. It assumes, as Ian Watt has explained, "a private and personal relationship . . . which could be carried on without leaving the safety of home."[20] Moreover, as women were generally the writers of familiar letters, they tended to be the subjects of their own correspondence—a position that would tend to oppose the elementary structural position of women as objects of exchange by men. In short, the familiar letter appears formally to correspond to an open system of exchange but to superimpose on it an idea of closure, much as the nuclear family can be said to have superimposed itself upon the open lineage family.

The combining of formal conventions with moral and affective concerns is, in fact, explicitly alluded to by Richardson in the full title of his *Familiar Letters,* which reads: *Letters Written to and for Particular Friends, on the Most Important Occasions. Directing Not Only the Requisite Style and Forms to be Observed in Writing Familiar Letters; But How to Think and Act Justly and Prudently, in the Common Concerns of Human Life.* Richardson's intention to combine the formal with the personal is also stated in his preface to the letters, where he says he hopes to "not only direct the *forms* requisite to be observed on the most important occasions; but, what is more to the purpose, by the rules and instructions contained in them, contribute to *mend the heart, and improve the understanding* . . . to inculcate the principles of virtue and benevolence."[21] Margaret Doody demonstrates how difficult it is to explain the blend of form and feeling in the letters when she associates Richardson's epistolary technique with stream of consciousness and then qualifies this association by pointing out that writing, as both Richardson and his characters practice it, is, after all, a highly self-conscious act. She then returns to qualify her qualification by noting that Richardson's stress on "writing to the moment" provides access to "thoughts in an unformed state."[22] Similar difficulties emerge when we try to grasp the implications of another critic's assertion that the familiar letter is a genre concerned with affirming a new subject-matter—that of the self.[23] By taking the self as its subject-matter, the form would seem to support a larger social matrix; for insofar as the self is understood as solid and consciously willed, it exists *for* society. But such self-consciousness can also be said to undermine the validity of social intercourse, since self-reflexivity raises questions concerning the boundaries of the self, its frankness and duplicity, its access to itself, and so forth.

Now in Richardson's novel *Pamela,* the contradictory impulses inherent in the genre of the familiar letter appear to be obviated by the nature of the plot. Open lineage relationships—the "forms," as Richardson puts it, associated with such letters—can be said to predominate. Writing from her place as servant in the home of Lord B., Pamela is part of that more traditional household of the lower classes that tended to apprentice its children (as did Richardson's family). Pamela's letters are about an especially tricky elaboration of a kinship structure: she is inserted into what had been a relatively endogamous system of aristocratic exchange. By getting Lord B. to marry her, she turns that system into one of more generalized exchange: turning an endogamous system into an exogamous one. We are still within an open lineage system, however, and for all her gumption, Pamela is an object of exchange; her letters are both metaphors of exchange and the means by which her value as an exchange object is dramatized.

Unlike *Pamela, Clarissa* begins by placing its heroine *inside* a family and making the drama focus not upon the heroine's transfer across families but upon the solidifying of her place within her family of origin—both her physical and figurative positioning in relation to it. After Clarissa elopes with/is abducted by Lovelace, the reader must locate her in two senses: where she is physically (what kind of home is she in? where is it located?) and how her action has defined her relationship to her family. In short, the letter-writing in the novel proceeds from within the context of a closed family system that breaks open and must be recontained in more complex and profoundly stabilizing terms. It is precisely this concern with the reformulation of an original family that Clarissa invokes continually throughout the novel, lamenting that her family "late so happy and so united" (1:22) has ceased to be so.

It should be noted that in her early letters, Clarissa is dealing with two different, though related, kinds of family trauma. First, her grandfather's will has left the family "strangely discomposed" (1:3). By bequeathing Clarissa his estate, her grandfather has wrenched the family out of a patrilineal conception of itself. This discomposure, however, symbolically reflects the advent of a new order of family relations that is also suffering trauma—or more correctly, is suffering the pain of formulation. For this new family order has never been fully realized; it exists as a potentiality that Clarissa both invokes and dislocates for us:

[T]he world is but one great family. Originally it was so. What then is this narrow selfishness that reigns in us, but relationship remembered against relationship forgot? (1:34)

Clarissa is not talking of a genealogical family here but of a family that essentially opposes patrilineage and that might be said to stand in direct opposition to the idea of marital exchange and hence of the splitting up of the original family into forbidden and permitted daughters for marriage (the distinction that Lévi-Strauss identifies as basic to civilization).[24] However, this idea of closure and solidarity, of the family affectively united, is still not feasible so long as the patrilineal ideology continues to hold sway, as it does in the form of Clarissa's brother James, the traditional heir, the person most upset by Clarissa's inheritance and willing to find every means of opposing it. Of course, James reflects a patrilineal ideology that already betrays its weakening status, if only because it no longer sees women as supports to the system (his grandfather's legacy simply reinforces his basic distrust on this score). As Clarissa explains to Anna Howe, to James, "daughters were but encumbrances and drawbacks upon a family.... chickens brought up for the tables of other men.... that, to induce people to take them off their hands, the family-stock must be impaired into the bargain" (1:54). For James, daughters continue to exist as exchange objects, but objects that have lost their value and become rather a drain to the family engaged in exchange than a source of profit and order. James's view reflects a view of the family that has lost the vitality once supplied by the exchange of the daughter in marriage but that, caught in patrilineal thinking, has not yet imagined a new kind of family in which the daughter's role would be different.

Clarissa has imagined such a family and such a role. We know, for example, that she has assumed many of the principal household chores and that one of the arguments she offers to support her refusal of the family's favored suitor, Solmes, is that she has "not, I hope, made myself so *very* unuseful in my papa's family" (1:77). Her mother, still subject to her husband and son's values, suggests that her daughter can be easily replaced by paid household help ("I have made inquiry already after a housekeeper" [1:78]), but Clarissa's energies are toward making such a replacement impossible. Her need to be "useful"—indeed, her cultivation in general of extraordinary virtue—can be read as a need to make herself unique and irreplaceable and hence to render undesirable her transfer to a new family. What seems most to offend her about Solmes is the way in which the family's support of that alliance implies her status as an object, a transferable possession, a creature without feeling ("To be given up to a strange man; to be ingrafted into a strange family;... to be obliged to prefer this strange man, to father, mother—to everybody" [1:153]). Lovelace, early discredited by her family as a suitor, becomes conceivable to her as a love object for two reasons: because he is not a possible one in family terms and hence can be sustained as a purely hypothetical object, and because he is not a prescribed one, and hence can reinforce the sense of uniqueness that she needs to feel herself safely tied to her family of origin.

In this context, Clarissa's remarks about an original "one great family" must be taken not as nostalgia for a lost unity that encompasses all but a wish concerning a unity for her own individual family that has not yet come into being—a unity that would not entail marrying out and being "ingrafted" into a strange family. The Harlowes, at the outset, have not yet internalized (incorporated as part of their interactive structure) a regulating dynamic by which the closure of the domesticated nuclear family can be conventionally defined and maintained. Clarissa, then, invokes a false origin while her story enacts a true one.

As already noted, the novel's movement to produce a regulating dynamic for the family as a closed system is also a movement to produce an individual psychology for the heroine that is not present at the beginning—the two movements are inseparable and mutually interactive. In reading *Clarissa*, critics have tended to psychologize the heroine and her world too quickly. Dorothy Van Ghent, who draws a sharp contrast between Defoe and Richardson, is typical of critical opinion: *Moll Flanders*, she writes, "offers a flat fictional landscape, uniform, unaccented, horizontal ... whereas *Clarissa* is a dramatically vertical world of fabulous heights and rank profundities."[25] However, by treating the psychological resonance of Richardson's novelistic world as its initial characterizing feature, critics like Van Ghent neglect the process by which the novel acquires this resonance.

To begin, it is helpful to look at Richardson's remarks on the key subject generally used as evidence for "verticality" in *Clarissa*: the heroine's unconscious desire for Lovelace. In the Postscript to the novel Richardson seems to state his intention unambiguously. "It is not intended that she should be in love," he asserts bluntly, "but in liking only, if that expression may be admitted" (4:558). In his letters, however, he complicates the issue:

> As to Clarissa's being in downright Love, I must acknowledge, that I rather would have it imputed to her, (his too well-known Character consider'd) by her penetrating Friend, (and then a Reader will be Ready enough to believe it, the more ready, for her not owning it, or being blind to it herself) than to think *her self* that she is.[26]

Yet, for all their apparent differences, the above statements are not, I think, incompatible. In the former, Richardson expresses his authorial intention in the creation of his character; in the latter, he takes a larger view of how the novel will tend to be read. The second statement is indeed a kind of a blueprint for the stages through which a reader can be said to pass in arriving at the conclusion that Clarissa is unconsciously in love with Lovelace. We start by reading her own assertion that she is not in love and acknowledging some reason for that assertion ("his too well-known Character consider'd"). We are then prompted to question this assertion owing to the assumptions of other characters, each of whom has a conventional reason to believe that Clarissa's "heart is not free": Anna Howe is convinced that Clarissa is in love based on Lovelace's superior qualities; Clarissa's family is convinced based on her unwillingness to accept their favored suitor, Solmes; Lovelace is convinced based on what he knows of the self-protective wiles of women. All of these characters base their assumptions on the idea that Clarissa is willfully hiding her love, that she does not mean what she says. This is where they are unconvincing, for the character that we associate with this heroine does not accommodate a lack of candor.[27] In *Pamela*, it was easy for us to understand the gap between the heroine's professed feelings and the final outcome as the result of a kind of hypocrisy. That novel permitted us to accept the premise that prudence and hypocrisy are inseparable in society. Yet because Clarissa is a character devoted not to integration into an open lineage society but to integration into a closed family ideal (an integration in which prudence does not appear to carry functional weight), it becomes impossible for the reader to accept that duplicity or guile or self-protection might motivate her actions. Thus, to preserve Clarissa's candor and yet to grant her desire for Lovelace, we arrive at the psychological reading that reconciles the professed feelings and the attributed ones in the form of a divided mind—a mind blind to itself, unconsciously in love.

Admittedly, the psychological reading is something that the novel must in some way be held responsible for, and Richardson, as I have already noted, predicted that we would psychologize his heroine and does so himself. But again, through the footnotes added later, and in the Postscript to the novel, he also appears to warn the reader to be wary of such response:

> [T]ake the word "love" in the gentlest and most honourable sense, it would have been thought by some highly improbable, that Clarissa should have been able to shew such a command of her person, as makes so distinguishing a part of her character, had she been as violently in love, as certain warm and fierce spirits would have had her to be. (4:559)

Richardson's comments here reflect the double sense that Clarissa should be taken at her word *and* that she should be attributed meaning and motives that exceed her words and actions.

In the changing emphasis that emerges in Richardson's instructions concerning his heroine, we can see that he is caught between being the author of his work and being yet another reader, made subject to the mystique of his heroine and already conditioned by the new thing he has brought into being. As for us, as modern readers, we have also been exposed to Clarissa's destiny, if not by literally knowing her fate before we read, at least by having been made subject to some kind of knowledge of it through our place in post-Richardsonian and, indeed, post-Freudian families. Thus, we cannot simulate an innocence that our position in culture must deny us. Still, I would like to suggest that by reading the novel with an eye on our own ideological conditioning we can understand its dynamic and realize that the novel is more about the *making* of psychological reading and psychological character than it is a psychological text with a heroine driven by her unconscious. For the purpose of demonstrating this, I should like to draw an artificial distinction: between the effect of the novel *as* we read it (pretending, that is, that we were reading outside of a contemporary ideological nexus) and the effect of the novel *after* we have read it. I will attempt to explain, through a family systems analysis, why a psychological approach to the novel and its characters is initially inappropriate, and how the novel leads us to assume this approach retrospectively.

Evidence for Clarissa's initial, unpsychological response can be found if we analyze the nature of her oscillating behavior in respect to Lovelace and her family. When she attempts to elucidate her feelings for her aristocratic suitor, she resorts to conditional explanations. To Mrs. Norton: "I will own to you, *that once I could have loved him—ungrateful man! had he permitted me to love him, I once could have loved him*" (3:345). And more tellingly still (since it is earlier in the action, before Lovelace has committed his irremediable crime), to Anna Howe: "one might be driven, by violent measures, step by step as it were, into something that might be called—I don't know what to call it—a *conditional kind of liking,* or so" (1:135). In the second statement, Clarissa has not yet hardened into opposition to Lovelace, and the movement of the sentence seems identical to the movement of response in its subject: Clarissa is driven not by powerful instincts within herself but by external "violent measures" (those measures on the part of her family that attempt to force her into marriage with the odious Solmes) to embrace a position of "conditional liking" for Lovelace. But the phrase also suggests that some other external force is present to force her back in the other direction. Indeed, in her very next letter to Anna Howe she refers, in what seems to be the complement to "conditional liking," to a "conditional willingness to give up Mr. Lovelace" to win "favour" with her family (1:136). What we have is an oscillation of her response as the direct result of external influence—of feeling transforming itself according to the conditions of the moment as dictated by her family. It is this oscillation that keeps Clarissa involved in a correspondence with Lovelace, continually breaking off and reaffirming the connection as her feeling for the respondent ebbs and flows with the quality of family pressure. It is just this oscillation that leads her to her fateful meeting with Lovelace in the garden and her subsequent elopement with him. Her need to disabuse him of her earlier professed willingness to leave her father's house combined with her fear that her father will discover them together (a fear that Lovelace exploits) give him the leverage necessary to carry her away.

But what, one must ask, are the conditions that differentiate an oscillating response from a response with unconscious content? Why is Clarissa's ambivalence initially comprehensible as a surface rather than a deep response? To answer this, we need to begin by analyzing the pattern of the characters' responses in the novel. What we find are a series of repetitive interactions—a kind of dance[28]—that Clarissa and her family perform as a function of their familial roles. Significantly, these roles are superficially reflective of older functions of family life—of a patrilineal ordering within an open lineage family system. Thus, Clarissa's father is the titular authority of the family who lays down laws. Her mother is the family go-between who acts as intermediary in the communication of the father's laws to the children (an elaboration of her role as exchange object). Clarissa's brother is the representative of the line of inheritance: he performs the role of social as well as historical emissary for the family in the world and supplies the father with information necessary for the framing of laws and the maintenance of authority. Finally, Clarissa's older sister is the representative of hierarchy *within* the family; she supports the brother's emissarial role and, as the female expected to marry first, takes priority in evaluating outsiders who seek admission to the family.

Within this family role topography, Clarissa is left to inhabit the role where power and self-definition are formally absent. As female and youngest child, her job is to provide other family members with power and self-definition through her own lack of status. In accordance with this role, she is supremely "good"—initially suggesting that she is humble, self-sacrificing, and self-effacing—in short, good in the service of others. As Clarissa explains to her friend: "They have all an absolute dependence upon what they suppose to be a meekness in my temper ... that the regard I have for my reputation and my principles, will bring me *round to my duty*—that's the expression" (1: 37). In a static system, Clarissa's role would indeed serve this end by being a fixed point in reference to which the role identities of the other characters could be perpetually reinforced. However, in a dynamic system (a system based on feedback), the continual use of Clarissa to strengthen the role identity of others becomes an escalating process. The extreme virtue associated with the daughter's role is relentlessly upheld in conjunction with the other family members' relentless performance of their roles. As a result, her role, originally the site of pliancy, becomes a locus of resistance, powerful in its own right.[29] The unassuming and self-effacing Clarissa is, through the very practice of her superior qualities, brought into relief. In Anna

Howe's words, she is "pushed into a blaze." It is this effect that Clarissa's sister describes with such bitterness:

> How often . . . have I and my brother been talking upon a subject, and had everybody's attention till *you* came in with your bewitching *meek* pride and *humble* significance; and then have we either been stopped by references to Miss Clary's opinion, forsooth; or been forced to stop ourselves, or must have talked on unattended to by everybody. (1:216)

As Arabella's hostile attitude demonstrates, once Clarissa's role becomes too well performed, it acquires a significance apart from those whom it was meant to serve. And where Clarissa ceases to serve her family, she can only antagonize them. Thus their love for her comes to alternate with resentment of her. This is the source of their ambivalence toward her—of a "pure" ambivalence, since it is not the result of something repressed but of an oscillation of response toward an object that is both yielding and assertive.[30] The novel records how this ambivalence, once generated, becomes self-propagating. The family's ambivalence toward Clarissa generates her ambivalence toward them, and this leads to her ambivalence toward Lovelace whom she sees by turns as a protector and as a seducer, depending upon which aspect of her family's response is most present for her. The duplicity of Lovelace's behavior is compatible with her oscillating response to her family, accommodating her need to shift back and forth between positions of conditional liking and distrust. The uncertainty concerning his intentions, in short, makes the relationship useful to her, and it is this uncertainty that she continually invokes and keeps alive: "If he has a design by this conduct . . . [she explains to Anna Howe] and were I to be sure of it, [I] should hate him, if possible, worse than I do Solmes" (1:124).[31]

Within this context, we can see how Lovelace's role in the novel serves to hasten a destructive process inherent in a family system in which a stabilizing dynamic has not yet been developed. Solmes, the man whom the Harlowes would have their daughter marry, is the embodiment of their will and values and represents a means of reproducing the family without having to alter familial roles. Lovelace, by contrast, represents a potential menace to family structure since, were he to marry Clarissa, he would elevate her to a higher class and thwart the Harlowes in their drive to define themselves at her expense.[32] However, Lovelace only becomes a genuine threat to the members of Clarissa's family when their pursuit of role-definition forces her into elopement with him.

By focusing Clarissa's ambivalence and thereby providing fuel for her family's ambivalence toward her, Lovelace simply feeds an escalating spiral of complementary behavior between the heroine and her family: Clarissa behaves like the angelic victim her role requires, while the Harlowes assert the rights of their roles. Their rigidity motivates her to behave even more like a victim, which inspires an increase in their rigidity, and so on, in escalating fashion. Ultimately, Clarissa's role as victim gets expressed in her representation as a weak, emaciated body—an anorectic body—that finally can no longer support life. Although the physician who attends her in the end prods her to eat "lest you should starve yourself," Clarissa makes it clear that she is not acting out of willfulness: "What, sir . . . can I do? I have no appetite. Nothing you call nourishing will stay on my stomach" (4:13). Her condition is the result of her exaggeratedly role-appropriate response to her family's equally exaggerated role-appropriate behavior. Together, they move the novel to its inevitable conclusion: the self-sacrifice/victimization of Clarissa for/by the family.[33]

Clarissa's death, so arduously arrived at and so elaborately prepared for, is a means of dramatizing not an individual death so much as the end of one family idea and the birth of another capable of preventing such deaths in the future. Clarissa's death destroys the Harlowes' former life as a family, but it also destroys the ambivalence that had set the destructive cycle in motion. What replaces ambivalence is familial guilt, the shared consciousness of a role in the death of a daughter. This new shared consciousness of guilt will now inform all subsequent family interaction:

These intelligences and recollections were perpetual subjects of recrimination to them: heightened their anguish for the loss of a child who was the glory of their family; and not seldom made them shun each other (at the times they were accustomed to meet together in the family way), that they might avoid the mutual reproaches of eyes that spoke when tongues were silent—their stings also sharpened by time; what an unhappy family was this family! (4:534)

The creation of this shared consciousness of guilt—this familial con-science—involves the introduction of depth—of an unconscious—into the Harlowe family. It allows the family to exist as a family even when dispersed and hostile toward each other. Prior to Clarissa's death, the Harlowes had been ambivalent toward their daughter: they hated her for the qualities of her role that threatened their roles within the family but, like her grandfather and like Lovelace, they alternately loved her too for these very qualities, which allowed them to define themselves. With Clarissa's death, the shifting pattern of response that constituted their ambivalence is stopped. Their now conscious response to the dead Clarissa is one of love, but we must suspect (indeed, we know through reference to what came before) that hostility has been substituted for or, in Freud's terms, repressed. The Harlowes can now become the amalgam of their hateful and their loving responses to their daughter, for the novel has led us to a place where hate and love can finally be imagined to exist, not alter-nately, but simultaneously, in the concept of a guilty mind—a mind divided between conscious and unconscious impulses. Similarly, Clarissa becomes for her family and for the reader the sum total of what she has told about herself and what others have told about her. This fixed subject, like the coffin with its elaborate emblems that she prepares to house her body in death, is now available for interpreta-tion and becomes a receptacle for her family's and our projected meanings. What had originally made Clarissa so elusive was her per-fect candor—the sense in which her language always corresponded to her immediate feelings. In death, she becomes elusive in a differ-ent way, through an opposite maneuver whereby her meaning be-comes overdetermined, perpetually unavailable in its totality.

This shift from Clarissa as part of a patterned surface to Clarissa as a whole whose depths are lost from view can be illustrated if we consider Lovelace's reaction to her following the rape from two van-tage points: from the point directly following the rape's occurrence in the novel, and from the retrospective point, after the principal events of the novel are over, when Clarissa is dead. From the first of these vantage points, Clarissa's situation and state of mind seem stark and unambiguous. Lovelace, having long sought to act as analyst to Clarissa—to uncover what he believes to be her hidden desire for him—has now admitted defeat, and the nature of his defeat seems clear: "And now, Belford [he confesses to his friend], I can go no farther. The affair is over. Clarissa lives" (3:196). At this juncture in the book, Lovelace's words indicate that his ultimate attempt to "uncover" Clarissa has failed because there is nothing to uncover. In seeming to peel away the layers of Clarissa's public self, both he and the reader find only more of the same. After a brief pause in Clarissa's correspondence following the rape, the letters continue, first in the form of mad scraps and finally becoming the coherent response of their author to her situation. What we see in this brief stumble and recuperation is a settling of the character into a linear trajectory as ambivalence is replaced by fixed response. Now that Lovelace has proven malevolent rather than protective and now that Clarissa perceives herself as definitively cut off from her family, there is no further reason for her to oscillate in her feelings. She can become utterly steadfast in her determination to refuse and evade Lovelace. In the famous penknife scene in which she threatens to destroy herself rather than endure his advances, this now unwavering, "fixed" opposition is dramatized. However, the shift from alternating to fixed response does not prevent both responses from being a matter of surface—of corresponding completely to external sources of influence. Clarissa's professed scorn for Lovelace following the rape cannot be construed as hiding an unconscious desire for him.

After her death, however, Clarissa's motives seem retrospectively to "thicken." When, in a letter written just prior to her death, she informs Lovelace that she is "setting out with all diligence for my father's house" where Lovelace "may possibly in time see me" (4:157)—a spiritual reference that Lovelace interprets literally as an invitation to visit her at Harlowe Place—she engages, for the first time, in double entendre. The letter anticipates what is in store not only for Lovelace but also for Clarissa's family and the reader; for her death will catalyze a "deeper" reading for everything that came before—doubling it, as it were. Thus, looked upon in retrospect following her death, Lovelace's declaration that he could "go no farther" no longer carries the "flat" meaning that it had before her death: that Clarissa simply did not desire him. Any interpretation of what she felt or did not feel has become presumptuous, a desecration of that precious selfhood that we now associate with the lost Clarissa.[34] Mrs. Harlowe relays this new sense of ineffability, of depth, associated with her daughter in death: "[Y]ou know not what a child I have lost! [she laments] Then in a lower voice, And *how* lost!—That it is that makes the loss insupportable" (4:393). These lines refer both to the irreparable quality of Clarissa's absence, which imbues her remembered person with unfathomable depths of meaning, and to the guilty memory that can re-create a new kind of family coherence, itself an ineffable bond, based on "insupportable" (and unutterable) grief around her absence. In her earlier elusiveness Clarissa escaped the family; in her present elusiveness, she becomes its foundation, the cohesive and coercive power of the family—in short, its unconscious.

* * *

Clarissa can be called literature's original anorectic daughter, and her story, a primal myth for the emergence of the "anorexia syndrome" for the family. As a result of her family's scapegoating, she is driven to self-starvation; by dying, she generates guilt that, had it existed earlier, would have checked her family's scapegoating impulses and prevented her death. The novel dramatizes what family therapists have demonstrated through their clinical research, namely that one motive in scapegoating is a need to conventionalize and strengthen the role identity of other family members and to repress external threats to the family; but that scapegoating unchecked is degenerative.[35] *Clarissa* is about the value of scapegoating but also about the need to check it through the generation of guilt. With the heroine's death, the least powerful member of the family gains power (albeit in death), and the most powerful family members have their power curtailed. The family system stabilizes itself, and the characters gain access to a psychology that complicates and "deepens" conventional role assignments. In its concern with a balancing of opposing forces, Richardson's story can be compared to Freud's story in *Totem and Taboo,* which postulates the origin of individual conscience as the result of the murder of a "primal father." Freud's narrative of murder and subsequent guilt, written in the style of fictional melodrama, is used to explain the origin of id and superego, which, in the "healthy" mind, according to Freud, exist as checks on each other.[36] The difference between Richardson's story and Freud's lies essentially in the focus of control. In Freud's story, the individual ego undergoes repression and, in so doing, becomes the psychological, the divided, self. In Richardson's story, the family as a system of mutually defining role identities is placed under restraint—undergoes a kind of repression—and, as a by-product, creates psychological selves for its members. It would appear that Richardson recognized that the family ideal that his society had embraced depended upon an underlying dynamic to support it and that this new family would need to find its temporary stability in a controlled dynamic focused on the daughter's role.

It must be said in concluding this chapter that *Clarissa* is ultimately about the forging of this dynamic in a hypothetical sense only. In the end, the dynamic is to be inferred based on what went wrong; it is postulated on an absence: the dead Clarissa. This allows Richardson to introduce role assignments associated with a patrilineal, open lineage family structure without ever having to revise them. Thus, throughout the novel, the family gets equated with a father who is not a substantive presence and who corresponds more to abstract notions of authority than to the more concrete notions of paternal presence that would begin to emerge as the ideology of the nuclear family became more entrenched. Likewise, Clarissa's brother James remains throughout a character defined by a genealogical imperative. Although both father and son are burdened with remorse following the heroine's death, because Clarissa is no longer there to be reckoned with, the scapegoating-guilt dynamic is never applied: we never see the adjustments in actual behavior that the nuclear family will require in order to achieve relative closure and equilibrium. For this, we must move forward in time. The next chapter will look at Jane Austen's *Mansfield Park*. In this novel, the new interactive dynamic *is* applied—if in simplified terms—to a family in which the regulating daughter is alive or at least less dead than Clarissa.

CHAPTER 3

Mansfield Park: Stabilization

Mansfield Park is Jane Austen's one novel in which the life of the family takes precedence over the life of the individual. Other Austen heroines spring into relief against the background of their families, but Fanny Price recedes. She shrinks, clings, and hides herself. Her "favorite indulgence" is "of being suffered to sit silent and unattended to."[1] She is stubbornly a part and not a whole. Lionel Trilling, among the first and most eloquent critics to recognize that Austen's concerns in this novel are different from those in her other novels, noted a resemblance between Clarissa Harlowe and Fanny Price.[2] Yet his conclusion that Clarissa and Fanny are in the mold of traditional Christian heroines ignores the historically determined family context within which these heroines acquire their value.

Historians have generally noted that the rise of the nuclear family was accompanied by a spiritualization of the home. Lawrence Stone explains, for example, that by the seventeenth century matrimony began to be imbued with the holiness once reserved for celibacy. The association of domestic life with spiritual refuge (an association that reached its apotheosis during the Victorian period) helped enforce the separation of private and public space and of expressive and instrumental function that assured the efficient operation of a competitive industrial economy. The family became the safe harbor, the place of spiritual nurturance, in counterpoint to the competitiveness and isolation of the workplace.[3]

Given the different, or rather the more partitioned, context in which spiritual ideas came to be located, the very nature of religious experience had to be affected. Philippe Ariès refers to the replacement of the sacred or eschatological aspect of religion by the moral aspect.[4] Family theorists Ivan Boszormenyi-Nagy and Geraldine M. Spark describe a more fundamental shift in the form and content of

religious feeling, arguing that to fill a vacuum produced by the loss
of a sense of divine justice, the family produced its own version of
Christian accountability in the form of a family "justice system"—
what they describe as a ledger of family debts and credits in which
"family debts function like a kind of 'original sin.'"[5] I have argued a
similar point with regard to Richardson's novel, *Clarissa*. That novel
is about the creation of a family justice system to replace a lost faith
in family lineage and divine historical guidance. Scapegoated to death
by her family, Clarissa becomes the source of a radical "debt" and
brings into being the greatest possible attempt at restitution through
guilt. In her role as martyr to the family, therefore, Clarissa enacts a
replacement of and not (as Trilling claims) a return to Christian belief
and values.[6] Moreover, the dynamic of scapegoating and guilt by
which Clarissa acquires meaning for the Harlowe family is the same
dynamic that would provide the domestic novel—the dominant literary genre of the nineteenth century—with a replacement for the
anchor of belief that gave previous literary genres their unity and
persuasive power. Tony Tanner, in examining the theme of adultery
in the novel, has observed that what "holds the great bourgeois novel
together" is "a tension between law and sympathy" toward the female's act of transgression.[7] If we pursue the ideological and psychological implications of his terminology we find that this coincides
with the scapegoating-guilt dynamic: "law," understood as patriarchal
law, scapegoats the female, and "sympathy" arises from the internalized guilt that the sternness of patriarchal law engenders in those who
wield it. In most nineteenth-century novels, the triumph of law or the
triumph of sympathy tips the balance to the tragic or to the conventional happy ending. In *Mansfield Park*, however, a perfect balancing
of these two forces produces a utopic ending that sets it apart from
other novels of the century.

* * *

Jane Austen began work on *Mansfield Park* in 1811, and the novel
was published soon after its completion in 1814. It is the fourth of
Austen's six completed novels and the first novel following her hiatus
from novel-writing, a period when, according to a recent biographer,
she emerged from a state of loneliness and depression with "a re-
newed sense of equanimity and stability."[8] It was also a period when

she existed in what must have appeared to her to be a fixed relationship to her family. In 1807, the last of her five brothers had married.[9] This meant that each had a household of his own that Jane and her also unmarried sister Cassandra could take turns visiting.

Further reinforcing her place in the family was the death in 1809 of her brother Edward's wife. He was left with eleven children, and this precipitated the move of Jane, Cassandra, and their mother to a cottage in Chawton, part of Edward's property and near his estate. Edward never remarried, and his mother and sisters assumed a kind of composite wifely role in relation to him. They had left Bath, which Jane Austen had detested, for Southampton following Mr. Austen's death a year or so earlier, but the move to Chawton seems to have had a decidedly settling effect on the author. Circumstances had arranged things in a remarkably felicitous way for a woman in Jane Austen's position. She now had a functional relation to her brother's family and need not feel herself on sufferance as his tenant. By the same token, her position did not require the degree of investment and responsibility that being an actual wife and mother would have entailed. She could also visit her other brothers and their families when she chose. It was a situation that seems to have given Austen the security and the freedom she needed to imagine a family ideal of the kind she depicts in *Mansfield Park*.

Not only does *Mansfield Park* mark a nodal point in Austen's personal history, but it also is a significant moment in the history of the novel. It stands as a kind of pure derivative of Richardson's *Clarissa* in its treatment of the dynamics of family life. If Clarissa plays Christ to the modern family, Fanny can be called her most adept imitator, one whose role is both less extreme and more deeply recessed in the family. Fanny is more colorless than Clarissa because, unlike her predecessor, she need not go "all the way"—her role as scapegoat has been integrated into a family interactive structure that knows how to check itself. Richardson's myth of the scapegoated heroine has been adopted in *Mansfield Park* not to produce a violent conclusion like that of *Clarissa*, but to prevent just such a conclusion.

In this chapter I will examine how Jane Austen in *Mansfield Park* fashioned a model of family life in perfect equilibrium. Her closing vision of the Bertram family as sealed and immutable is what the nuclear family, insofar as it defines itself as a closed system, aspires to be. The history of the nineteenth-century family and of the nine-

teenth-century novel is, I believe, a struggle to achieve this equilibrium. *Mansfield Park* is that unique moment in Austen's canon and
arguably in the literature of the century when such an equilibrium is
(and indeed, could be) successfully imagined.

*   *   *

Fanny Price is brought to Mansfield Park at the beginning of the
novel as the result of a transaction between the Bertrams and the
Prices. Sir Thomas and Lady Bertram have offered to "undertake the
care" of a child from the "large and still increasing" brood of Lady
Bertram's poor, overburdened sister, Frances Price, who had long
ago married beneath her and moved from the neighborhood. The
offer is a gesture of reconciliation between households that had been
estranged for many years. It is conducted in writing, with Mrs. Norris, the energetic, intrusive sister, serving as epistolary intermediary.
She stipulates that the eldest Price daughter be the object of negotiation (to Mrs. Price's surprise "that a girl should be fixed on, when
she had so many fine boys" [48]). In all of these particulars, the
introduction of Fanny into the Bertram household bears comparison
to a marriage transaction as Lévi-Strauss describes its function in the
creation of an elementary kinship system. As already discussed, the
exchange of women in marriage can be understood as the basic transaction of patriarchal culture, the means by which a structured relationship between families was established, opening each family to a
wider community.

However, there are also important differences between the transaction that begins *Mansfield Park* and the one described by Lévi-
Strauss's model. The transaction in Austen's novel, while it involves
the relocation of a female, is an inversion of the lateral and historical
extension created through elementary kinship exchange. Although
Fanny is sent to live with virtual strangers, she nonetheless goes from
her mother's house to her aunt's and, in this sense, is sent not *across*
families but *within* her own family. She is also a child of ten, not a
marriageable young woman, at the time of the transaction, and she
enters the Bertram family under the express admonition that a marriage *not* take place. (When Sir Thomas voices concern about the
danger "of cousins in love, &c," Mrs. Norris assures him that the
prohibition of incest will operate to prevent a marriage of cousins

who have lived together as children. "It is morally impossible" [44], she says.)[10]

As it happens, of course, Mrs. Norris's pronouncement concerning the impossibility of a marriage between cousins is a prophecy in reverse. She does not foresee a new affective order for the family in which a marriage between cousins, far from being impossible, will perform a much-needed structural role. To understand the structural role of incest in this novel, it is helpful to refer to Lévi-Strauss's analysis of the incest prohibition in primitive society as the point "where nature transcends itself." The prohibition, he explains, initiates "the formation of a new and more complex type of structure [that] is superimposed upon the simpler structures of physical life through integration."[11] This is the first-order change, the premise that underlies patriarchal civilization. *Mansfield Park* dramatizes the application of the next, the second-order, leap in structuration, the blueprint for which I have already discussed in *Clarissa*. Fanny's move from her mother's house to her aunt's is an exchange occurring *within* the family, and it superimposes upon the first-order change that Lévi-Strauss describes a second-order change: a new level of complexity through integration. The order based on the prohibition of incest thus yields to a newer order in which incest is structured into family relations.

Georges Bataille has written that "the taboo does not alter the violence of sexual activity, but for disciplined mankind it opens a door closed to animal nature, namely, the transgression of the law."[12] The taboo, in other words, links desire to transgression. Fanny enters the Bertram family under terms that suggest both marriage and its prohibition—a set of contradictory injunctions that recalls the dynamic of the Oedipus complex. This dynamic will, in fact, produce Fanny's desire and anchor her securely to the family. The Bertrams, for their part, will discover that the dynamic of scapegoating of and guilt toward Fanny as the weakest, most unassertive family member ultimately becomes necessary to the stability of their life as a family. As we shall see, the personal dynamic and the family dynamic interlock to reinforce each other.

Fanny's move from her mother's house to her aunt's is also a move from one style of family life to another. The Prices are a large, loosely knit family characterized by conventional role requirements and a porous connection with society. Life in the Price household is noisy, disorderly, and continually disrupted as members leave and return, and as messages from the outside are sent and received. Mr. Price has authority not in himself (he is drunken and largely absent) but in his *title* as father. His place at the domestic hearth is as often occupied by one of his cronies as by himself—all are privileged in a limited sort of way by simple reason of age and sex. In the Price family, Fanny's role is also defined according to traditional conventions: as eldest daughter, she serves as mentor to the younger children and helps with the chores. Yet her usefulness does not prevent her mother from valuing only the male children (and, predictably, favoring the eldest son). When Fanny returns to Portsmouth after her long absence, she finds that her mother's interest in her is short-lived. "The instinct of nature was soon satisfied," explains the narrator, and Mrs. Price's attachment "had no other source" (382).

As this maternal response demonstrates, "the instinct of nature" would have little binding power in the Price family were it not for the conventional roles by which family members come to know and relate to each other—and marriage supplies the essential structural foundation for the development of these roles. Furthermore, were daughters not to marry (and sons go off to sea), caring for so many lives would be too great a burden for a harried, incompetent Mrs. Price and a drunken, irresponsible Mr. Price, whose personal inadequacies become calamitous on a small income. By turning their daughter over to others, the Prices therefore gain the practical advantages of a marriage transaction: they lighten the daily load of familial responsibility. At the same time, however, by exchanging Fanny *within* the family rather than waiting to forge a link with a new family, they undermine the elementary kinship structures that make families like their own possible. In this sense, Fanny's passage from her mother's house to her aunt's is historically significant and expresses that shift in the nature of family life actually occurring at the time Austen wrote. The Bertrams, Fanny's new family (though really an extension of her old one), are the kind of insular and inbred (nuclear) family fated to replace outer-directed families like the Prices.

Superficially, wealth and social position are what separates the Bertrams from the Prices. At Mansfield Park the responsibilities of housekeeping and education lie with the servants and the governess, and the family members (with the exception of the father) are left

free to engage in less functional pursuits and to cultivate more orna-
mental personal accomplishments. In this context, the play that the
Bertram children stage during their father's absence is a form of
conspicuous consumption and a means of demonstrating the family's
separation from lower-class families like the Prices through what
Thorstein Veblen termed "vicarious leisure."[13] Yet what originates
in class difference also corresponds to more far-reaching changes in
the structure of the family as a social institution. Thus the play is not
only an expression of the vicarious leisure of upper-middle-class children, it also denotes the "surge of sentiment" that Edward Shorter
cites as responsible for the formation of the nuclear family itself.[14]
Although the artificial and unbridled emotion of the play is an example of sentiment lacking a suitable object, the affective tendencies
that the play celebrates (and carries in its wake among the actors)
nonetheless connect it to a more modern set of values. When Tom
Bertram asserts that he "can conceive of no greater harm or danger
to any of us in conversing in the elegant written language of some
respectable author than in chattering in words of our own" (151), he
recognizes a relative equivalence in the two discourses that suggests
an analogy between the play and his own life in a modern family.[15]

It is no wonder, then, that at Mansfield Park, Fanny's familial role
is substantially altered. Whereas at Portsmouth she occupied herself
through being useful, she now finds only the facsimile of useful
work: performing trivial messenger duties between the house and the
parsonage or holding Lady Bertram's yarn. Ultimately, it is not these
attempts at literal usefulness that bind her to the Bertram family but
the *relational* role she comes to perform among them—a role that,
given the closed system of Mansfield Park, favors the development
of affective ties. When she visits her original family toward the end
of the novel, she is less disturbed by their lack of affection for her
(this does not surprise her given her long separation from them) than
by their lack of "curiosity to know her better" (383)—the necessary
foundation for affection. It is not so much that time and distance
have brought about a shift in loyalties, but that her new family, by
virtue of its interactive structure, induces emotional loyalty where her
original family, with its easily permeable surface relationships, does
not: "in her uncle's house there would have been a consideration of
times and seasons, a regulation of subject, a propriety, an attention
toward every body which there was not here" (376).[16]

The differences between the Bertrams and the Prices thus have implications that transcend the differences in economic and class status that separate them (although the development of a more modern family structure can be seen to issue out of conditions associated with wealth and privilege). The Prices, though occupying a lower socioeconomic position, still conform to the traditional conventions of title and status; the Bertrams, though still technically linked to primogeniture, are in the process of establishing a new, internalized "justice system." They operate according to the terms that Fred Weinstein and Gerald M. Platt have defined as characteristic of the nuclear family: "the ability to manipulate is based not only on one's legitimate status in the system but on one's special relationships to other members of the system."[17] Thus, Sir Thomas looks to Edmund, his younger but more judicious son, whenever a question of judgment arises. We see these new values expressed by Fanny herself who, in opposition to Mary Crawford's insistence that "Mr. Bertram" sounds well, counters with her preference for the proper name:

> To me, the sound of *Mr.* Bertram is so cold and nothing-meaning—so entirely without warmth or character!—it just stands for a gentleman, and that's all. But there is nobleness in the name of Edmund. It is a name of heroism and renown—of kings, princes, and knights; and seems to breathe the spirit of chivalry and warm affections. (224)

Although her language suggests nostalgia for an imagined past, Fanny's preference really places her in advance of Mary, for it connects her to the affective world of individual and familial as opposed to social relations, and denotes a refusal to accept the traditional hierarchy by which the eldest son is favored (since "Mr." and "Miss" affixed to the last name were reserved for eldest children). Significantly, Maria—"Miss Bertram"—will be literally canceled from the family and replaced by Fanny despite the conventional precedence she holds as eldest daughter, and Tom—"Mr. Bertram"—will be thematically canceled from the novel by the very persistence with which his position and his life are preserved without being infused with value. Not only will Tom Bertram's illness lack any element of heroism or drama, but his recovery will rob him of even the limited distinction of dying and giving value to the status of eldest son by bestowing it upon his younger brother.

The valorization of younger over eldest children reflects a general tendency in this novel to favor the displacement of a linear historical model of the family expressed through blood and inheritance by a systems model expressed through personal interaction. Where the former would necessarily concern itself with the individual as the latest in an evolutionary line (in *Pride and Prejudice,* for example, this concern persists insofar as Elizabeth and Darcy can be viewed as the best "stock" available from their respective classes), the latter conceives of the individual as part of a system, and hence gaining value only in relation to others (thus Fanny Price's "price" goes up as the novel progresses and her context of relations changes). Ruth Bernard Yeazell has similarly observed that the novel's impulse is to supplant what she calls "temporal ordering" with "spatial frameworks," but she finds in this drive to deny history a resemblance to a pre-Christian tradition, to "the domestic religion of ancient Rome."[18] When viewed within the context of a history of the family, however, the spatial frameworks that Yeazell notes describe a relational system that, far from being ancient, is decidedly modern.

Indeed, throughout the novel, Austen calls our attention to the internal laws that govern the Bertram family system, and these laws bear comparison with the laws (or "norms" as they are often referred to by family therapists) that have been discerned in modern nuclear families struggling to maintain their equilibrium as relatively closed systems. When Julia accompanies Maria on her marriage trip, we are told that there opened "a chasm which required some time to fill up. The family circle became greatly contracted" (218). In referring to Edmund's imminent taking of orders and settlement at Thornton Lacey, Sir Thomas notes that "his going though only eight miles, will be an unwelcome contraction of our family circle" (255). Edmund Bertram's primary objection to the theatricals, and the spur that makes him agree to take part, is the fear that an outsider will be asked to join the group and be "domesticated among us—authorized to come at all hours—and placed suddenly on a footing which must do away all restraints" (175). His object, he explains, is "to confine the representation within a much smaller circle than they are now in the high road for" (176). Edmund understands that the family's successful operation depends upon restraints related both to the limited number of members and to the patterned quality of their interaction. What he fails to see is how profoundly the family circle has been disrupted already, first through his father's absence, and then, in an attempt to fill that void, through the introduction of the Crawfords. Similarly, when Sir Thomas hears of Maria's engagement, he fails to deduce its negative effects. Instead, he rationalizes his daughter's impending marriage as a gain for the family:

> A well-disposed young woman, who did not marry for love, was in general but the more attached to her own family, and the nearness of Southerton to Mansfield must naturally hold out the greatest temptation, and would, in all probability, be a continual supply of the most amiable and innocent enjoyments. (215)

Like Edmund in the case of the play, Sir Thomas views the family's continued integrity with too much complacency; he can justify Maria's marriage as being, not the loss of a daughter, but the gain of a strengthened and enriched family system. But an introduction of new material like that represented by either the Rushworths or the Crawfords can only be disruptive, since it fails to take into account the interactive structure of the family for which any change must have important consequences. No change, in other words, is "amiable and innocent."

If life at Mansfield Park is experiencing disruption, however, it is also struggling to establish equilibrium. The mistakes in judgment and interpretation on the part of Edmund and his father are like the random attempts at combination and exchange of any unstable system. They reflect a movement through trial and error toward the goal of stability. Thus every change that affects the family gives rise to a counteraction and, as that action fails to establish the desired balance, another alternative is sought: Sir Thomas's trip to the West Indies leads to the introduction of the Crawfords to the family; his return results in their temporary expulsion and the marriage of Maria to Rushworth; this leads to the absence of the daughters (Julia accompanies Maria on her marriage trip), brings Fanny into prominence, and sets in motion the courtship of Fanny by Henry Crawford; Fanny's rejection of Crawford then precipitates his return to Maria and their elopement, which provokes the rupture of Edmund and

Mary, which leads finally to the union of Edmund and Fanny—the point at which the family—and the novel—stops, having achieved its goal of stability.

The drive to achieve the stability of a closed system is a drive to "improve" the family. Unlike the superficial attempts at landscape improvement that the novel presents as the latest fad among families of the period, this familial improvement is not superficial or faddish but occurs on a deep structural level. Mary Crawford, who *is* superficial and faddish but at bottom thinks patrilineally, is on the wrong track when she declares that "every generation has its improvements" (115). On the contrary, familial improvement in *Mansfield Park* can be viewed as a kind of *relational* eugenics that focuses on the quality of the interactive bond rather than the quality of the bloodline. What is sought is a core dynamic that is perfectly controlled and supremely durable. The achievement of this stable dynamic is a slow, painful process as Fanny Price is assimilated to the Bertram family system.

Fanny is first introduced into the Bertram family as if to mark her exclusion from it. Her attic room, her sitting room without a fire, and her neglect and abuse at the hands of family members are constant reminders to her that she is, in Mrs. Norris's words, "the lowest and the last" (232). Nor is this role simply imposed upon her. When Fanny first meets her new family, she graphically acts out the part of outsider: "Afraid of every body, ashamed of herself...she knew not how to look up and could scarcely speak to be heard, or without crying" (50). Yet by virtue of her outsider status, Fanny immediately establishes a role for herself in respect to the Bertram family. "Small of her age," "exceedingly timid and shy," her difference from her "well-grown," "forward" cousins places their privilege and their handsomeness into relief. This difference of person and address is the starting point from which other, more subtle differences can be discerned and cultivated. It soon follows that she becomes the means by which the Bertram girls can measure their accomplishments, Mrs. Norris can express her ingenuity, Lady Bertram can refine her lethargy and dependence, and Edmund can practice the moral theories of his chosen vocation. At the same time that she helps define these individual identities, she also serves to define the family as a family. Where she is one and alone, they have an identity in combination;

where she has been torn from her relations, they are secure in each other and rooted in their home. In this sense, Fanny's failure to fit in at Mansfield Park is in itself a functional role and makes her valuable to the Bertrams from the outset. What remains for us to discover is a value for *her*. How does she profit from her role in this family?

What Fanny gains from her position in the Bertram family becomes apparent when we examine her relationship with Edmund. Early on, when Edmund comes across her sobbing on the attic stairs, she forms the connection that will sustain her for most of the novel. From this moment, Edmund supplies one part of the dynamic by which she will be anchored to Mansfield Park: he feels guilty for his family's part in neglecting and exploiting her. In short, he seems to have a sense of the "debt" incurred by his family in relation to Fanny and strives to make up the balance. However, it also must be said that his attentions are usually short-lived and are never really enough to prevent others from continuing to treat her badly. Moreover, when Mary Crawford appears on the scene, Edmund ceases to act solely to reduce the family debt in relation to Fanny; he now contributes to that debt and hence enacts the scapegoating-guilt dynamic in himself. The episode in which he lends Fanny's horse to Mary Crawford and forgets to return in time for his cousin's morning ride is a typical example. When he finally discovers that during their time away Fanny has been overtaxed by her aunts and has developed a headache, his guilt is immediate: "Vexed as Edmund was with his mother and aunt, he was still more angry with himself. His own forgetfulness of her was worse than anything which they had done. Nothing of this would have happened had she been properly considered" (103). Yet the guilt he feels does not prevent him from performing a similar act of thoughtlessness again. On a subsequent outing, he leaves Fanny alone on a bench while he and Mary take a leisurely stroll. His earlier guilt seems to function more as a payment for the right to scapegoat Fanny again than as a deterrent against the repetition of the crime.

Curiously, however, the dynamic in which Edmund makes Fanny suffer, then suffers guilt for her pain so that he can be free to make her suffer again (a pattern to which, as I have noted, other family members also contribute), proves to be precisely the pattern calculated to attach Fanny to the family. The narrator goes to some length to explain this:

[T]hough her motives had been often misunderstood, her feelings disregarded, and her comprehension under-valued; though she had known the pains of tyranny, of ridicule, and neglect, yet almost every recurrence of either had led to something consolatory; her aunt Bertram had spoken for her, or Miss Lee had been encouraging or what was yet more frequent or more dear—Edmund had been her champion and her friend—he had supported her cause, or explained her meaning, he had told her not to cry, or had given her some proof of affection which made her tears delightful—and the whole was now so blended together, so harmonized by distance, that every former affliction had its charm. (173–74)

As this passage makes clear, it is not pleasure alone, but pleasure as the consolation for pain that combines to produce the "charm" that binds Fanny to Mansfield Park. Thus, with each instance in which she is neglected by Edmund in favor of Mary Crawford, Fanny feels envy, and for each crumb of compensating attention she is overwhelmed with a surge of gratitude that acts to cancel the envy and balance her negative feeings. In the incident with her horse, for example, Edmund's "sudden change" from neglect to solicitude brings Fanny such joy that it "made her hardly know how to support herself" (104).

In keeping with this pattern, Fanny repeatedly finds her pleasure throughout the novel not in unconditional gratification but in something far more mixed. When asked by Sir Thomas to begin the dance given in her honor, she shrinks back: "The distinction was too great. It was treating her like her cousins!" (281). When offered a necklace from Mary Crawford's collection, she instinctively chooses the one that "Miss Crawford least wished to keep" (265); and when she inadvertently beats her brother at cards, her disappointment prompts Edmund's exclamation: "Poor Fanny! not allowed to cheat herself as she wishes!" (252). Even when Sir Thomas grants her her wish to breakfast with her brother on the morning of his leave-taking and then, against her inclination, invites Henry Crawford to join them, she cannot be disappointed. As the narrator explains, she "was more disposed to wonder and rejoice in having carried her point so far, than to repine at the counteraction which followed" (285).

At this point, a Freudian argument would postulate the psychic structure from which Fanny's masochistic behavior could be said to spring. An argument based on family systems theory, however, is concerned not with postulating deep structure but with analyzing its source in surface pattern: how Fanny's need to experience pain so as to savor consolation allows her to fit into the family and makes her increasingly valuable to its operation. As I have already noted, Fanny is initially "fixed" at Mansfield Park under conditions that at once suggest desire for something (marriage with her male cousins, resemblance to her female cousins) and assert the forbidden nature of such desire. Early in the novel, Sir Thomas makes plain these conditions to his sister-in-law in arranging to take Fanny into his home:

> There will be some difficulty in our way, Mrs. Norris . . . as to the distinction proper to be made between the girls as they grow up; how to preserve in the minds of my daughters the consciousness of what they are, without making them think too lowly of their cousin; and how, without depressing her spirits too far, to make her remember that she is not a Miss Bertram . . . . It is a point of great delicacy. (47)

The attitude toward the family that Fanny must be taught, according to Sir Thomas, is simply the mirror image of the family's attitude toward her. Both scapegoating and guilt on the part of the family with respect to Fanny, and desire and the injunction against desire in Fanny herself, are mutually reinforcing attitudes that assure a controlling balance. Little does Sir Thomas know at this point that his "delicate" idea will end by fashioning for him "the daughter that he wanted" (456) and will result in the usurpation of his natural daughters.

Mary Crawford perceives a paradox in Fanny's position when she observes that Fanny seems, socially speaking, neither "in" nor "out." But Mary's emphasis is wrong in assuming that the ultimate goal for Fanny lies in social rather than familial relationships (that she must move from being "in" to being "out"). As an outsider who nonetheless occupies a place in the Bertram family system, Fanny is both "out" and "in" at this point in the novel, but the direction in which her role tends (inconceivable to a social creature like Mary Crawford) is not toward the outside but toward the inside, through the forging of internal ties and the binding together of the family. The novel traces the conventionalization and assimilation of this outsider role to the point at which it becomes part of the central, internal dynamic of the family system, supplanting the priority of the natural daughters and eventually driving one of the daughters out of the system altogether. In this, the novel can be said to reverse the terms that we associate with the Cinderella story; for the stepdaughter eclipses the "legitimate" offspring. Although the nuclear family still assumes a basis in some kind of blood kinship, the ultimate concern of this family model lies not in the defense of blood at all costs, but in the preservation of the interactive patterns that have come to define the family as a family. As a system stabilized through a constructed interpersonal dynamic, the nuclear family is the beginning of the triumph of art over nature—of relationship taking predominance over blood.

For such a system to stabilize itself at Mansfield Park, Fanny and Sir Thomas, the weak and the powerful, the outsider and the insider, must achieve an interactive relationship. Prior to the father's return from the West Indies, Fanny is confined to the periphery of the family system, interacting with individual family members to strengthen their role identity, but not functioning within the family in a consistent way. But a relationship to the father must be forged for Fanny's place in the family system to take on comprehensive meaning.

Almost immediately upon his return, Sir Thomas's relationship to Fanny is placed in the foreground. For one thing, his sudden arrival fortuitously saves her the embarrassment of once again responding to pleas that she act in the play. This coincidence functions symbolically in the novel: she has lost her original champion, Edmund, to the sway of Mary Crawford, and the father will now replace the son as savior and protector. Sir Thomas, for his part, shows a new consideration for and awareness of Fanny upon his return. "'But where is Fanny?',"he demands after greeting his family, "'Why do not I see my little Fanny?'; and on perceiving her, came forward with a kindness which astonished and penetrated her, calling her his dear Fanny, kissing her affectionately, and observing with decided pleasure how much she was grown" (194). To her, we are told, "his manner seemed changed; his voice was quick from the agitation of joy, and all that had been awful in his dignity seemed lost in tenderness" (194). He asks about her family and comments upon her looks ("he was justified in his belief of her equal improvement in health and beauty"), and she in turn registers him: "when, on having courage to lift her eyes to his face, she saw that he was grown thinner and had the burnt, fagged, worn look of fatigue and a hot climate, every tender feeling was increased" (194–95). This scene of greeting signals the new interactive balance toward which the family will move for the remainder of the novel. There is a mutual acknowledgment on the part of Fanny and Sir Thomas of their roles as daughter and father while the conventional nature of these roles is undermined by new elements of awareness: hence the weak and yielding daughter is presented to Sir Thomas's eyes as "healthy" and "pretty"; the strong, authoritative father appears to Fanny as "thin" and "worn." The physical appearance of the two characters counters the conventional symbolism of their roles in this mutual recognition scene, as it displays the weakness that must accompany power and the power that must accompany weakness for the family system to exist in equilibrium. One is reminded of Nina Auerbach's thesis that the Victorians' tendency to ascribe vital and threatening powers to women was connected to their support of a frail and passive female stereotype.[19] If Austen can ever be said to imagine vampirism it is in this scene, where the timid daughter presents a rosy face to the wasted visage of patriarchal authority. Only it is not clear who stands in the position of victim and who is the vampire. Both characters, in a sense, inhabit both roles.

For as we read this novel, the terminology of "above" and "below," of "inside" and "outside," by which we might at first place Sir Thomas and Fanny if we were locating them within a more traditional family hierarchy, become ambiguous, ineffective at locating power or its absence. As the novel progresses, we begin to see Sir Thomas and Fanny as engaged in a dialectic of above and below in which these positions have relative meaning and are always shifting. When Sir Thomas begins to scapegoat Fanny concerning her rejection of Henry Crawford, he can only go so far; her timidity makes him averse to tyrannical dictation. Fanny, on her side, is left "in a glow of gratitude" (321) from having escaped the severest treatment. Thus, her stubbornness arouses his severity, but the timidity with which she expresses her stubbornness inspires him to yield, and his yielding inspires her gratitude and a greater willingness to do his bidding. Had Henry Crawford not disqualified himself as a marriage partner for Fanny, one wonders what the outcome would have been, since the mutually accommodating interaction of Sir Thomas and Fanny would have moved each closer to acceptance of the other's viewpoint. This self-correcting dynamic reflects that "improvement" upon familial role behavior that allows the Bertrams to preserve and strengthen themselves as a family despite the loss of Maria (unlike the Harlowes, for example, who are shattered by the loss of their daughter).

In other ways, Fanny and Sir Thomas are a perfect fit. While her cousins are bored by the quiet evenings at home that their father favors, Fanny enjoys just this kind of insulated domesticity. "The evenings do not appear long to me," she confides to Edmund; "I love to hear my uncle talk of the West Indies. I could listen to him for an hour together. It entertains *me* more than many other things have done—but I am unlike other people I dare say" (212). Her "unlikeness," which had at first marked her as an outsider to the family, now appears to make her the character most like (and liked by) the father, and hence the one nearest the center of the family. Fanny herself suspects that she risks taking such a central place and holds back the expression of her interest in Sir Thomas's stories. "I thought," she explains, "it would appear as if I wanted to set myself off at their [her cousins'] expense, by shewing a curiosity and pleasure in his information which he must wish his own daughters to feel" (213). She has now implicitly exchanged the outsider's role for the insider's, and instead of "setting off" her cousins, is set off by them.

With Sir Thomas's new attention, Fanny's life in the family also changes appreciably: she gets a fire in her sitting room, she is allowed to dine out, she is given a ball in her honor. All these concrete advantages demonstrate the difference between acknowledgment by the son, who has no real power, and acknowledgment by the father, who can make Fanny an integral part of the family system. In fact, it is through the father's interaction with Fanny as a daughter that the son's interaction is validated and his marriage to her made possible. The patriarchal sense of justice in this novel therefore passes from son to father—that is, from the periphery to the center of the family system.

The shift from son to father is also significant in that it reverses the order assumed by the Oedipal model. In a Freudian family romance, the law would pass from the father to the son as the final marriage approaches. But the central interaction in this novel is not between father and son but between father and daughter, since the daughter, as conventionally weaker and less consequential, can accept a position of power in weakness that complements, rather than usurps, the father's place of weakness in power. We are not dealing, then, with the production of a new family and a new order as we would if we were assuming an Oedipal *quid pro quo* (the son gives up his desire for his mother in exchange for not being castrated so that he can one day create his own family and replace his father in a new context). Fanny and Sir Thomas are brought together in this novel to actually make over (in improved form) the family that begins the novel: the idea of the family as the generational extension of an original family has been discarded in favor of an idea of the family as a reconstituted family of origin. Although Fanny and Edmund marry, it is under the eye of the father who, we are told, was "chiefly anxious to bind by the strongest securities all that remained to him of domestic felicity" (455). It is indeed he who has the idea for the marriage, he who "had pondered with genuine satisfaction on the more than possibility of the two young friends finding their mutual consolation in each other for all that had occurred of disappointment to either" (455).

In its reference to consolation for pain, Sir Thomas's reasoning also suggests that the married couple fits into the family system in the same way that Fanny did alone: Edmund is subsumed within the daughter's role. At the same time, there is a curious blending of the son into the father as the narrator finds it hard to distinguish where Edmund's joy ends and Sir Thomas's begins:

> ... the joyful consent which met Edmund's application, the high sense of having realised a great acquisition in the promise of Fanny for a daughter, formed just such a contrast with his [Sir Thomas's] early opinion on the subject when the poor little girl's coming had been first agitated, as time is for ever producing between the plans and decisions of mortals, for their own instruction, and their neighbors' entertainment. (455)

Syntactically, Edmund's relation to Fanny in the sentence is swallowed up by his father's relation to her, as Sir Thomas finds not his true heir but his eternal complement in a daughter who can remain attached to the family. The tie that binds Sir Thomas and Fanny, the result of a constructed rather than a natural father-daughter relationship, is the basic dyad around which the "improved" family system is formulated at the end of the novel.

If improvement involves the assimilation of the good daughter, Fanny, it also involves the purgation of the errant daughter, Maria. Maria's ultimate fate contrasts interestingly with her original role in the family. Like Arabella in *Clarissa,* Maria occupies a position of relative precedence at the beginning of the novel. It is a precedence that comes out of an old-style family order in which the eldest daughter is the mirror and support for the eldest son. Edmund attempts to recontextualize Maria's positioning early on when he beseeches her to act as his moral confederate in condemning the play ("[I]n this matter it is *you* who are to lead. *You* must set the example" [164]). Instead of representing her as an analogue for the dissolute Tom Bertram, whose privilege is a matter of blood, not merit, Edmund seeks to highlight her relationship to himself—since eldest daughter and second son occupy places in the family that can be said to be analogous also. However, Maria stubbornly refuses such a role. Edmund, despite being temporarily misled by Mary Crawford, always redirects his desire back to the family; its integrity is paramount to him and he accepts the role of surrogate and intermediary for his absent father. Maria, on the other hand, directs her desire away from the family. Her marriage to Rushworth is an expression of rebellion against the conventionalized relationship with her father that Edmund and Fanny embrace so willingly: "She was less and less able to endure the restraint which her father imposed. The liberty which his absence had given was now become absolutely necessary" (216). Liberty from the father is presented here as a pathological desire that first propels Maria into an unsuitable marriage and then into an adulterous affair. In committing adultery, she refuses both the original daughter's role and the incestuously structured form of marriage in which the son/son-in-law can be made a surrogate and intermediary for the father (as happens not only with Edmund but eventually with Julia's husband, Yates). In this sense, Maria is the real threat to the family in the novel, since she disregards its boundaries and seeks new, unauthorized alliances.

In another sense, however, Maria's transgression is not threatening but empowering to the family. To see this it is necessary to look beyond the more superficially obvious differences between Maria and Fanny to a deeper point of resemblance. When Fanny hears of Maria's adulterous elopement, she reacts with revulsion: "the whole family, both families connected as they were by tie upon tie, all friends, all intimate together!—it was too horrible a confusion of guilt, too gross a complication of evil, for human nature, not in a state of utter barbarism, to be capable of!" (429–30). The imagery Fanny uses to express her revulsion suggests that Maria has engaged in incest, precisely the "crime" that Fanny will eventually commit with impunity. Although Maria's adultery seems the very opposite of incest—a turning away from the family rather than toward it—Fanny's reaction helps expose the link between them. Social theorists such as Michel Foucault and Richard Sennett have stressed the ways in which resistance and separation in modern society are merely the counterpoints, the supports, for power and attachment. Murray Bowen has similarly observed in his work with families that "the person who runs away from his family of origin is as emotionally dependent as the one who never leaves home."[20] Maria, who was "less and less able to endure the restraint which her father imposed" and for whom "the liberty which his absence had given was now become absolutely necessary," defines herself as completely in relation to her father as Fanny does. Her self-definition simply depends on a position of opposition to her father, on the idea of his repression evaded, rather than on his presence and his restraint. Her concept of "liberty" therefore relies upon the father to mark it as liberty. Maria is thrown (throws herself) outside the family, but this "outside," far from being a cauldron of primal passions, is a place that the family—expressed through the mutual fit of patriarchal authority and daughterly devotion—defines as the outside. It is an id to which the family assigns what is no longer of use.[21] By this reasoning, the outer-directedness by which the primitive family, according to Lévi-Strauss, is opened up now takes on the appearance of "barbarism." The only "civilized" relations have come to be those contained within the intimate enclosure of the family. If the taboo of the traditional family was incest, the taboo of the nuclear family is disloyalty—Maria's "barbarous" crime.

There is still another connection to be drawn between Fanny and Maria. At the beginning of the novel, Frances Price, Fanny's mother, had been expelled from the family system much as Maria is at the end. Mrs. Price is the original "insider" turned "outsider," whose outsider child is brought back inside the family. Maria, then, symbolizes the possible recurrence of the cycle (did she perhaps have a daughter by Henry Crawford?). Yet almost as soon as such a possibility enters our minds, it is canceled out, for what might have been left

open is closed. The place in the Bertram household that Maria va-
cates is immediately supplied by Fanny's sister Susan, whose function,
I believe, is to mark where a gap could have been and to fill it up.
Austen does with Maria Bertram what Tony Tanner says nineteenth-
century bourgeois society tended to do with the adulterous female
who so threatened its family model. He explains: "the unfaithful wife
is, in social terms, a self-canceling figure, one from whom society
would prefer to withhold recognition so that it would be possible to
say that socially and categorically the adulterous woman does not
exist."[22] It seems more accurate to say that the adulterous woman
does not so much disappear as wear the mark of erasure—as Hester
Prynne wore the mark of her shame. Her disappearance is a conspicuous one, for she must mark the place outside the family just as
prominently as the good daughter must mark the place within. Indeed, the two positions are dynamically complementary: while Maria's identity seems to diminish as she embraces new roles—retreating, as it were, from daughter to wife to mistress to social exile—
Fanny's identity enlarges as she comes at the end of the novel to
occupy the trinity of roles of daughter, sister, and wife.[23]

Significantly, the novel's conclusion fails to be explicit about another role—the maternal role—that one might expect Fanny to occupy. It seems part of the novel's triumphant conclusion that any
possibility of projecting the family system in time, whether forward
or backward, has been obscured or eliminated. Not only are children
absent from the final scene, but the memory of childhood is symbolically obliterated as Mrs. Norris, the busy-body aunt whose idea
Fanny's adoption originally was, is expelled with Maria from the family system at the end of the story. With Mrs. Norris gone, Fanny's
"outsider" childhood self can now be effectively forgotten as the thematic extension of the family system beyond its immediate, integrated
form has been edited away. Finally, the family is shown to contract
geographically as well. Not long after Fanny and Edmund's marriage,
the Mansfield parsonage becomes vacant and the couple settles in
immediate proximity to the great house occupied by Edmund's parents. The last paragraph of the novel records a vision of perfection
as the heroine sees the final transformation of pain into consoling
pleasure: the parsonage, "which under its two former owners, Fanny
had never been able to approach but with some painful sensation of
restraint or alarm, soon grew as dear to her heart, and as thoroughly

perfect in her eyes, as every thing else, within view and patronage of Mansfield Park, had long been" (456). With this final transformation, the dynamic of pain and consolation, and reciprocally, of scapegoating and guilt, collapses into itself. We arrive at that point of convergence of opposites that makes the closing image of the novel seem a transcendent vision of the homely conventions of family life: "the happiness of the married cousins . . . secure as earthly happiness can be" (456). The family as it emerges at the end of *Mansfield Park* appears to be in such a perfect state of equilibrium and to have closed itself off so completely to the outside as to become a static configuration. A generational succession has given way to a system of fixed relations.

* * *

In positing a fundamental shift in the mechanisms of power from the classical to the modern age, Michel Foucault describes a move from an order of law and lineage to a technology of sex in which sexuality polymorphously saturates all relations. Foucault also observes that it is in the family that the older relations based on alliance and the new relations based on sexuality come together, bolstering each other by means of the incest taboo. The prohibition of incest, he claims, is a "means of self-defense, not against an incestuous desire, but against the expansion and implications of this deployment of sexuality which had been set up, but which among its many benefits, had the disadvantage of ignoring the laws and juridical forms of alliance."[24] What Foucault's analysis neglects, however, just as Lévi-Strauss's did before him, are the alternative defenses that the nuclear family was able to erect so as to gradually supplant the order of alliance. Incest, when it is not conceived as the product of a proliferating sexuality but as a structured emotional investment in a family of origin, is not barbarous at all. Freud said as much when he posited the Oedipus complex as the experience of an interfamilial desire necessary to individual socialization. Unlike Freud, however, who concentrates on the relationship of father and son in order to assert the continuation of a patrilineal succession, Austen depicts a family scene in which the essential bond is between father and daughter—a bond that stabilizes the family as a closed relational system in space and, in so doing, opposes a patrilineal model of the family in time.

The vision that emerges at the end of *Mansfield Park* is the expression of a wish to remain anchored to the family of origin, to annex all needs to this nuclear family and close off all access and egress. For Jane Austen, this is hardly a surprising wish. Living at home in a family that social conditioning had taught her to love above all else, having lost all hope of—or more correctly, having come to terms with a lack of desire for—marriage (we know that she received proposals and rejected them), Austen was also a member of a society that gave status only to married women. The logical solution to this double bind would be to marry inside the family, a wish approximately realized in her life through the role she acquired upon the death of her brother's wife a few years before she began writing *Mansfield Park*. At the same time, the structure and closure afforded by fiction provided her with a space in which this wish could be imaginatively depicted in the form of a perfectly closed nuclear family, uncontaminated by outside influences. In this sense, Jane Austen's vision of familial interaction at the end of *Mansfield Park* corresponds to what Max Weber, in his effort to establish the equivalent of a scientific method for sociological study, termed an "ideal type," one of those "forms of human behavior, which . . . involve the highest possible degree of logical integration because of their complete adequacy on the level of meaning." Weber compares such logically integrated forms to "a physical reaction [calculated] on the basis of an absolute vacuum."[25] The Bertram family in its final, circumscribed representation exists as if in such a vacuum: it possesses that "highest possible degree of logical integration" only achievable when all external and extraneous factors have been eliminated.

In her critique of Lévi-Strauss and Freud, Gayle Rubin notes that both offer interpretations of the sex/gender system that assume a fundamental asymmetry between the sexes, with women occupying the lesser role.[26] In Lévi-Strauss's kinship model, the woman is seen as a gift between families and hence powerless in respect to the male giver and receiver; in Freud's Oedipal model, the woman is seen as castrated and hence diminished in relation to her brother. However, an examination of the ideal type of the family system as Austen renders it in *Mansfield Park* demonstrates the beginning of a transformation in male-female power relations that we will see working itself out over the course of the nineteenth century. Fanny's weakness is shown to contain elements of power, and Sir Thomas's power is shown to contain elements of weakness. At the conclusion of the novel, they are made to complement each other in a dialectic that makes them virtually equal in power and weakness. This complementarity tends to cancel not only sexual asymmetry but generational asymmetry as well. When traced to its logical end, moreover, this tendency toward the equalizing of forces between father and daughter must introduce a new asymmetry in the relations of brother and sister and of husband and wife in which the female position gains dominance.[27] Indeed, it can be argued that Freud intuitively grasped the asymmetry implicit in the structure of the nuclear family (in which the daughter gains precedence over the traditional son and heir) and, as a spokesman for a patriarchal culture that he saw threatened, introduced the notion of castration, a physically-based theory of female subordination, to cancel and reverse this newly emerging asymmetry.[28] (That Freud's own legacy was passed on through his daughter becomes especially ironic in this context.) One might also argue that while Freud grasped the incestuous structure that the nuclear family had brought into being, by concentrating on the Oedipal triangle that encoded patrilineal succession into the structure of the family, he conveniently ignored what was lurking elsewhere—a counterforce to patrilineage in the developing daughter who was being conditioned *for* the father. Yet such attempts to counter or ignore the daughter's potential power can also be said to have contributed indirectly to the slow emergence of this power (although, as I shall explain, "power" is not really the right word to apply to this process of feminization). Deprived of all means of emotionally separating herself from her family of origin, the daughter was, from one point of view, kept down, thwarted in her opportunities, deprived of a wider arena for growth and development. From another point of view, however, her confinement made her an increasingly important imaginative and emotional force within the family.

* * *

I have said that Austen produces an ideal type of the nuclear family in *Mansfield Park.* In bringing this chapter to a close and as a prelude to the next chapter on *Wuthering Heights,* I would like to consider what such an ideal really means both in terms of the author and her canon and in terms of more general concepts of self and family.

I have said that the ideal type of family experience depicted in *Mansfield Park* is a wish-fulfillment on the part of its author. However, this wish certainly does not reflect a wish on Jane Austen's part to *be* Fanny Price. Austen's other heroines, as critics have long pointed out, are the antithesis of Fanny. The qualities that appeal to us in Austen's greatest heroines, Elizabeth Bennet and Emma Woodhouse, are strikingly individual qualities: even when they are wrong, these women appear to possess an assertive selfhood that makes them attractive. To acknowledge the difference between Fanny Price and these great heroines is to acknowledge, then, that Austen's interest in *Mansfield Park* is in an ideal of family that does not accommodate the self. Indeed, in *Mansfield Park* the selfhood of Fanny Price is ultimately merged with the (male) other—with Edmund, with Sir Thomas—and they, by the end, have merged with her: all pain is transformed into pleasure, all difference into resemblance. This process of submersion and diffusion of identity might be likened to Christian self-renunciation or, in Freudian terms, to a pre-Oedipal oneness with the mother (Mrs. Bertram's cosmic lethargy has metaphorical significance in this context). However, if we continue to think in terms of the family system, then the movement to self-reflexive stasis is the product of a perfectly closed and equilibrated family system.

It becomes interesting at this point to compare the ideal family produced at the end of *Mansfield Park* with the attempts by modern families to achieve such perfect closure and to merge the identities of their members. Therapists refer to these families as "enmeshed," "undifferentiated," or "stuck-together" and note that in such families someone invariably suffers from a psychosomatic illness. In order to maintain an equilibrated, closed family system (when external tension and internal change always threaten), one member must develop symptoms, serving as the regulating focus for deviant behavior *in* the system and as the register for stressful external effects *on* the system. This homeostatic solution is precarious; as stress and change besiege the family, the equilibrium of the family is continually strained, and the symptomatic member must experience further degeneration.

Austen, however, can produce in her novel a static scene of control and order of the kind the psychosomatic family desires but can never achieve. In *Mansfield Park* all unmanageable and inconvenient elements are progressively eliminated: Maria and Mrs. Norris are banished; the Mansfield living becomes vacant; and the unruly Price household, with the exception of the self-improving Susan, is placed safely at a distance. All tensions that might have been expected to accompany the shift from one love object to another and, specifically, from the transformation of fraternal love into conjugal love are glibly eliminated. Within this sterile context, the core dynamic—the relationship of Fanny and Edmund (and later Sir Thomas)—appears controlled and not degenerative. Indeed, guilt and scapegoating balance each other so perfectly that at the end they disappear into each other to produce a static "happy" family. But a static equilibrium is, of course, the illusion produced by the form. It is achieved just as the novel conveniently ends.

If we accept this systems analysis of the real versus the ideal implications of nuclearity, then *Mansfield Park* becomes more comprehensible within Austen's canon. It is now possible to situate the other Austen novels as corollaries or other sides to this family ideal. Instead of presenting an ideal type of the family, the other novels present a series of ideal types of the female character as the product of unstable, disequilibrated families. In other words, Austen's other novels place the emphasis on the heroine much the same way that sick families place emphasis on the symptomatic individual—only Austen fashions admirable character traits out of what, in the context of the contemporary psychosomatic family, would realistically produce symptoms.

In her early novels, Austen had been specifically concerned with her heroines' individuality as the counter or antidote to their families. Both Elinor Dashwood and Elizabeth Bennet must develop their strong personalities because their families are so impossibly weak and irrational. When Darcy tells Elizabeth that he likes her despite her family, he might also be explaining why it is possible for him to single her out from among so many insipid women from good families. Her "impertinence," he later admits, attracts him, and certainly this is a trait bred at home. *Emma* and *Persuasion* are concerned with the selfhood of their heroines in something closer to what we think of as psychological terms. Emma's manipulative and aggressive sense of self-importance seems to derive from her dependent, indulgent father, and Anne's silent wellspring of sometimes debilitating feeling from her father's callous dismissal of her. In clinical terms, Emma's tendency is toward delinquency while Anne's is toward depression and psychosomatic illness of the kind suffered by her friend Mrs. Smith. Although marriage to reasonable, good men promises to correct these imbalances, no reader believes that Emma will succumb wholly to Knightley's law or that Anne will not brood when Wentworth goes off to sea. Fanny Price begins with the symptoms of invalidism and gradually loses them as she blends into the fabric of the family, but the prospect of Emma or Anne losing her symptomatic traits seems unlikely. They are, as Trilling remarked of Emma, formed characters confronting their destinies, not partial representations or props, and not girls undergoing their first formative experiences.[29]

The irony, of course, is that the notion of formed character takes on a different aspect when we see it as both the function of and the compensation for a disequilibrated family system. It means that the heroine's selfhood is really the result of the strain placed on her as she regulates the values and behavioral tendencies of her family. Since the family's values, usually embodied by the father and elaborated in other family members, are trivial or selfish, the daughter-heroine assumes the burden of reason or at least, as in Emma's case, of energy. (The theorem holds perfectly well for the fatherless Elinor Dashwood, whose sense extends even to money matters; she is the most reasonable of Austen's heroines, I would suggest, because she must complement paternal absence.) Of course, in becoming the repository of all that her father lacks, the heroine ultimately becomes interesting in herself. She springs into relief against the background of her family in a way that Fanny Price (whose surrogate father is essentially a reasonable and moral man) never does. However, the structural similarity between Fanny and Austen's other heroines lies in the fact that they are all fundamentally complements of their fathers, even when—and indeed, especially when—their fathers are fools or tyrants.

This complementary structure, which determines the novels' outcomes, may be further understood in terms of game theory. Von Neumann and Morgenstern, in their work on the logic of games, postulated stability among three perfect, nonhuman players as a coalition of two against one—in essence, of a dyad relationship plus an outsider to the dyad: "If A and B are in alliance, there is nothing C can do about it. . . . A and B will necessarily develop conventions (supplementary to the rules) which will, for example, forbid them from listening to C's approaches."[30] This is the situation depicted at the end of *Mansfield Park,* in which Sir Thomas and Fanny form the perfect dyad with Maria as the player banished in perpetuity to the outsider position. The other players in the game are either negligible or support the dyad: Mrs. Bertram is a vegetable presence and Edmund acts as the surrogate and tool of his father.

Von Neumann and Morgenstern's mechanical model is misleading, however, if we are led to assume from it that the characters in *Mansfield Park* are robotlike. They are certainly less psychologically complex than the tortured souls we find in more modern literature (even in literature written a generation later). Yet what we may tend to call nonhuman and abstract may also be a function of the gap between Austen's structural positioning in relation to the ideology of the nuclear family and ours. In other words, the frozen stability that is achieved at the end of *Mansfield Park* may be the result not only of the artifice of Austen's fiction but also of the absence in her family and in the culture more generally of certain instabilities that would be inherent in later forms of family function. I have already noted, for example, that according to contemporary studies of family interaction, a dyadic relationship in a family is not likely to remain stable for even a relatively short period without producing pathological symptoms; it will tend instead to reconstitute itself quickly as a triangle made up of continually shifting alliances. One triangle will, in turn, quickly generate other triangles involving other family members and, eventually, reaching beyond the family.[31] Perhaps owing to the fact that the nuclear family was not yet a central and entrenched part of the ideology of English culture at the time Austen was writing, structure and idea were as yet loosely rather than intricately linked, and triangular interaction had not yet become a built-in, predictable function of family interaction. Thus, Austen did not have it in her power to explore the contradiction between the daughter's regulating role within her family of origin and her disruptive role as a desirable wife, a role that would make possible the reproduction of her family in a new generation. The contradiction is between the affective order of the family as a closed system and the more traditional patrilineal order of the family based on alliance. It is also a contradiction between the two faces of the daughter as regulator within the family system: the daughter as Fanny Price, who blends into the fabric of her family as she stabilizes it, and the daughter as Elizabeth Bennet, who seems to spring free of her family as she stabilizes it. Austen could not imagine these impulses at work together in one character. Emily Brontë could. *Wuthering Heights* elaborates a dynamic of family interaction that tries to accommodate in its volatile heroine these two faces of the daughter. I hope to demonstrate in the next chapter how Brontë sought to manage both in her novel and in her life the contradictions generated by an ideology of the nuclear family that had now taken hold in the culture.

CHAPTER 4

Wuthering Heights: Elaboration

In a survey of the nineteenth-century English novel, *Wuthering Heights* is often excluded or set apart. The assumption appears to be that while other novels are grounded in a "realistic" model of nineteenth-century English life, *Wuthering Heights* resists such a model.[1] The first-generation story that dominates the plot is said to exist outside of a recognizable context of motivations and values. One critic expresses a representative attitude when she writes that in Heathcliff and Cathy "we see the childhood of the race" and that these characters and their story cannot be made "convenient to culture."[2]

In this chapter, I will argue that the first-generation story *can* be made "convenient to culture," that, indeed, its extreme convenience to the culturally constructed relationship system of the nuclear family is what accounts for its problematic nature. My reading should connect the novel not only with a social context but also with a literary context, by tracing patterns that, once their historical relevance is understood, can find analogous or responding patterns in other novels of the period.

In *Mansfield Park*, the central structural configuration was the dyad. In *Wuthering Heights*, it is the triangle. This shift can be said to reflect a structural evolution in the form of both the novel and the family. In other words, the elaboration of the idea of closure (the evolution of this idea into a fully articulated and pervasive ideology for the nineteenth century) carried with it a corresponding elaboration of the structure needed to support it.

The triangle, "a three-person emotional configuration," is a fundamental concept in family systems theory. It is "the molecule or building block of any relationship system," according to family theorist Murray Bowen.[3] As I have already noted in chapter 1, the triangle as a basic structural unit for the family makes sense in a historical context as the means by which companionate marriages, which began to be favored in the seventeenth and eighteenth centuries and which formed the basis for the nuclear family, were more securely anchored. To assist the fragile romantic tie, a third person was necessary, in the form of the couple's child, who could serve as a more enduring means of unity.

However, the concept of the triangle as the stabilizing figure for the nuclear family still requires a dynamic explanation. When we speak of a triangle involving human beings, we are speaking not of a static configuration but of a living system. The triangle becomes comprehensible in family systems terms when we recognize that, for the figure to exist, someone is always "triangled"—used as a stabilizing focus or "scapegoat" for the other two individuals in the system.[4] According to family systems theorists, pathological symptoms result when one family member is *chronically* triangled. In "healthy" families, they say, the triangled member constantly shifts so that stability is not maintained at the expense of one individual all the time.[5] However, a so-called healthy family in which the triangled member always changes is a family whose continually shifting internal relations are liable to become easily confused with external relations. In other words, shifting triangulation runs counter to the definition of the nuclear family as a closed relationship system based on conventionalized roles. It would seem that if an individual family were to remain compatible with the ideology of the nuclear family—separated from an outer world while maintaining durable emotional ties among its members within—it would need to engage in some form of chronic triangulation.

Wuthering Heights is a novel about such chronic triangulation. The triangulating process occurs first within the family system at Wuthering Heights and then within the combined family system of Wuthering Heights and Thrushcross Grange. The triangled element is the daughter of two successive generations. The first daughter is destroyed; the second daughter escapes destruction and is rehabilitated. Yet despite the novel's effort to regularize character and relationships in the end, Brontë's elaboration of the dynamics of the daughter's role reveals basic structural problems in the nuclear family as it attempts to maintain its stability as a relatively closed relational system.

* * *

Catherine Earnshaw is the daughter of the family at Wuthering Heights, and Edgar Linton is the son of the family next door at Thrushcross Grange. The existence of the two families with no competing families nearby would appear to support the requirements of what anthropologists call "dual organization," in which the son in one family must seek his partner from the daughter of the other.[6] In the novel, however, this elementary exchange is complicated when, during Cathy's childhood, an outsider, Heathcliff, is introduced into her family of origin. Nelly Dean, the family servant, provides insight into Heathcliff's disruptive role when she recounts a seemingly insignificant scene just prior to Mr. Earnshaw's death:

> Miss Cathy had been sick, and that made her still; she leant against her father's knee, and Heathcliff was lying on the floor with his head in her lap.
>
> I remember the master, before he fell into a doze, stroking her bonny hair—it pleased him rarely to see her gentle—and saying—
> "Why canst thou not always be a good lass, Cathy?"
> And she turned her face up to his, and laughed, and answered—
> "Why cannot you always be a good man, Father?"
> But as soon as she saw him vexed again, she kissed his hand, and said she would sing him to sleep.[7]

Nelly begins her account with a frozen tableau whose iconography (Heathcliff's head on Cathy's lap, Cathy's head on her father's knee) describes a triangle in which Cathy inhabits the intermediary position between her father and Heathcliff. But only when the scene is animated by dialogue does this positioning take on functional meaning. By posing the accusatory question of his daughter ("Why canst thou not always be a good lass, Cathy?"), Mr. Earnshaw demonstrates his tendency to scapegoat her, while Cathy's response ("Why cannot you always be a good man, Father?") reflects her willingness to respond to his blame with reciprocal blame. Out of context, this might seem like a simple inversion of the kind of daughterly behavior we encounter in *Mansfield Park*, where Fanny Price's timidity complements Sir Thomas's severity. Within the context of this scene (and the novel as a whole), however, Cathy's resistance to her father is shown to be a sporadic function: her rebellion alternates with daughterly devotion. This alternating response can be explained if we interpret the father-daughter exchange as part of a larger interaction in which a third party has a temporary alienating effect on the daughter's devotion to her father. The third party here is, of course, Heathcliff. Though silent, Heathcliff exerts his influence, pulling Cathy into temporary alliance with his outside position and instigating her hostile response to her father's accusatory remark. Once there, however, she is immediately contrite and moves back into alliance with her father (kissing his hand, volunteering to sing him to sleep). (At the same time, the content of her previous rejoinder ["Why cannot you always be a good man, Father?"] implies that her father too inhabits the outside position on occasion—a point to which I will return.) Read in the context of this triangular interaction, the exchange between Cathy and her father becomes revealing less of her relation to her father than of her mediation of her father's relation to Heathcliff.

The daughter's mediating role represented in this scene can perhaps be more logically understood if we analyze and elaborate upon Bowen's concept of the triangle as the "smallest stable relationship system." "A two-person system is basically unstable," explains Bowen. "In a tension field, the two people predictably involve a third person to make a triangle." He continues by describing the dynamics of triangular interaction: "In calm periods, the triangle consists of a two-person togetherness and an outsider. The togetherness is the preferred position.... In tension states, the outside position is preferred, and the triangle moves are directed at escaping the tension field and achieving and holding the outside position.... The moves in a triangle are automatic and without intellectual awareness."[8] The triangle has already been discussed as the stabilizing figure for the nuclear family within a historical context, and the triangle of parents and child can be viewed as an initiating structure. However, for the nuclear family to be stabilized as a socially viable entity, the mother's role had to quickly recede or become obliterated—an operation either literally effected through the mother's death in childbirth or figuratively effected as the result both of the mother's subordinate status in relation to her husband and of her tendency to continue to define herself according to her role as a daughter in her family of origin.[9] Thus, it would follow that the son and daughter would quickly become situated in relation to the authoritative presence of the father, and the shifting moves that Bowen attributes to human relations within a triangle would become a pattern involving the father and son with respect to the daughter. These moves are crucial to the identity of both father and son, for they describe the passage back and forth, from coalition to autonomy, by which each is both tested in relationship with the daughter/sister and affirmed when removed from this relationship. In other words, male identity can be dynamically defined as a matter of being, by turns, in and out of coalition with a daughter/sister—of being in an alliance with her and being an outsider to such an alliance.[10]

By building on this model for male identity formation, we can also suggest a model for how the nuclear family as a whole has been able to test and affirm its identity as a system. For the pattern of leaving home and returning home in the case of the father (while the son remains at home) and of leaving home and forming new relationships as a suitor/husband in the case of the son (while the father remains at home) expresses a movement between autonomy and relationship on the level of family function. Moreover, in the son's movement outside his family of origin to court his future wife, we have the means by which the original family triangle can be propagated. In systems terms this coincides with Bowen's final proposition that "when tension in the triangle is too great for the threesome, it involves others to become a series of interlocking triangles" (where "tension" would be translated as the reproductive need of the family system itself).[11]

If father and son are taken as two positions in the triangle that alternately require alliance, the daughter's role within the triangle becomes clearer. She must be available for alliance whenever one member of the triangle has moved outside. She must be "at home" for anyone who wants her. Ultimately, of course, the reproductive assumption built into this model dictates that she must be at home for the son of another family who, in his passage outside, comes to court her and make her a wife in a new family. Here is where this model of family interaction, which attempts to reconcile family stability with a genealogical imperative, runs into difficulty.

If the daughter were purely an object, a gift to be exchanged within and between families, the model would remain compatible with the concept of reciprocity (the exchange of women) that Lévi-Strauss connects to the basic functioning of society. However, when

triangulation serves not only as a system by which the family is organized and reproduced but also as a system by which male identity is
forged, the daughter in the nuclear family cannot simply be an object
of exchange. In order for her role in the family triangle to be effective she must also be a *mediating consciousness* and become defined
not only externally (as an object) but internally (as a subject, through
those whom she mediates).[12] Formed under such circumstances, the
daughter must be both irreparably divided as a function of her mediating role and profoundly identified with her first experience of
mediation. It is precisely these complications, posed by the daughter's
place in the family triangle, that appear to determine the course of
action in the two-generation story of *Wuthering Heights*.

As already noted, most critics of *Wuthering Heights* have viewed the
novel as a kind of primal myth, a fiction cut off from history, in
which the relations described bear no apparent resemblance to a
conventional paradigm for the nuclear family. A reading of the novel
within a narrow context bears out this view, and I shall begin with
such a reading. Having done this, however, I will return to interpret
the patterns traced within a much broader context—one that reveals
their paradigmatic nature.

In the first-generation story, the daughter's problems appear to
arise out of exceptional circumstances that disrupt the smooth course
of her youth. The story begins with a conventional family scene. Mrs.
Earnshaw is still alive, and we are given a glimpse of a short-lived
family configuration in which the children appear to be allied with
her: they remain with her when Mr. Earnshaw goes on his journey
and, when he brings Heathcliff back with him, they initially side with
her in ostracizing the strange child. But Heathcliff soon disrupts the
standard course of family interaction, as outlined above, by creating
an early alliance with the daughter, Cathy. Thus, instead of moving
into a triangle involving her father and brother following her
mother's death, Cathy forms a premature triangle with her father
and Heathcliff (a truly nondomestic male figure), a triangle that
excludes her brother Hindley. She is pulled into alternating alliance
with the outside (Heathcliff) and the inside (her father) when she
would otherwise have remained in alternating alliance with the inside
(her father and brother).

Indeed, Cathy's early alliance with an outsider can be used to explain (more comprehensively than can the requirements of exogamy) both her marriage to the exaggeratedly domestic Edgar Linton and the subsequent undermining of that marriage. Events can be traced systematically as follows. After the father's death, the drive to regain the relative stability of triangular interaction is manifested as Heathcliff and Cathy immediately become involved with the formerly ignored brother, Hindley (who, according to a "normal" family model, now enters the triangle at the wrong time, belatedly). Hindley replaces his father as a third but, as Cathy puts it, "is a detestable substitute—his conduct to Heathcliff is atrocious" (62). Hindley becomes an especially detestable substitute for his father because he soon ceases to occupy himself with Heathcliff and Cathy at all. His marriage, occurring soon after his father's death, essentially results in his abandoning the triangle for an exclusive relationship with his wife. Left to themselves, Heathcliff and Cathy grow "more reckless daily" (87)—for their relationship now lacks a stabilizing third.[13]

The escalating recklessness of Cathy and Heathcliff is stopped, however, through an accident that transforms the uncontrolled dyad into a new triangle. The accident happens one day when the pair, in the course of their ramblings, decide to spy in at the window of Thrushcross Grange. They are observed in this act of mischief, an alarm is sounded, and they are forced to flee, only to be thwarted by the Linton dog, who fastens his teeth to Cathy's ankle and pins her to the spot. This image of violent restraint initiates a series of images that depict Cathy's arrest and placement within a scene that reproduces her earlier position in relation to her father and Heathcliff. No sooner is she inside the Linton home than she is recognized for who she is, and is propped on the sofa, fed, and coddled. Through these positionings, she is made accessible to Edgar (who "stood gaping at a distance" [92]), while remaining within sight of Heathcliff (who "resumes [his] station to spy" [91] from outside). The relational configuration that preceded this scene—of Heathcliff and Cathy rambling unattended on the moors—has changed radically. Instead of the couple wandering aimlessly, we now have Cathy fixed in place and gazed at from two opposing vantage points—one inside (Edgar) and one outside (Heathcliff). Thus, Edgar does not replace Heathcliff in Cathy's world but rather becomes the balancing other side to Heathcliff's outsider status in relation to her. Edgar inserts himself into the position in the triangle that Hindley had vacated through his marriage, and thereby becomes the substitute for Hindley in a triangle in which Hindley himself had served as a "detestable substitute" for his father. Cathy appears to have a dim awareness that Edgar is needed in this role—to help stabilize and define the increasingly unstable, undifferentiated dyad of Heathcliff and herself—when she explains to Nelly her rationale for marrying him: "did it never strike you that, if Heathcliff and I married, we should be beggars? whereas, if I marry Linton, I can aid Heathcliff to rise, and place him out of my brother's power" (122). In fact, her tie to Edgar *does* have the effect she describes, though not through the means she intended: it spurs Heathcliff's ambition to become a gentleman and make his fortune, putting him outside her brother's power. In the process, however, a new and more violent antagonism is created between Heathcliff and Edgar, which places more extreme demands on Cathy, and eventually results in her death.

To understand how the achievement of temporary stability (Edgar's insertion into the Heathcliff-Cathy relationship) gives rise to a destructive outcome (Cathy's death), it is necessary to examine the form Cathy's mediation takes in the novel. Her mediating role appears to begin soon after her father brings Heathcliff home. Initially, she, along with her mother, Hindley, and Nelly, rejects the strange child. However, the father's displeasure at their response seems to influence Cathy (and, to a less intense degree, Nelly). She crosses over to the other side; or, more correctly, she alternates in her allegiances, serving as mediator between the domesticity of the family and the wildness of the outsider's character. In the scene quoted earlier, in which Cathy is positioned between her father and Heathcliff, we see her mediating function represented as she acts both the good daughter and the antagonist to her father.

If Cathy's role in the family can be understood as formed to reduce stress in—to regulate—the family system, it must itself become the locus of opposing forces. Given the extremes of behavior she must regulate, it is not surprising that she should become symptomatic—and not just in one direction but in two. Cathy's poor health is not a simple debilitation but a wildly oscillating movement with hysteria and anorexia as its poles. Each of these illnesses represents itself as an exaggeration of an acceptable though opposite mode of behavior: hysteria often resembles a pathological excess of robust spirits; anorexia, a pathological excess of delicacy.[14] Thus, while Cathy recalls her childhood as "savage and hardy," the scene with her dying father also describes her as recovering from an illness (significantly mimicking his enfeeblement at this point in the story). Following her father's death she reverts to recklessness as Heathcliff's companion, but in the course of their adventures she has the accident at Thrushcross Grange and temporarily occupies again the invalid role among the timid and sedentary Lintons. When Heathcliff runs away, she experiences her first serious illness, a mix of hysterical and anorectic behavior—of fits and fasting—which, once Heathcliff's disappearance and her marriage to Edgar become established, gives way to a state of uneasy quiescence. (As Nelly recalls: "for the space of half a year, the gunpowder lay as harmless as sand" [131].) During this period, not only do Cathy's symptoms go into remission but also her personality seems to experience eclipse—as though her symptoms and her distinctive character are equivalences that disappear when she loses her mediating role. When Heathcliff returns, this mediating role is activated again, and her former character returns in more explicitly symptomatic form. In greeting Heathcliff, the clinical observer Nelly reports that Cathy is "breathless and wild, too excited to show gladness; indeed, by her face, you would rather have surmised an awful calamity" (134); she laughs, continues Nelly, "like one beside herself" (136). As the conflict between Heathcliff and her husband escalates, Cathy retreats into invalidism punctuated by occasional hysterical attacks. The alternation between the two extremes of her condition becomes shorter in time, and the intensity of the symptoms in both directions increases. Her final scenes with Heathcliff and Edgar are a curious amalgam of both extremes—of being torn apart by the drive "to adopt a double character without exactly intending to deceive anyone" (107). She is hysterical to the point of animal ferocity and helpless to the point of unconsciousness.

The difference between the "reckless" Cathy and the invalid ("no better than a wailing child" [162]) is a difference in regulatory strategy. Both forms of expression can be read in relation to the two men who trigger them as adjustments of a system through a directing of the uncontrolled element onto the self. In her hysterical mode, Cathy symbolically allies herself with Heathcliff; in her invalid mode she allies herself with Edgar. These alliances are also forms of mediation. As she grows more hysterical, she complements Edgar, who becomes more docile and controlled (she "frightens" [156] him in that state), while in her invalid mode, she complements Heathcliff, who grows more fierce and wild (she enrages him with the sense of his own impotence). She not only mimics each man in her relation to him but "fills out" his identity through her relation to the other man, making each more himself and more antithetical to the other. In short, she moves back and forth within the Bowen triangle, providing each man with coalition and each with outsider status. A consistent identity is achieved for each while her own identity becomes increasingly strained as the bridge between them.

What is especially noteworthy about this dynamic is the way it distances us from a traditional ideology of the family, which depended upon the exchange or interchangeability of two women. In *Wuthering Heights,* one woman is torn between two men. The female position has now become the locus of great tension, with the conflicting claims of that position made manifest through the stressful effects on the heroine's mind and body. But Cathy's case also involves the valorization of the female position in a way unimaginable in the traditional open lineage family. For instead of being a nonindividualized object of exchange, Cathy is valuable in herself; she has acquired a unique subjectivity through her mediating role that makes her irreplaceable. When Heathcliff takes Isabella Linton for his wife because he cannot have Cathy, it is a parody of exchange: he takes Isabella to hurt his rival rather than to have a debt paid. In other words, female subjectivity, however it can be said to arise, must thwart Lévi-Strauss's model of social organization as structured alliance.[15]

Thus far my reading of the novel has confined itself to a literal examination of the case of Catherine Earnshaw Linton. From this limited perspective, the case seems exceptional. If, however, we examine the patterns of relationship just described within a larger metaphorical context, they no longer appear to be aberrations. Through such a reexamination of the first-generation story, we can see how the heroine's dilemma reflects a conflict between elementary exchange and the superimposed structures of the nuclear family.

I have already noted that the Earnshaw family, as it is briefly described during the period before Heathcliff's introduction, seems to conform to a conventional model for the nuclear family. The mother and children are seen bidding farewell to the father as he leaves for a tedious trip on an unspecified errand: the father in his instrumental role moves outside to perform functional pursuits; the mother and children remain behind in an emotional nexus to which the father will eventually return. Thus, for the father, the scene metaphorically enacts the identity-making process—from relationship, to separation, to confirmation in relationship: Mr. Earnshaw, inside the family, moves outside, only to return again to the security of his home.

If the father's voyage and return can be read as a metaphor for the process by which male identity is formed, his adoption of Heathcliff becomes a metaphor for the end product—for formulated male identity. By depositing the boy in the bosom of his family and making him a favorite, Earnshaw merges outside with inside, or rather he asserts, through the adoption, a split of himself into patriarch and vagabond—relational self and autonomous self—and demands the mediation of both within a domestic context. This mediating role must fall to the daughter, who alone in the family is in the position of being formed *for* the father. In Earnshaw's final scene in the novel (quoted earlier), Cathy's role as mediator between the two positions, inside and outside, is explicitly rendered. She is both good daughter and wild thing. She serves both men, who represent both parts of her father's identity.

When viewed as the mediation of a split in her father, Cathy's behavior begins to look comprehensible in social terms. Talcott Parsons has noted that the father's position in the conventional nuclear family "is the one which is most strategically important as linking the earlier familial experience with the role structure of the wider society."[16] In short, the ideology of "separate spheres" stipulates that the woman has her place, while the man has two places. Through the father's dual role as outsider on the one hand and insider on the other, the family as a closed system of conventionalized roles is supported and sustained within a larger social context. In the psychological terms represented by triangular interaction, this requires that the father's identity be split. His role-effectiveness and, by extension, the personal sense of identity that the role engenders depend upon his putting in abeyance one aspect of his role function at any given time.[17]

By comprehending Mr. Earnshaw and Heathcliff as two parts of the father, we need no longer approach the novel as the case of a singular family whose introduction of an outsider wreaks havoc on a genealogical succession; we can now read it as a more general study of how the father's split identity in the nuclear family might tend to affect the formation of the daughter's identity. What is revealed is that the daughter's effort to achieve a perfect dyadic relationship with her father (an effort for which the vulnerability and conventional associations of her age and sex fit her) would cause her to mediate the two parts of her father's identity—the relational and the autonomous, the expressive and the instrumental, the inside and the outside. Insofar as the daughter is taught to serve as her father's complement, her complementarity must be not single but double, a complementarity that alternates between the two parts of her father's identity. Thus, the father-daughter dyad must function like a triangle. With this triangle behind it, the more conventional triangle of father (or brother)-daughter-suitor that Lévi-Strauss posits as the basis for elementary kinship exchange would be both prepared for and undermined: prepared for, in that all future relations would mimic the original relation to the father and be mediating ones; undermined, in that all subsequent mediation, having moved outside the single person of the father, would become unsatisfying and unreconcilable substitutes for this original relationship.

Cathy's original splitting of loyalties occurred between her father and Heathcliff, a split that can be understood metaphorically as representing the duality of her father's identity. Although this original relationship is not without difficulties of its own, as Cathy's verbal interaction with her father (cited earlier) demonstrates, it becomes for her the idealized site of an integrated identity ("Why am I so changed?" [163], she laments, nostalgically recalling her childhood self) and the model for all subsequent mediation. Her splitting of loyalties is then repeated with Heathcliff and her brother (her father's "detestable substitute"), and again with Heathcliff and her husband (Hindley's substitute). All of these split loyalties are in a sense superimposed upon each other, producing a confusing welter of splits and substitutions that incorporates past and present. Cathy expresses this confusion graphically when she tries to explain to Nelly Dean the images that come to her at night:

> I thought... that I was enclosed in the oak-panelled bed at home; and my heart ached with some great grief which, just waking, I could not recollect... I did not recall that [the past seven years]

had been at all. I was a child; my father was just buried, and my misery arose from the separation that Hindley had ordered between me, and Heathcliff—I was laid alone, for the first time, and, rousing from a dismal doze after a night of weeping—. . . memory burst in—my late anguish was swallowed in a paroxysm of despair—I cannot say why I felt so wildly wretched—it must have been temporary derangement for there is scarcely cause— But, supposing at twelve years old, I had been wrenched from the Heights, and every early association, and my all in all, as Heathcliff was at that time, and been converted at a stroke into Mrs. Linton, the lady of Thrushcross Grange, and the wife of a stranger; an exile, and outcast, thenceforth, from what had been my world— You may fancy a glimpse of the abyss where I grovelled! (163)

The images Cathy invokes reverberate with loss and separation, for in each case the pain lies in that which escapes her: the dead father, the banished Heathcliff, and even the "stranger" husband. These are all references to the men in her life when they are outside of alliance with her, as they must temporarily be when she is in alliance with another. What is more, she cannot situate the problem since it is precisely a series of superimposed oppositions that she must mediate: her father-Heathcliff, Heathcliff-Hindley, Heathcliff-Edgar. This series of superimposed conflicting coalitions, which come into being through her mediation, are what Lockwood inadvertently confronts when he discovers her name scribbled inside the bed closet with three male names affixed to it: "*Catherine Earnshaw;* here and there varied to *Catherine Heathcliff,* and then again to *Catherine Linton*" (61). This series of names, which reflects the heroine's role as a mobile signifier within an elementary system of exchange, is pathetically at odds with the emotional loyalties resulting from her role as her father's complement in the nuclear family. (The intensity of this emotional investment is also dramatized for Lockwood when, during that same night, he experiences the powerful grip of the child-Cathy's hand on his.) To be a good *generic* daughter (a willing mediator), and to be a good *particular* daughter (an emotionally invested complement) is to occupy contradictory roles once the daughter ceases to relate exclusively to her father.

Furthermore, while male identity in the nuclear family involves a self that seeks alternately confirmation in relationship and autonomy in outsider status, female identity is never outside of relationship and thus never autonomous within it: the daughter is always performing mediation for her father or his substitutes. In trying to grasp her identity outside of mediation, therefore, Cathy can only conceive of her condition by means of male alienation or as the by-product of her relationship to a man. Thus, she invokes her father's death, Heathcliff's banishment, her marriage to Edgar. These references can be related to those "outside" places in the novel: to the un-specified place that the father goes when he makes his lonely journey from home and returns with Heathcliff early in the novel; to the shadowy place outside Wuthering Heights from which Heathcliff comes and to which he temporarily returns to make his mysterious fortune; and to the life of Thrushcross Grange, Edgar Linton's home, before Cathy enters it. This unmediated position outside (even when the outside is an inside as in Edgar's case) is the unallied aspect of the father and his substitutes. It represents the daughter's exclusion from autonomy and thus becomes the symbolic expression of autonomy not available to her directly.

The wave of nostalgia that breaks from the adult Cathy in the throes of one of her fits takes on profound meaning in this context. "I wish I were a girl again," she cries, "half savage and hardy, and free . . . and laughing at injuries, not maddening under them!" (163). What the words call for is an idealized freedom that is also, implicitly, an idealized relationship: a savage and hardy girlhood describes a freedom that falls under the protection of the father. This is where all loyalties would indeed be unconflicted—where the daughter would exist in a dyadic equilibrium with the father that would incorporate the contradictions of triangular relationship. Cathy seems to be grasping for just such an ideal of freedom in relationship when she rejects the real Heathcliff for a better, imagined ideal. "That is not *my* Heathcliff. I shall love mine yet; and take him with me—he's in my soul" (196), she confides to Nelly. If only, she complains, Edgar would understand and sanction her friendship with Heathcliff, all would be well. If only, in other words, she could be allowed to integrate freedom into relationship (much as her father did in intro-ducing the alien child into his family), she would be resolving the conflicts of selfhood versus family and autonomy versus alliance. Yet because her notion of freedom is never really autonomous but simply another form of alliance, such integration is impossible. While the father could integrate these through the daughter's mediation, the daughter can only do so through her own mediation, by enacting the mediation on her own body. Self-mutilation—"break[ing] their hearts by breaking my own" (155)—becomes her only form of regulating power in a system whose elements are so radically at odds with each other. "[T]hough everybody hated and despised each other, they could not avoid loving me" (159), explains Cathy as she thinks back over her relationships in the final stages of her illness. Mediation becomes the supreme form of power, but a power that, to maintain itself, must ultimately destroy itself. Thus Cathy can picture her death as a form of transcendent power—of absolute and final control: "I shall be incomparably beyond and above you all" (197); and, in the same breath, accuse the others of murder: "You have killed me—and thriven on it, I think" (195).

Death becomes the only solution to the double bind presented by a life in which neither real autonomy nor unconflicted alliance seems to be available. From this perspective, Cathy's self-starvation, already interpreted as one part of a mediating dynamic, takes on a more comprehensive metaphorical meaning. "Anorexia nervosa isn't an attempt to make yourself suffer," explains a contemporary anorectic patient, "it's an attempt, from a postlapsarian vantage point, to recapture Eden.... It isn't that I wanted to be a child again. It's that I wanted to feel the way I felt when I was a child in this asocial life, centered on my home."[18] Cathy's nostalgia for her own girlhood as "savage and hardy and free," a childhood in which she imagines perfect security and perfect freedom to exist simultaneously, echoes the words of the anorectic girl who explains her nostalgia for the past as the pursuit of a place where the contradiction of being a self in the family is reconciled. In refusing to eat, Cathy manipulates her body into solving her divided loyalties within the family triangle and returning her to an imagined simpler state. Anorexia is the ultimate enactment of mediation: all contraries are collapsed into the mediator who then wastes herself away to nothing.

In the next-generation story that follows Cathy's death, we begin with what looks like a perfect father-daughter complementarity—that which had remained tragically out of reach in the first generation. Edgar Linton is rarely away from home (a contrast to the nomadic Mr. Earnshaw), and unlike Cathy Sr., who frequented the moors in complementary relation to her nomadic father, Cathy Jr. exists in corresponding seclusion with her father: "Till she reached the age of thirteen, she had not once been beyond the range of the park by herself. Mr. Linton would take her with him a mile or so outside, on rare occasions" (224). The family, in its drive for closure, seems to collapse and to approach a static dyad of the kind that concluded *Mansfield Park;* for not only is the daughter being formed for the father, but the father now molds himself to the daughter (Cathy Jr. "wielded a despot's sceptre in [Edgar's] heart" [219][19]). Within the context of this new father-daughter relationship, the original split in the father has become inverted: the outside position has become a more recessed inside. Edgar's only retreat from domestic relations is to his library and the pleasures provided by books rather than by the kind of first-hand experience away from home enjoyed by Mr. Earnshaw. Similarly, Linton Heathcliff, who can be said to stand metaphorically for one part of the father (as Heathcliff did in the earlier generation), now embodies an "other" that is a more fragile and sensitive version of Edgar's domestic function. Thus, the two men whom Cathy Jr. must mediate—the ailing father and the ailing boy— are more similar than they are different, and Linton Heathcliff's presence at Thrushcross Grange becomes the symbol not of the daughter's exchange across families but of her stasis within her family of origin. To nurture such "milk-fed calves" (as Heathcliff would call them) entails no reckless wandering on the moors, no wandering from home at all; it is simply a matter of remaining at home, reading, and spooning medicine. This is the static ideal the structure of the nuclear family would tend to engender in the female imagination. It seems finally to reconcile the daughter's conflicting need to mediate both the father and the family, collapsing father and suitor into one extended body to be ministered to. As a fantasy of fixed, unconflicted relations, it also significantly implies the end of the family in its regenerative capacity.[20]

However, this atemporal idyll is not sustained in the novel. It is quickly and violently disrupted as Cathy Jr. is forced into a painful conflict of interest that seems to mimic the conflict her mother experienced. Heathcliff removes Linton from the Grange, then inserts him into the role of Edgar's rival, and finally completes his plot by trapping Cathy at the Heights and marrying her to his son.

Heathcliff, in other words, enforces difference between Edgar and Linton and engineers an exogamous marriage for Cathy Jr. that would not have taken place otherwise or, if it had, would have had an endogamous rather than an exogamous value.

Although Heathcliff's original role in the novel is both literally and figuratively to block patrilineal succession, his manipulation of relationships at this point provides an excellent metaphor for what Lévi-Strauss, in his discussion of the endogamous impasse to which complex kinship systems can lead, refers to as "a sort of sociological *clinamen,* which, whenever the subtle mechanism of exchange is obstructed, will, like a *Deus ex machina,* give the necessary push for a new impetus."[21] In other words, Heathcliff's desire to inherit Wuthering Heights may be read as a metaphor for society's desire to open up property and bloodlines beyond the unit of the family. In primitive society, the prohibition of incest functioned to this end. In a more evolved society dominated by the nuclear family, the taboo of incest begins to lose its efficacy as family love and loyalty gain dominance over exchange; hence, the increasing need for social pressures to detach daughters from the families in which they might otherwise wish to remain. Indeed, it could be argued that the more the prevailing social ideology favored marriage the more likely that there had begun to exist tendencies on the part of women themselves to oppose it. However, given the emotional nature of the daughter's loyalties to her father, arbitrary pressures to effect marriage must be stop-gap measures at best.[22] In this sense, Lévi-Strauss's mechanical model for reestablishing elementary exchange in complex kinship structures fails to account for the introduction of a female point of view—a subjectivity—which, having emerged out of complex kinship structures, must permanently change the nature of all future social function. If the daughter can be tricked into marriage, her mind cannot be permanently manipulated within it. For Cathy Jr. (and for Isabella Linton, another victim of Heathcliff's machinations), the passage into marriage is effected, but the marriages are also soon revealed to them as bad trades for their original situations. As a result, they are neither good wives in the traditional sense nor functional autonomous individuals. This is why Linton Heathcliff's death, which might seem to liberate Cathy Jr. from the horrors of marriage, leaves her with only a more complete sense of desolation: as she explains, "I'm free ... I should feel well—but . . . I feel and see only death! I feel like death!" (325). Since the daughter's identity is dependent on shifting alliances fueled by a nostalgia for her original mediation of her father, pure freedom—where she is not called upon to mediate another identity—can only be a form of death.

Still, the image of Cathy Jr.'s living death is not the novel's final word on her destiny. It serves as a kind of holding pattern while the first-generation story gets told, and it generates an expectation in us that she be revived and reintegrated at the end. Cathy Jr. *is* ultimately revived and made subject to what seems like the requisite happy ending. However, in order to provide this ending, the novel must deviate from the logic of family relations that it has supported up until this point; it must support a new kind of logic as the basis for relationship. What is this logic? How is the novel's ending reached?

After her forced marriage and her husband's death, Cathy remains at Wuthering Heights, positioned between two male figures: her father-in-law, Heathcliff, and her cousin and potential suitor, Hareton. This positioning is, until the end of the novel, an inert triangle. Although it amends one aspect of the difficulty attached to Cathy's original position between her father and Linton Heathcliff by ridding her of any sense of divided loyalty (since her original loving father has been replaced by a repulsive father-in-law), it involves no romantic lure either, since there remains no incentive for Cathy to alter her hostile attitude toward Hareton or loosen her emotional investment in past relationships. For the novel to achieve a happy ending, therefore, Cathy's loyalties to the past and to her dead father in particular must be made to recede and her hardened attitude toward Hareton must be softened. Since the novel has already taught us that the past haunts, that original emotional investments cannot be replaced and only gain power over time, the ending, in which obstacles are dispersed and the heroine is revived from her metaphorical sleep, is bound to jar the reader.[23] At the same time, the ending, for all that it contradicts the earlier lessons of the novel, has a logic of its own, one that has the power to illuminate the future form of the family and of the novel.

Where Cathy Jr.'s first marriage had been engineered by Heathcliff and may be read as a metaphor for society's engineering of its daughters' marriages through social norms, Cathy Jr.'s second marriage has been engineered also, although this time it seems that another kind of plotting is in effect. This final plotting cannot be fully explained as the logical outgrowth of the relationships themselves nor solely as the result of imposed social or fictional norms. Instead, the source of change appears to be the result of plotting that occurs at the intersection of these two modes of organization. Occupying the position where family and fiction intersect is Nelly Dean. Nelly is both a participant in the structural imperatives of family life and a character who remains emotionally undebilitated by them and is able to stand apart and tell the story.

Like the Cathys, Nelly figures in a shifting series of alliances. Beginning with Hindley, she is by turns the ally of Heathcliff, Hareton, Cathy Sr., Edgar Linton, Isabella, Cathy Jr., Linton Heathcliff, and Lockwood. What distinguishes Nelly from her mistresses, however, is her ability to move from one alliance to another. Free from any anchorage in a family, with no apparent tie to a father or lover of her own, she is always available to any relationship in distress. She functions, in other words, not as a self but as a signifier (where a self can be defined as a construction that possesses a deep or unconscious structure of desire, and a signifier is a surface element that carries and adjusts meaning from one context to another). Memory for Nelly Dean is an image (she recalls the child Hindley playing at the crossroads), but not a debilitating nostalgic longing as it is for her two mistresses.

In Nelly Dean, we have the author's notion of the female role retaining its mediating abilities but not paralyzed by emotional investment. In this, the character might be construed as a throw-back, the product of traditional kinship structure: a society in which the porous, extended family served as the context for identity formation. However, unlike her foremothers, she does not function as an object of sexual exchange, the role assigned to women according to the laws of elementary kinship structure. It is not her body that is circulated but her access to information.

Nelly tells the story where the others are either too emotionally invested or too disconnected to do so. And in telling the story, she also functions as a teacher to Lockwood, the reader's surrogate. When the novel begins, Lockwood, on an interpretive level, cannot read: he mistakes dead rabbits for cats, and Cathy Jr. for Heathcliff's wife; he fails to register the true incivility of the occupants of the Heights and returns for a second visit. Nelly teaches him (and us) to comprehend these signs: to place them in a coherent relation to each other and turn a group of hostile co-habitants into a family system whose past makes their present behavior comprehensible.

But Nelly's function goes beyond the ability to interpret signs passively. It is also transformative: it affects the shape of experience. For it is through her presence that Cathy Jr. is reintegrated into the human community, Hareton is raised from his brutish existence, and the stalled narrative is set back in motion. From mediating a narrative of events to Lockwood, Nelly glides effortlessly into mediating the enactment of its ending. She effects this not through direct persuasion or manipulation, but through her existence on the scene as a "third" through whom Cathy Jr. and Hareton can begin to communicate.

Family theorists have noted the value of inserting random "noise"—new, undirected behavior and communication—into a relationship system in order to effect a structural change.[24] Nelly's presence in the novel is like such noise. Through Nelly's presence, Cathy is roused from the death-in-life in which she appears to be suspended and is eased into a relationship with Hareton. Their alliance causes Heathcliff to lose some of his emotional grip on Hareton, thus activating a triangle out of a once static dyad. Ultimately, a new dyad is created as Hareton and Cathy emerge as a kind of reconstructed Adam and Eve, "afraid of nothing" (366), with no ghosts to haunt them. Nelly's presence has worked magic: it has obliterated the past. In the wake of the forgetfulness that imbues the conclusion to the novel, the reader too is obliged to forget; any reminder of Cathy Jr.'s former life becomes curiously inappropriate. If one does happen to recall Cathy's earlier declaration—"I should never love anybody better than papa" (271)—it is to associate the speaker of those words with another story and another life, with the first-generation Cathy who could not extricate herself from the emotional investments of childhood.

Critics have tended to view the conclusion of *Wuthering Heights* as the enactment of a standard scene of Victorian domesticity, with Cathy's schooling of Hareton serving as the passage through which he can emerge as a conventional Victorian patriarch and she can settle into the role of docile helpmate.[25] But if my reading is accepted, then the ending must also be seen as the beginning of yet another spiral leading to that degenerative conclusion embodied by the Cathy-Heathcliff story. In other words, Hareton and Cathy are not so much the "pale replicas of their elders," as Thomas Moser has argued,[26] as they are the pale progenitors. Just as the schizophrenic is said to emerge after some number of generations of increasingly distorted family interaction, so Cathy Sr. and Heathcliff can be said to be the (patho)logical product of that conventional family dynamic described in the second part. In this sense, we cannot say that Emily Brontë revised in her conclusion the family idea that fueled the first-generation story. She simply patched it up, rehabilitated it, as it were, through the intervention of Nelly Dean.

Ultimately, then, Nelly Dean must be viewed as herself a kind of *clinamen*, a *deus ex machina* whose intervention allows for the rehabilitation of the degenerated system that the novel depicts in its first half.[27] She obviates what would otherwise logically have led to the death of the family. As conventional as she is in the content of her values, therefore, Nelly's formal role affords us a glimpse of another organizational idea for culture and of a potentially new female role, even as she helps to reinstate an old order. To be sure, Brontë does not provide this character with an arena in which her qualities can be admired. Nelly is not portrayed as heroic; her role is presented as peripheral and menial. We therefore tend to discount her despite her indispensability to the novel's conclusion. In *Literary Women*, Ellen Moers made the observation that a difference between Jane Austen and George Eliot lay in their respective treatment of class disparities—that the former confined the lower classes to the periphery of her novels while the latter brought them to the center.[28] The same can be said in comparing the use of the freely mediating female consciousness in Emily Brontë and Henry James. Brontë confines her use of this consciousness to the periphery of her novel in the character of the servant, Nelly Dean, while James brings this consciousness to the center by elevating it to the status of "central intelligence." The difference in approach is not surprising. James was positioned within a changing family ideology and within a personal family structure that made possible his appreciation of the unencumbered female consciousness, a positioning that I will discuss in chapter 6. Brontë was situated within an ideological and personal context that made any other use of Nelly's qualities inconceivable.

* * *

It seems appropriate to end this chapter with a few comments on Emily Brontë's own family experience, trying to apply some of the patterns discerned in her novel toward a better understanding of what has generally been viewed as a mysterious, though superficially uneventful, life.

The strangeness associated with Emily Brontë's life is an impression cultivated by Charlotte Brontë, both in her preface to *Wuthering Heights* and in the recollections about her sister that she provided in her letters.[29] The image of the weirdly independent sister and family genius appears at once to have provided Charlotte with a focus for idolatry after Emily's death and with a defense against emotional resentments and rivalries that she may have harbored against her sister alive. We can begin to demystify this portrait of Emily when we situate her within the context of an enmeshed family system of the kind I have described as evolving out of the ideology of the nuclear family.

A comparison to Jane Austen is helpful here. Austen's role in her family at the time she wrote *Mansfield Park* supported the creation in her fiction of an ideal type of the nuclear family. A certain orderliness and ease seem to have characterized her life as the unmarried sister of married brothers that fostered the perspective necessary to produce such a vision of the family. Emily Brontë, by contrast, seems to have lived far more intensely in her family than Austen did—owing to the difference in her relationship to her siblings and also, perhaps more tellingly, to the different time in which she lived: her position at a later point in the evolution of the ideology of the nuclear family. Thus, Austen envisioned a model of family stability; Brontë envisioned a case study in family trauma, anticipating the strain, the elaboration of accommodating measures, and the ultimate revision of structure that the institution of the family would undergo in subsequent generations.

Emily Brontë's mother died when she was three, and Emily was believed to have been her father's favorite and the most like him of all his children.[30] The father, Patrick Brontë, was born into a poor Irish family but succeeded in making his way to England, getting himself admitted to Cambridge, and forging a career as a clergyman-intellectual. As one critic has noted, he appears to have had "remarkable will and stamina, driving himself to overcome great hardships and achieve ambitious goals."[31] However, this energy was not sustained; as he settled into a quiet life as a country curate, "his strivings ceased." The conflicting forces at work in the man come through in family anecdotes. Mrs. Gaskell was told horror stories of Brontë's severe treatment of his wife and children that seem at odds with the playfulness and humor attributed to him in other accounts. Richard Chase, in his centennial essay on the Brontës, addresses this duality in the father, making him out as alternately "maudlin and fanatical"—a kind of caricature of the nineteenth-century patriarch.[32] It is just such a patriarchal caricature that Emily Brontë depicts in Mr. Earnshaw, a man who is increasingly tyrannical in his treatment of his family but who still fondly strokes his daughter's hair in his calmer domestic moments.

A characterization of Patrick Brontë as split between aggression and passivity, between tyranny and benevolence, between life outside the family (his past history of "striving") and his role as the purveyor of domestic order within may help explain the seemingly paradoxical aspects of Emily Brontë's character. Emily was both the wild child (playing all day on the moors with her sister Anne in tow, cauterizing a dog bite with a hot iron, and refusing to consult a doctor in her last illness) and the domestic angel who baked bread and kept house for her father while her sisters were away at school (she herself could not bear being away from home for any extended period). A corresponding split is discernible in her diary papers in which mundane references to turnips and dogs alternate with descriptions of her fantasy world of Gondal. Given my analysis of the daughter's regulating role in the nuclear family, the duality of Emily's nature can be understood as the by-product of a profound emotional investment in her father. This supports a reading of her character that fills out David Daiches's conclusion that "ultimate passion is for [Emily Brontë] rather a kind of recognition of one's self—one's true and absolute self—in the object of passion"[33]—where the object of passion is the original familial object of authority: the father.

What further elucidates Emily's relationship with her father is the implicit role played in that relationship by her only brother, Branwell. One anecdote that Mrs. Gaskell was told by Patrick Brontë seems especially illuminating. It concerns a ritual in which he asked his children questions meant to develop their moral character. The question he recalled posing of Emily was not about herself but about her brother: How should Branwell be treated when he is naughty? "Reason with him," was Emily's reply, "and when he won't listen to reason, whip him."[34] The response reflects the daughter's mediating position between father and son—a mediation that recognizes the power of the father and implicitly shares in it. Since Emily makes reference to the recourse of whipping Branwell and recommends it to her father as the last resort, this places her in the position of being the moderating influence that is aware of its power to unleash more severe punishment. She is her father's respondent and tool in one sense, and, in another, she holds the reins to her brother's destiny. *Wuthering Heights* dramatizes a similar situation. Young Catherine asks her father to bring her a whip as a gift when he returns from his journey early in the novel. He brings her Heathcliff instead, who will serve metaphorically as the whip to her brother Hindley and later to her husband Edgar. The whip destroys these two men and, significantly, it also destroys the one who wields it, Catherine herself.

For all that Emily was not the passionate soulmate of her brother (critics have had little success tracing a resemblance between Branwell and Heathcliff), Branwell nonetheless appears to have played an important role in her life, as Hindley and Edgar did in Catherine's, and seems ultimately to be linked to her early death. We know, for example, that she would get up late at night to let him in, helping to hide his usual state of drunkenness from her father. His death from deteriorated health brought on by alcoholism appears, if not to have precipitated Emily's decline, at least to have destroyed her will to live: she died of tuberculosis less than a year after he did, refusing all attempts at medical treatment and experiencing a physical wasting, attributed as much to an anorectic refusal to nourish herself as to the natural debilitation of the disease.[35] If she both restrained and wielded the whip that was her father's judgment regarding her brother, it was a whip that struck both ways, destroying both of them.

The triangular interaction that included Emily, Branwell, and their father may also cast light on the roles played by Charlotte and Anne in the family and on how these roles may have affected their emotional and creative development. As they were the excluded, or at least the less directly triangled, daughters, this may account for their greater ability to engage in employment and pursue creative outlets not directly linked to the family. No doubt these daughters paid for their relative freedom by suffering a sense of paternal neglect and by acting out in other, substitute, relationships the familial role occupied by Emily.[36] This hypothesis could elucidate a recurring theme in Charlotte Brontë's fiction: the heroine, an orphan or outsider to a family system, seeks acceptance from a paternalistic lover while engaging in an oblique competition with a more privileged female character. If, in childhood, Charlotte did desire to usurp the role occupied by Emily, this may account for her need to mythologize Emily in death. The myth that Charlotte created and nurtured of her sister as a willful, mysterious genius seems to me to have given Charlotte a degree of detachment from a figure who in life was probably the object of intense resentment.

Admittedly, I have also created a biographical myth of Emily—and of Charlotte too—for my own purposes here. If Jane Austen tends to invite underreading (a casualness of interpretation, a tendency to take the life and the work at face value), Emily Brontë tends to invite overreading, and I have simply followed the lure of *Wuthering Heights*.

The following chapter on George Eliot continues to explore the dynamics of triangulation begun in this chapter. Like Catherine Earnshaw, Maggie Tulliver in *The Mill on the Floss* is destroyed when her original role in a family triangle ceases to be viable. Although Eliot seems to have been able to negotiate for herself a place in relation to her family where she was protected from its more debilitating effects—where she was, in fact, empowered as a writer and as a woman—her life and work resonate with many of the same interactive patterns that I have traced in *Wuthering Heights* and in the life of its author.

CHAPTER 5

The Mill on the Floss: Substitution

The other novelists treated in this study lived lives that seem—emo-tionally, at least—compatible with patterns traceable in their fiction. George Eliot at first looks like an exception. Critics have long been baffled by the way in which her life appears to deviate from the lives she permitted her heroines. Her heroines never aspire to do the kind of work or achieve the kind of success of their creator; not one ever considers living with a man to whom she is not legally married, as Eliot did. Critical response to George Eliot from the nineteenth cen-tury through to the present has reflected an ongoing attempt to connect the novelist's work with her life, but the attempt has always been a struggle. Indeed, in surveying the history of this response, one is more impressed with the shifts in judgment than with any one argument in itself.

Critical response to Eliot has essentially moved through three phases. Early readers tended to see intellectual and rational elements as ascendent. They focused on the novels' detached narrative voice and wealth of learned allusion as evidence both for Eliot's greatness and for a certain aberrance in her female nature that seemed in keeping with her unconventional life. As Elaine Showalter has ar-gued, female readers (and aspiring female novelists especially) saw Eliot as an intimidating and unsympathetic figure: "Her very superi-ority depressed them."[1] Not far into this century, however, critics began to recognize an emotional side to Eliot. Virginia Woolf, writing in 1919, was perhaps the first to break through the official portrait. In Eliot, Woolf writes, "the ancient consciousness of woman, charged with suffering and sensibility, and for so many ages dumb, seems...to have brimmed and overflowed and uttered a demand for something."[2] F. R. Leavis translated this perspective into less laudatory, esthetic terms in 1937 when he argued that Eliot

115

overidentified with some of her heroines and showed a lack of artistic control in the conclusion to *The Mill on the Floss*. Dating more or less from Leavis, critics also began to portray the novelist's life differently. Instead of the calmly stoic and sybilline figure of the early portrait, Eliot began to be depicted as a rather desperate woman, struggling to maintain respectability against the opposing tide of a passionate nature.[3]

Recently, the critical perspective on Eliot has shifted again as judgments based on biographical and esthetic considerations have yielded to critiques of the novelist and her work as these relate to ideology. For feminist critics, who have contributed most substantially to this perspective, Eliot's self-renouncing heroines are not moral exemplars but victims of patriarchy, capitulating to the forms of Victorian convention. These critics have sought to find in the novels a repressed counter-message that opposes their more conventional moral message. Hence, Eliot's emotional excesses and failures at balance criticized by Leavis and his followers have ceased to be viewed as expressions of artistic failure but have become clues to the hidden story behind the ideological cover. Contemporary critics have also used the facts of the author's life in new ways, as part of their proof that she was not at ease with the diminishment she enforced upon her heroines. Phyllis Rose, for example, countering the previous generation's tendency to construe Eliot as a needy woman striving for respectability, has rediscovered the author's assertiveness, pointing out the strategies by which she took control of decisions and events while employing the language of emotional fragility and dependence.[4]

Despite the ongoing effort to bring Eliot's life into line with her work, these shifts in critical perspective suggest that a gap still remains between the world Eliot created in fiction and the world she made possible for herself through writing. I think it is possible to bridge this gap and to explain the disparity of past critical perspectives as well by situating George Eliot in the context of a history of the family. A study of the dynamics of the nuclear family as it relates both to the representation of Eliot's heroines and to what we know of her own life can help us see how tied Eliot was to the ideological patterns of a stereotypical daughter's role within a nuclear family, and how her personal and professional achievements were the result of elaborate substitutions within this family configuration. Ultimately, it is to see Eliot as an extremely ingenious regulating daughter, bound to an ideological system already in decline, but effecting extraordinary variations within the limitations bequeathed to her.

Of all her novels, *The Mill on the Floss* seems the best focus for this kind of study. Although its heroine follows the typical self-renouncing trajectory of the Eliot heroine, it is the novel closest to personal memoir. It is also the novel most explicitly concerned with the dynamics of family life as a shaping force in the development of individual character. In this chapter, I shall begin with an analysis of *The Mill on the Floss* that traces the ideologically determined patterns of family interaction that shape the identity of the heroine, Maggie Tulliver, and then move to an examination of the life of the author, using these patterns to help gain a better understanding of Marian Evans (the character who is antecedent to but also, as I shall argue, contiguous with the character of the professional author, George Eliot) in her role as a daughter in a nuclear family. Finally, by explaining how Eliot was able to use the dynamics of her daughter's role to build on her formative identity, I shall show how she was able to arrive at a freer, more creative life than that which she made available to her heroine. My understanding of Eliot as a regulating daughter both for her own family system and for the ideology of her age at a historical moment when that ideology was beginning to unravel makes her a point of transition and of contrast to Henry James, the subject of the next chapter, who would grasp the emergence of a new ideology and describe a new structure and dynamic to support it.

*   *   *

> A wide plain, where the broadening Floss hurries on between its green banks to the sea, and the loving tide, rushing to meet it, checks its passage with an impetuous embrace.[5]

The first line of *The Mill on the Floss* is a syntactical fragment and functions as a kind of directorial note for the novel. It situates us in a natural landscape and depicts the relationship of two natural forces in dynamic equilibrium: the River Floss rushes to the sea; the tide seeks to be united with the river. Hurrying toward each other, river and sea effect a loving, if "impetuous," merger in which the river's momentum is checked by the reciprocal, opposing movement of the tide. This image has metaphorical significance with regard to the heroine's "source" relationship in the novel—her relationship with her father. Yet the complicated and fragmented syntax in which the image is expressed may warn us that this will be neither a simple nor a complete metaphor for the human relationship.

For one thing, the image of river meeting sea depicts a reciprocity that appears to ground the novel in elemental natural forces that exist in an eternal present. The human relationships in the novel, by contrast, are introduced so as to emphasize their existence in time and their grounding in the conventions of gender enforced by the nuclear family. In the first chapter, the narrator recalls a shadowy figure gazing at the river—"that little girl" who seems at once to be the nascent fictional character, Maggie Tulliver, and the narrator's childhood self remembered. In the second chapter, we leave the larger natural landscape and the frame of memory behind and enter the Tulliver household, where we encounter Mr. and Mrs. Tulliver in conversation. Theirs is the first human interaction that we see, and it establishes a context within which the life of "that little girl" will need to be understood. In other words, the novel proceeds to juxtapose the ahistorical, "felt" image of reciprocity associated with the natural scene with a scene in which a husband and wife are clearly positioned within a historical and social context.

The actual conversation between Tulliver and his wife that opens the second chapter also underscores the distance we have traveled from the harmonious natural image that begins the novel. While the river and sea are sublimely compatible, merged in an "impetuous embrace," the husband and wife are engaged in mundane talk that reflects a very prosaic incompatibility. Their exchange is reminiscent of stock scenes of married life: she literalizes his figurative speech ("I meant it to stand for summat else," Tulliver explains to his wife in exasperation about one such misunderstanding, "but niver mind" [58]); and she comprehends his concerns with lawsuits, arbitrations, and their son's education only as they refer to her storage of linens, the "couple o' fowl [that wants] killing" for dinner next week, and the likelihood of being able to do Tom's laundry if he goes away to school. Because they operate on different logical levels (she is literal and domestic; he, more abstract and publicly political), their incompatibility expresses itself not through outright confrontation but through gaps and dislocations: by benign neglect on his part ("he had the marital habit of not listening very closely" [58]); and by her "facility of saying things which drive him in the opposite direction to the one she desired" (135).

Ironically, we learn in the very next chapter that Tulliver had selected his wife carefully: he "picked her from her sisters o' purpose 'cause she was a bit weak . . . a pleasant sort o' soft woman" (68). The stock quality of their opening scene now becomes attributable to his having chosen her according to the superficial conventions of male-female role-playing in the nuclear family, i.e., according to the doctrine of "separate spheres" in which the wife is stereotypically weaker and softer than the husband and occupied with the literal duties of the household while he is engaged with the larger, more abstract concerns of the world. However, even as Tulliver explains the rationale for his choice according to conventional notions of family life, he exposes the faulty logic of this kind of conventional thinking:

> But, you see, when a man's got brains himself, there's no knowing where they'll run to; an' a pleasant sort o' soft woman may go on breeding you stupid lads and 'cute wenches, till it's like as if the world was turned topsy-turvy. (68–69)

What this speech both obscures through its biological terminology and brings into relief once we begin to focus on the inadequacy of the stereotypical husband-wife relationship is the sense in which the "crossin' of breeds" (at least as regards the daughter) can be understood as the structural remedy for conventional marriage. Indeed, the daughter's identity is developed so as to serve the father as a far more perfect complement than his wife ever could. While the relationship of Maggie's parents is founded on physical and conventional characteristics that have long ceased to convey a mutual attraction, the relationship of Maggie and her father reflects a profound structural complementarity that endures. This "fit" of daughter to father makes comprehensible why Tulliver is Maggie's most ardent defender and admirer, why he "craves" her presence in his illness, and why she remains always the "delight of his eyes," despite her numerous failings in the eyes of others.[6]

The difference between the husband-wife relationship and the father-daughter relationship is illustrated when we move from the scene between Mr. and Mrs. Tulliver in chapter 2 to the scene in chapter 3 in which Tulliver meets with his business advisor, Riley, while Maggie sits reading in a corner. We shift from a depiction of two people at cross-purposes to a depiction of three in apparent equilibrium. Riley, Tulliver, and Maggie form a triangle in which Maggie's place in the corner positions her in the role of mediator between two sites that symbolically refer to the two aspects of paternal identity we have already discussed as a structural principle in *Wuthering Heights*. The father in his internal, domestic role is represented by Tulliver himself in this scene. He is presiding over his own hearth in entertaining Riley, taking proprietary enjoyment in the comforts of his home, his daughter's cleverness, and his wife's buxom appearance. Moreover, his primary concern at this moment—arranging for his son's education—is a familial concern. At the same time, the father in his external capacity (as mill-owner, breadwinner, man of worldly animosities and schemes) is assisted here by Riley, "a man of business," whose talents Tulliver draws on for counsel in his legal affairs and, in this instance, for advice on preparing his son for the world. Riley, in this sense, is Tulliver's surrogate and extension in the community of St. Oggs. The scene explicitly depicts the duality of Tulliver's role, which, like Mr. Earnshaw's in *Wuthering Heights,* links domestic experience with the larger world outside.

In accordance with her father's dual identity—a duality required by the structure of the nuclear family, discussed in the previous chapter—Maggie's complementary relationship to her father cannot involve a simple balancing of his character through opposing characteristics (a balancing doomed to failure, as Tulliver and his wife demonstrate in their interaction). It must involve instead a harmonizing of the two sides of her father's nature in relation to domestic space and outer world. As her father's mediator, Maggie must therefore reflect the contradictions of her father's dual nature, transforming these contradictions into their complementary female form. By being a child as well as a female, she offers her father the physical evidence of complementing his strength with her weakness (improving upon her mother's subordinate status by being, as it were, doubly helpless in relation to him). At the same time, Maggie also complements his intellectual energy with imaginative energy—with a feminine "[a]'cuteness."[7] When, in the same scene, Maggie offers her interpretation of the picture in Defoe's *The History of the Devil* to Riley and her father, she in effect glosses her own role:

[T]hey've put [the woman] in [the water], to find out whether she's a witch or no, and if she swims, she's a witch, and if she's drowned—and killed, you know—she's innocent, and not a witch, but only a poor silly old woman. But what good would it do her then, you know, when she was drowned? Only, I suppose she'd go to heaven, and God would make it up to her. (66–67)

In order to survive, Maggie must, like the woman in the water, be both the good woman (confined to a domestic space and a subordinate role) and the witch (the emotional and imaginative complement of her father, whose elaborate defensive schemes and virulent animosities reflect the intensity and potential destructiveness of his external interests). And she *can* manage to occupy both roles so long as she relates solely to her father. As she suggests herself in her solution for the woman in the picture, "God," the metaphorical father figure, is the site of all solace, the place where contradiction gets reconciled. Maggie's father, as shall be seen, does serve this magical function of resolving conflict and contradiction for his daughter during her early life.

If the story that Maggie tells about the picture in the book is an allegory for her own case, her devotion to books in general serves as a broader metaphor for the dynamic inherent in her relationship with her father.[8] As an avid reader, Maggie is a passive receptacle for another's words: a daughter confined within the order of the text and, metaphorically, subject to the authority of the father. However, she is also (as her focus on picture over words in this scene dramatizes) an extrapolator, capable of embroidering and extending a story, and hence of following her father's flights outside the known domestic sphere through emotional and imaginative empathy. In short, the act of reading, by being both a passive, receptive act and an act inspiring of the imagination, appeals to Maggie, I would suggest, because it involves training in the opposing impulses of self-abnegation on the one hand and imaginative self-indulgence on the other—impulses that she is called upon to exhibit in her mediating relationship with her father. We see the results of this training at the time of Tulliver's bankruptcy when she defends her father against the harsh judgment of the rest of the family. Her defense is at once an expression of intense loyalty, reflecting her willingness "to do or bear anything for his sake" (284), and a passionate articulation that fearlessly opposes the viewpoint of others (what Tom perceives as her "hectoring, as-suming manners" [285]). She is the devoted, good daughter and the unruly, bold daughter—the innocent woman and the witch—but only insofar as these two personas serve the two sides of her father.

From this structural reading of the father-daughter relationship, we can conclude that Maggie's traits (like Catherine Earnshaw's in *Wuthering Heights*), so highly individual out of context, derive their form and meaning through the very thoroughness with which they were originally formed to fit the contradictory needs of the father's identity. If Maggie does not possess a "well-balanced mind" (494), as the narrator tells us at a later point, if she is ultimately viewed by St. Oggs as "dangerous to daughters" (621), this is because she has been educated to the complex function of mediating a father like Tulliver. In combining a large fund of domestic generosity with an equally large fund of energy directed outward toward commercial schemes and defenses, Tulliver is a father especially liable to produce a daugh-ter of distinctly unconventional and erratic character. Indeed, the other father-daughter pair in the novel, Mr. Dean and Lucy, seem designed to contrast Mr. Tulliver and Maggie, and to demonstrate how a more routinely operating father-businessman would tend to produce a more conventional daughter. As shall be shown, however, Tulliver, and Maggie too by extension, are far more the realistic products of the ideological conditions of family life of the period than are the more stereotypical Deans.

I have concentrated thus far on the father-daughter relationship in a vacuum without reference to the larger context within which the relationship operates. But the functional nature of Maggie's identity relates not only to her father but also to her family as a whole as it exists at the beginning of the novel as a relatively closed, stable sys-tem. Mr. Tulliver determined the origin of this family (he chose his wife; she didn't choose him), thus becoming the template upon which his daughter's identity and hence the improvement of the original relationship between himself and his wife was forged. This improve-ment constituted not only an improvement for Tulliver, but a bal-anced core relation around which other family members could then be assigned positions.

The temporary stability of a relatively closed (nuclear) family re-quires that family members engage in a repetitive dynamic that at once reinforces their assigned roles and maintains the boundaries of the family by preventing individuals from exceeding the limits of these roles. This, I have argued, was the lesson of *Clarissa*. The harsh treatment Maggie experiences at the hands of her mother, brother, and aunts during her early years serves as one part of this dynamic. Through scapegoating—that tendency of others to find fault with Maggie for qualities and behavior that they come to associate with her essential nature—her difference from her persecutors is brought into relief (her femaleness in contrast with the maleness of her brother Tom; her "Tulliverness" in contrast with the "Dodson-ness" of her mother and aunts). This setting off of difference also serves to emphasize her special relation to her father. His appreciation of her makes him feel uniquely discriminating ("He seldom found any one volunteering praise of 'the little wench': it was usually left entirely to himself to insist on her merits" [139]), and his sympathetic response to her, so unlike the response of others, makes her value him all the more ("Her father had always defended and excused her, and her loving remembrance of his tenderness was a force within her that would enable her to do or bear anything for his sake" [284]). Thus Maggie reinforces the identity of all family members, including herself, by being the focus of everyone's scapegoating *except* her father's.

Tulliver supplies the other part of the family dynamic. The scapegoating of Maggie (efficacious up to a point but destructive to the family if uncontrolled) is kept in check initially through his intervention. Time and again, Maggie is placed in a situation where blame is heaped upon her, only to be raised from ignominy by her father; his interference protects her from further humiliation and brings the family as a whole back into temporary harmony. Two examples illustrate how the father's response keeps the family in balance. In one scene, Maggie, in a fit of anger and frustration as the result of scapegoating by her mother and aunts, cuts off her hair during a family gathering. Luckily, her father is present to intercede: "Give over crying: father'll take your part" (125), he assures her. Here, the scapegoating is checked, and she is not driven to more violent action. In a subsequent scene at Aunt Pullet's, however, the father is temporarily absent. Now, the scapegoating escalates, and Maggie is made desperate: she pushes Lucy into the mud, then runs away to the gypsies. Only after she is returned to her family is her father able to intercede ("Mr. Tulliver spoke his mind very strongly when he reached home that evening, and the effect was seen in the remarkable fact that Maggie never heard one reproach from her mother or one taunt from Tom about this foolish business of her running away to the gypsies" [180]). The dynamic of these scenes resembles the dynamic in *Mansfield Park,* in which Fanny Price, the scapegoat of the Bertram family, has her scapegoating checked first by Edmund and later and more effectively by her adoptive father, Sir Thomas. However, the guilt that inspires Edmund and Sir Thomas to intercede on Fanny's behalf is a shaping force in the family, whereas Tulliver's sympathy for his daughter reflects a structural relation already set. (Indeed, one might argue that guilt, once it has become fully incorporated into one's relationship to another and has ceased to be reactive to a particular injustice, takes the form of sympathy.) Unlike Austen's novel, then, the plot of Eliot's begins with the family in temporary equilibrium and charts the inefficacy of the original family dynamic in the context of later life.

In analyzing the patterns of the schizogenic family, Gregory Bateson writes that "any self-correcting system which has lost its governor ... spirals into never-ending, but always systematic, distortions."[9] In *The Mill on the Floss,* all the relationships in which Maggie becomes involved are substitutions that systematically distort the original balanced relationship with her father. These distortions superficially appear to issue from Tulliver's bankruptcy, but, as we shall see, they have their source in the family itself as a temporarily self-correcting system destined to lose its "governor."

We can trace the process by which the Tulliver family moves from stability to a spiraling instability by analyzing the nature of Maggie's relationship with her brother Tom. Maggie comprehends her love for Tom as rooted in her earliest memory: "the first thing I ever remember in my life is standing with Tom by the side of the Floss while he held my hand" (402). As many critics have noted, however, Maggie's feelings concerning her childhood relationship with her brother are contradicted by the friction and unhappiness recorded in the early scenes between them. Maggie's sense of her past with Tom seems to reflect her tendency (and a tendency of her creator as well) to confuse the facts she relates with the feelings that are evoked in her in relating them. We can account for this confusion if we recognize that Tom's relationship to Maggie, while it appears to remain constant (to reflect disharmony and misunderstanding from the beginning), changes not in itself but in its context. What changes is the balance of the family system within which Tom and Maggie interact, and this radically affects the way in which the heroine experiences her relationship with her brother.

In effect, Tom plays two distinct roles in relation to Maggie: one, the more antecedent role, includes the father; the other substitutes for him. (Although one role appears to be subsequent to the other, the substituting role must be understood as always present, "embedded," so to speak, in the original role.) Tom's original role is represented in the sequence of events in chapters 4 and 5 dealing with his return from school for the holidays. In chapter 4, Maggie, in excited anticipation of Tom's return, is confronted with the appalling knowledge that the rabbits he had asked her to care for during his absence are dead because she has forgotten to feed them. Tom arrives home in chapter 5 and is predictably furious when he learns what has happened. He announces that he will not take her fishing with him the next day. His anger and the prospect of punishment plunge Maggie into a misery so acute that she arouses the attention of her father. He quickly enters on her side: "Be good to her, do you hear?," Tulliver orders Tom when he notices that Maggie has retreated to the attic, "Else I'll let you know better" (90). The next scene depicts the reunion of brother and sister, engaged in "one of their happy mornings" (the only really harmonious interaction recorded between them in the novel). The idyllic fishing expedition then leads into the final paragraphs of the chapter, in which the narrator muses on the powerful attachments of childhood that enrich all later experience.

The episode contains a number of key components: Maggie's original misdeed in neglecting the rabbits; Tom's anger at her for her neglect; their father's intervention, which causes Tom to forgive Maggie and brings the children into harmony; and the narrator's nostalgic response to their reunion. We see in this chain of occurrences that, despite Maggie's undeniable negligence in failing to feed the rabbits, her alliance with her father serves to cancel her crime in relation to her brother and make possible their "happy morning." In other words, the daughter's privileged relation to the father gives her special immunity, a kind of added power that, after a brief struggle, brings the son into a harmonious (if short-lived) complementary relationship with her. Not the last scene alone, then, but the whole dynamic (which makes the last scene possible) can be understood as the reference for the narrator's nostalgic commentary. It should also be noted that despite the reality of Maggie's negligence, which precipitates the chain of events, she sees herself as being scapegoated by her brother ("O, he was very cruel! Hadn't she wanted to give him the money and said how very sorry she was? . . . she had never been naughty to Tom—had never *meant* to be naughty to him" [89]). Thus, Maggie's sense of being treated unjustly (her expectation that good intentions and a guilty conscience should cancel a crime), by turning Tom's justified if severe reproof into scapegoating, makes her father's ability to bring Tom into line seem that much more like an act of natural justice in her eyes.[10] The facts of the case appear to have little relevance for the participants, whose responses have been conditioned by their roles in an already established family drama.

A very different configuration, though derived from the above, is represented in the subsequent chapter—the episode in chapter 6 in which Tom and Maggie are sharing jam puffs. This time, the scene begins idyllically with the brother and sister swinging on the boughs of the elder tree and lazily eating from the store of jam puffs that they have carried away from their mother's kitchen. As they arrive at the last jam puff, Tom cuts it into two parts (of slightly unequal size) and insists that the pieces be assigned "fairly." Maggie would prefer to let Tom have the bigger half, but he orders her to shut her eyes and "choose":

> So she shut her eyes quite close, till Tom told her to "say which," and then she said, "Left hand."
>
> "You've got it," said Tom in rather a bitter tone . . . handing decidedly the best piece to Maggie.
>
> "O, please, Tom, have it; I don't mind—I like the other: please take this."
>
> "No, I shan't," said Tom, almost crossly, beginning on his own inferior piece.
>
> Maggie, thinking it was no use to contend further, began too, and ate up her half puff with considerable relish as well as rapidity. But Tom had finished first and had to look on while Maggie ate her last morsel or two, feeling in himself a capacity for more. . . .
>
> "O, you greedy thing!" said Tom when she had swallowed the last morsel. He was conscious of having acted very fairly and

thought she ought to have considered this and made up to him for it. . . .

Maggie turned quite pale. "O, Tom, why didn't you ask me?"

"I wasn't going to ask you for a bit, you greedy. You might have thought of it without, when you know I gave you the best bit."

"But I wanted you to have it—you know I did," said Maggie in an injured tone.

"Yes, but I wasn't going to do what wasn't fair, like Spouncer. He always takes the best bit, if you don't punch him for it, and if you choose the best with your eyes shut, he changes his hands. But if I go halves, I'll go 'em fair—only I wouldn't be greedy." (99–100)

Examined out of context, this scene depicts a double bind—what Bateson and his colleagues have described as the impasse produced when two mutually exclusive messages, occurring on two logical levels, are relayed to an individual who is not in a position to critique their inconsistency.[11] Maggie, whose helplessness and credulity before her brother provide the scene with much of its dramatic power, is subjected to two contradictory messages here: the primary injunction that she behave "fairly" and choose according to the rules is contradicted by the secondary injunction that she be "generous" and act spontaneously to give up what she has won. Not only are the notions of fairness and generosity contradictory notions in the context of Tom's original requirement that Maggie "choose which hand," but also Tom's subsequent condemnation of Maggie for selfishness, in attempting to make generosity subject to his rules and his sense of justice, is a more abstract contradiction since, for an act to be truly generous, it must be spontaneous and unlegislated. Given these two levels of contradiction, there is no way in this situation that Maggie could have made the right choice. Her subsequent experiences with Philip Wakem and Stephen Guest reenact the dynamic of the jam puff episode. Each of these relationships becomes the site for Maggie of the same kind of mutually exclusive injunctions: one invoking "fairness" (in the form of her duty to her father and to Lucy), the other invoking "generosity" (in the form of Philip's neediness and Stephen's passionate desire). Her relationship with Philip ends the first time with a simple act of renunciation that returns her to her brother. It leads the second time to her elopement with Stephen, but, ultimately, it comes to the same end: renunciation and a return to her brother. In this sense, the elopement and return seem to serve her only as a means to a more intense re-creation of the familiar opposition between her brother and herself. After fleeing from her lover and arriving at her brother's house in shame, the narrator explains, "she almost desired to endure the severity of Tom's reproof, to submit in patient silence to that harsh disapproving judgment against which she had so often rebelled" (612). In her compulsion to locate herself at the crossroad of irreconcilable choices, Maggie would seem, then, to be the tragic victim of her brother. Her life would seem to be the acting out of patterns to which she was conditioned by the chronic double-binding Tom imposed upon her during her childhood.

But this conclusion is incomplete. Maggie is no simple victim of Tom. Although the patterns described above do indeed structure the life of the heroine, a more comprehensive reading is required to show how the brother's messages have themselves been conditioned within a family system that has a father-daughter complementarity at its center. If we read the dynamic of the jam puff episode against that earlier dynamic of scapegoating and sympathy that we discussed as necessary for maintaining the closure and stability of the original family (in which the brother-sister relationship was balanced through the intervention of the father), we can see that the double bind that Tom imposes on Maggie in the jam puff scene is the residue of that earlier dynamic. Now that the father has disappeared, Maggie and Tom's relationship has spiraled out of control; the stable triangle has become an unstable dyad. Maggie continues to experience an acute sense of injustice at Tom's scapegoating but now lacks the means by which to check his persecution. Tom, unencumbered by paternal authority, is now permitted to scapegoat his sister unchecked. What drives their interaction, in other words, are patterns from early experience that exist in systematically escalating and distorted (substitute) forms.

The increasing frustration and alienation that characterize Tom and Maggie's relationship can be traced to the difference between male and female identity formation in the family. According to the terms of nuclear family structure already outlined in the preceding chapter, the daughter mediates the father, complementing the two aspects of his identity, inside and outside. The son, on the other hand, imitates the father and expects to be mediated in turn.[12] Once the father has dropped out of the dynamic, the brother-sister relationship becomes one in which the brother continually expects to be mediated by the sister, and the sister continually attempts to mediate the brother.

As the products of this model of family interaction, Tom and Maggie are fated to be "dispositions . . . not in sympathy" (406) and to see each other in ways that are out of step with the roles they played in their family of origin. Despite the desire for a mutual fit, they are thwarted by an essential structural incompatibility. Maggie, formed to mediate her father, appears to Tom to be perpetually in oscillation between "extremes"—a nature lacking in "consistency" and "utterly untrustworthy." Tom, for his part, formed to imitate his father, adopts the outline of his father in assuming the conventional forms of his authority but cannot become the man himself. Hence, Tom appears to Maggie as a two-dimensional justice figure: "below feeling those mental needs which were often the source of the wrongdoing or absurdity that made her life a planless riddle to him" (504–5)—needs that her father was always quick to understand. The residue of the family dynamic that included Maggie, Tom, and their father now gets expressed through that sense of superiority Maggie feels toward Tom and the more intense scapegoating to which Tom is driven in his attempt to place his conventional authority above the emotional superiority that his sister carries as the legacy of her early complementary relationship with her father. "You're always setting yourself up above me and every one else," complains Tom bitterly, ". . . you should leave it to me to take care of my mother and you and not put yourself forward. You think you know better than any one, but you're almost always wrong. I can judge better than you can" (319). However, such lectures are doomed, like the behavior itself, to a kind of repetition compulsion: "You think you know best . . . you will never give way," Tom repeats later in frustration. "Yet you might have sense enough to see that a brother, who goes into the world and mixes with men, necessarily knows better what is right and respectable for his sister than she can know for herself" (503–4).

Tom's efforts to control Maggie and her efforts to please him are bound to fail. This is because the dynamic by which she is controlled and he is made powerful cannot satisfy either one. While Maggie is continually punished by Tom for being wrong, she also continually feels herself to be unjustly accused by a harsh and unfeeling brother ("it seemed," explains the narrator, "... as if he were a prophetic voice predicting her future failings—and yet all the while, she judged him in return: she said inwardly, that he was narrow and unjust" [504]). Tom, on his side, is placed in the position of always seeming to be disobeyed by his sister, so that even his final, sovereign act of patriarchal power—his banishing of her from his sight—galls him as the reminder of her insurrection: "the thought of it made his days bitter to him" (630). Both Tom and Maggie base their actions on a desire to restore some stability to their relationship but succeed only in establishing more profound instability.

Ironically, what I have analyzed as a chronic pattern of conflict (leading ultimately to complete alienation between Maggie and Tom) is also the pattern that constitutes the form of Maggie's attachment to her brother, and that links her to him until death. I have argued that the father-daughter relationship is the lost origin—both for the stable nuclear family and for Maggie's identity—since the father constituted the mind upon which the daughter's identity was molded and where contradictory messages were reconciled. With her father gone, any relationship that promises success, support, and harmony must be experienced by Maggie as a transient and illusory substitute. She must ultimately come to see failure, frustration, and alienation—that which her brother represents—as the realistic and indeed inevitable fruits of adult relationship. Since she cannot reproduce the form of the original relationship, she seeks, again and again, the experience of the substituting one, the insoluble double-bind represented by her brother, whose "mind" she "can never mould [herself] upon, and yet ... cannot endure to alienate ... " (611–12).

With this paradigmatic model of family interaction established, we can now return to a consideration of the discussion between Tulliver and Riley in chapter 3. We can now see in Tulliver's concerns a historically conditioned view of the family that is emotionally if not intellectually supported by the author. Tulliver's discussion with Riley centers on two issues that are of pressing importance to him: the lawsuits and arbitrations with which he is embroiled, and his son Tom's education. The former involves him in external action, namely the defense of what he takes to be encroachments upon the land and river that provide him with his source of livelihood. He interprets the "dykes and erigations," improvements that his neighbors wish to perform on their land, as "an infringement on [his] legitimate share of water-power" (225)—a threat to the ecological balance of his business. By the same token, the decision to have his son properly educated is also a defensive action, although here the territory being defended is more personal than commercial; as he explains:

> [W]hy, if I made him a miller an' farmer, he'd be expectin' to take to the mill an' the land, an' a-hinting at me as it was time for me to lay by an' think o' my latter end. Nay, nay, I've seen enough o' that wi' sons. I'll niver pull my coat off before I go to bed. I shall give Tom an' eddication an' put him to a business, as he may make a nest for himself an' not want to push me out o' mine. (65)

This defensive argument resembles the rationale he gave for his choice of a wife ("I picked her from her sisters o' purpose 'cause she was a bit weak, like; for I wasn't a-goin' to be told the rights o' things by my own fireside" [168]). In both cases, Tulliver has in mind an image of family life frozen and closed around himself. Moreover, the domestic defense that spurs his concern for Tom's education will, he believes, help him hold the line against his neighbors ("he'll be even wi' the lawyers and folks, and put me up to a notion now an' then" [128]), and hence, it will also contribute to his external defense.

Tulliver's defensiveness about his property and his personal identity situate him in relation to a prevailing ideology of family life. Although he is described by the narrator as a representative of "traditional" opinions, it is easy to see how far we have moved from the view of family life depicted in *Mansfield Park*. In Austen's novel, the nuclear family as an institution is in the process of being conventionalized and a new groundwork for tradition is being laid. In Eliot's novel, the ideology associated with the nuclear family has hardened and is now being eroded by a new order. It is clear early on that Tulliver is engaged in a losing battle. His effort to preserve the family as a closed, stable system appears doomed as soon as we acknowledge that, if nothing else, time must unseat him and disrupt the stable configuration to which he is committed. The disruption he attributes to unscrupulous lawyers is, to some extent, implicit in the very fact of his mortality. However, his entanglement in an ideology that can only conceive of relationships as balanced and closed around himself prevents him from acknowledging this.

From the historical viewpoint, Eliot has simply widened the context in which the chain of substitutions, already noted in the personal relationships of the heroine, is carried on. The novel contains scattered remnants of an earlier tradition of family life. This is a tradition (suggested by certain Dodson family traits) that defines itself through an extended network of kin and through patrilineal succession (Aunt Glegg's will, which divides the property left to her by her father among all her relations, embodies the now democratized remnants of this succession). But the fabric of this tradition has been rent long before the novel begins, and the pieces that remain are the stuff of folklore ("There's a story as when the mill changes hands, the river's angry" [352]) or of trivialized household ritual (Mrs. Tulliver's fixation on the fact that her linen and china remain in the family following the bankruptcy). This kind of family tradition has been substituted for by a style of family life that is a matter not of bloodline but of spatial pattern—of that stability and closure embodied by the nuclear family. Tulliver is thus a Januslike figure. Not only does he stand in opposition to the lawyers, who represent the future in the form of disruption of home and family, but he also opposes the Dodson clan, who represent the past in the form of the extended, patrilineal family (in dismissing the notion of his daughter's marriage as a "poor tale," for example, he betrays his distrust for the system of marital exchange that Lévi-Strauss posited as the organizing principle of elementary kinship structure).

With Tulliver's bankruptcy, however, the bulwark that he had erected aginst both the past and the future gives way. On the one hand, with the loss of his business and his reputation, Tulliver's drive to restore his good name and, symbolically, to restore himself in his old role seems to ally him with the restoration of a linear succession. Indeed, Tom's success in paying his father's debts and regaining the mill suggests that the family has returned to an old-style patriarchal order—an appearance of return that appropriately gains the applause of the Dodsons. On the other hand, the traditional forms of this achievement belie its more modern content. Tom's refusal to accept his sister into his home (a decision that the kin-oriented Aunt Glegg opposes) and the solitude and one-sidedness with which he carries on his life ("I want to have plenty of work. There's nothing else I care about much" [511]) reflect a profound disregard both for affective relations and for the perpetuation of bloodline (a disregard that is the vanguard of a new order to be discussed in the next chapter, on Henry James). As the narrator explains: "aunt Glegg found a stronger nature than her own [in Tom]—a nature in which family feeling had lost the character of clanship in taking on a doubly deep dye of personal pride" (631). The terms of this assertion highlight the systems quality of the change—the evolution of a pattern into a new form. Tom seems to side with the lawyers in what they symbolized for Tulliver of dislocation and fragmentation of home and family. He substitutes for his father, then, both in his relationship to Maggie, where he becomes the purveyor of failure, frustration, and pain, and in his relationship to society, where he has come to replace the tradition of family closure and stability embodied by his father (itself a substitution for the linear tradition of family embodied by the Dodsons). His is a version of that "letting go" that Dr. Kenn describes as "the substitution of wayward choice for the adherence to obligation which has its roots in the past" (625). Appropriately killed off by the author so as to make the possibility of a Tulliver succession impossible, Tom is the anticipation in Eliot's work of the modern, alienated man, symbolizing both the end of genealogical succession associated with the patrilineal family and the failure of closure and balance associated with the nuclear family. He is the individual who has ceased to find a place either in a linear tradition or in a relational one.

All this being granted, Tom is nonetheless not at the center of this novel. Although the logic that drives his character leads to the frontiers of modernism, Eliot is ultimately unsympathetic to this logic. Similarly, the final scene in the novel, a kind of modernist apocalypse, although mapped out by Eliot with precision (we know that she had this ending in mind even before she began to write the novel[13]) seems an inappropriate resolution to a novel whose emotional loyalties lie in an earlier tradition. The natural imagery that she so often incorporates into descriptions of the relationship of Maggie and her father reveals that for the author *this* constitutes the original relationship: this is the "felt" origin of the daughter's identity—both Maggie's and Eliot's own. To be sure, the novel tries to convince us that Tulliver's appeal is a matter of perspective (the scene between Tulliver and his wife in chapter 2 exposes the social conventions of sexual complementarity that stand behind the seemingly natural father-daughter relationship) and that Tom's viewpoint is not altogether without its own contextual logic. There is even the suggestion that the author knows that Mrs. Tulliver's portrait is only a partial one, that the woman's story may lie elsewhere in a relationship with a father that we never see (Aunt Glegg, the strongest Dodson sister, is the one significantly made to invoke her "poor father" repeatedly throughout the novel). Yet ultimately Eliot does not render the mother's portrait with any complexity, just as she does not render Tom's perspective as anything but limited. Both characters remain outside the core relation within the nuclear family that determined the identity of both Maggie Tulliver and her creator.

Emotionally, then, the dynamic of Maggie's early life with her father stands immovably at the center of this novel. It is the relation for which all subsequent relations attempt to substitute. If the novel's ending is, formally, the enactment of fragmentation and destruction, the emotional loyalties of the author imbue it with the feeling of return and restoration.[14] And if an intellectual analysis of the novel yields the insight that the past (like the present) is only a substitution in which the origin recedes infinitely, a poetic analysis of the novel counters this insight, producing a conviction that the origin resides at the source of our own identity, at the place where we "feel" our most basic loyalties to be. As the narrator wistfully puts it: "heaven knows where that striving might lead us, if our affections had not a trick of twining round those old inferior things, if the loves and sanctities of our life had no deep immovable roots in memory" (222). The line can serve as a segue into a consideration of how this novel (an exploration of the roots of identity that ends by revealing the author's profound entanglement in the process she uncovers) can be reconciled with the author's life, whose "striving" only seemed to lead away from "those old inferior things."[15]

* * *

Because George Eliot's own life reflects an especially interesting relation to the ideology of the nuclear family, it is useful to consider at some length how the facts of that life correspond to and deviate from the patterns of family interaction described in *The Mill on the Floss*.

Before doing so, however, I must change the way I refer to my subject. In discussing her life, it is no longer appropriate to refer to "George Eliot," the professional pseudonym that she adopted relatively late in life, but instead to use the proper name, Marian, by which she was familiarly known to her friends and relatives. I also use only the first name, not to fall into the trend of earlier critics who often referred to female subjects by their first names and male subjects by their last, but to avoid referring to a last name that could be "Evans" or "Lewes" or "Cross," depending on the period in question (names that, for me, recall the triumvirate of last names for Cathy Sr. that Lockwood found carved inside the bed closet).

Marian's mother appears to have been a withdrawn and ailing figure.[16] When she died, Marian was sixteen, and there is no recorded reaction to the death. By contrast, Marian's father, Robert Evans, played a prominent role in her emotional life. One biographer postulates that the relationship between father and daughter was a troubled one, pointing to the conflict that erupted between them in 1842 when Marian refused to attend church.[17] But she was already 23 when the "Holy War" (as she termed the conflict in her letters) occurred, and it seems more convincing to take the word of her husband and first biographer, John Cross, that she was her father's "pet," and to see the 1842 rupture as gaining intensity from the fact that she and her father had enjoyed an especially close bond up until this point. When we consider the interests and talents of father and daughter and even the course of their respective careers, this conjecture gains credibility. We can discern in them a complementarity that resembles that of Maggie Tulliver and her father. "My father did not raise himself from being an artisan to be a farmer," Marian explained in a letter to her friends the Brays, angered that they had referred to her as a simple farmer's daughter, " . . . he raised himself from being an artisan to be a man whose extensive knowledge in very varied practical departments made his services valued throughout several counties" (3:168). Gordon Haight contends that Evans was proud of his daughter's intellectual precocity, noting that he indulged her in the purchase of books and made sure that she had tutors in Italian and German. Throughout her childhood, she traveled with him across the county, chatted with the servants as he surveyed the estate under his management, and served as his housekeeper after her mother's death, often reading to him from Walter Scott in the evenings (a pastime that she would later repeat with George Lewes). Like Maggie, she seems to have experienced an almost sublime satisfaction in caring for her father during his last illness: "I feel that these will ever be the happiest days of my life to me. The one deep strong love I have ever known has now its highest exercise." "What shall I be without my Father?" she wrote on the day of his death. "It will seem as if a part of my moral nature were gone" (1:283–84).

If the relationship were indeed one of complementary knowledge and feelings, the "Holy War" of 1842 becomes a significant event. It suggests not an ongoing tension between father and daughter but a temporary disruption of a profound tie. To surmise the cause and true nature of that disruption it seems worthwhile to note the places where Marian diverged from her fictional creation, Maggie Tulliver, and to examine the patterns of interaction that made the divergence possible.

Like Maggie, Marian was an avid reader, but her interest in writing had also begun early (no such interest is associated with the fictional character). When asked later about the precipitating cause of the religious doubt that brought her into conflict with her father, Marian attributed the change to Walter Scott, a response generally understood to mean that she had received ideas from this solidly historical author that did not fit into the Evangelical creed she had embraced in the 1830s. However, Scott also happens to be connected with an early anecdote concerning writing. Recounted by Edith Simcox to Cross and recorded in the opening motto of the fifty-seventh chapter of *Middlemarch,* the story tells how the eight-year-old Marian, frustrated at having to return a borrowed volume of *Waverley* before she had finished reading it, sat down and transcribed from memory what she had read ("The book and they must part, but day by day, / In lines that thwart like portly spiders ran, / They wrote the tale, from Tully Veolan"). It may seem strange that the future novelist would try to reproduce what she knew had happened in the novel rather than fashion an ending of her own. Yet this is precisely the solution that makes sense within the pattern of Marian's life. The act of writing from memory placed her in the position of mediating Scott's story by means of her transcription, duplicating the position that we have discussed as proper to the daughter's role in relation to the father in the nuclear family. But the mediation is also with a difference. By re-creating the story from memory and in her own hand (the vivid metaphor of "portly spiders" calls special attention to the distinctiveness of the writing), the child could bring into being an image of herself in the role of scribe and interpreter. I have discussed how Maggie, in the act of reading Defoe, practiced her role as a mediating daughter, continually oscillating between literal subservience to the text and imaginative extrapolation on it while remaining tied to the text for the extremes of this process; Marian, by contrast, seems to have practiced a different kind of mediation in recording Scott's story from memory, relying not on the original text alone but on that text and a now textualized self, substituting for the original. If we refer back to the model of father-daughter interaction as the basis for female identity formation in the family, then the textualized self can be said to substitute for one part of the father, while the text undergoing transcription substitutes for the other part. The original mediation of the father by the daughter remains, as it were, behind these substitutions.

Marian's ability to create a textualized self-persona and insert it into the mediating process is, I believe, the key to her unique development as a woman and a writer. Not only is it the pattern implicit in her earliest relationship to writing, it also appears as an underlying dynamic and source of ambivalence in the letters of her adolescence and early womanhood.[18] Her first substantial correspondences are probably represented in the first letters available to critics. These were written in her early twenties to Maria Lewis, a former teacher who had inspired her conversion to Evangelicalism, and to a classmate, Martha Jackson, who shared her Evangelical views. One of the more revealing attitudes she expresses in these letters is on the subject of music. In one letter, after having informed Martha Jackson that she attended a church concert the week before, she goes on to speculate:

> I think nothing can justify the using of an intensely interesting and solemn passage of Scripture, as a rope-dancer uses her rope, or as a sculptor the pedestal on which he places the statue, that is alone intended to elicit admiration. I think, too, that it is the duty of Christians individually to throw their weight, however dust-like, into that scale which as Christians they must profess to wish to preponderate; not to take the low ground of considering things merely with relation to existing circumstances, and graduating

their scale of holiness to the temperature of the world; but to aim as perseveringly at perfection as if they believed it to be soon attainable. And if so, I ask myself can it be desirable, and would it be consistent with millennial holiness for a human being to devote the time and energies that are barely sufficient for real exigencies on acquiring expertness in trills, cadences, etc.? (1:9)

This commentary reflects a distaste not for music itself, but for performance.[19] The distinction can help us understand the conflict between mediation and self-personification that would lead to Marian's religious conflict with her father four years later. Implied in her critique above is the assumption that music in the abstract, before it is degraded by the artifice of performance, is a pure medium for the divine spirit. As such, it can be compared to the female self in its mediating relationship to the father. But music is also hard to differentiate from performance (it is impossible to imagine how else we would come to know and love it), and hence its appeal becomes suspect. Evangelical religion reflects a similar paradox. It conceives of the pious daughter as a filter (often conceiving her as literally the mouthpiece through whom God speaks), but by allowing her to serve as the mediator of spirit, it also encourages the cultivation of a self-persona for the daughter—turning her into a locus of interest in her own right, like the pedestal for the statue referred to in the letter as "alone intended to elicit admiration" (Marian's later treatment of the subject of women preachers in *Adam Bede* suggests that she continued to be concerned with this issue). Finally, the letter form itself reflects the paradox, as can be seen if we trace the reasoning in the lines quoted above. First, as proper to the informational function of correspondence, Marian relays to her friend the neutral fact of her attendance at a concert. She then launches into the speculative discourse on music, which fills the longest paragraph in the letter. Finally, she checks herself and concludes with an apology:

But I am running on very selfishly with my own thoughts, without regarding the trouble I am giving you in expecting you to read what I dare say neither your theory nor your practice needs. I do know full well the variableness of mind and affection of which you speak; it is suited to humble and distress us, but may also quicken us to an increased ardour of exertion during our wakeful hours when eternity is realised by us in its awful nearness and importance; if such be the effect we shall have the joy of finding that as persons of riper years gradually lose that soundness and excess of sleep observable in growing children, so our intervals of spiritual drowsiness will decrease.... (1:10)

In these closing lines, the writer is expressing her wish that the letter be a "pure" medium, a place where she can practice obedient service to God through an analogous obedience to the desires and needs of her correspondent. But the letter form prevents this, as the paragraph preceding this apology demonstrates. The writer must indulge in "intervals of spiritual drowsiness" (even when those intervals appear to deal with pious subjects), for these are inherent in the act of intimate letter-writing: neutral details must inevitably give rise to speculative discourse produced less for the correspondent than for the writer herself.

This basic dynamic also seems to be behind Marian's habit in the same letters of signing off with an apology, sometimes for the content of what she has written as in the case above, but more often and more prosaically for her penmanship: "I need scarcely apologize for the disgraceful untidiness of my note..."; "In reading my letter I find difficulties in understanding my scribble that I fear are hopelessly insurmountable for another"; "pardon me if I have sent you many illegible words" (1:3, 24, 47)—such comments occur chronically until about 1850, when Marian's professional life more or less begins, at which point they become less frequent. Reading according to the systems terms set up here, these apologies reflect yet another attempt to emphasize the text's existence as a concrete entity produced by her hand. The focus on handwriting, like the "portly spiders" in the Scott anecdote, calls attention to the fact of authorship and asserts the existence of the work as a fixed entity—the embodiment of a unitary self-persona—detached from a fluid, mediating self. At the same time, by claiming that her handwriting is illegible, she can also deny responsibility for her words, pretending either that the reader will be unable to decipher them or that, written in haste, the letter is not a just reflection of her intention.

Finally, a salient characteristic of the early letters is the variety of nicknames and name variations that Marian employed in them. Between 1840 and 1850, she signs herself as "Clematis" (Greek for "mental beauty"), "Apollyon," "Pollian," "Polly," or "Minie"; and in

1840, during her correspondence with Maria Lewis, she first drops the "e" in "Mary Anne" that she had been using up until 1837. (In a notebook dated 1834, she had already varied the spelling of her name to "Marianne," influenced by her study of French, says Haight). She would become "Marian" in 1850 during a sojourn in Switzerland, and of course, the names "Mrs. Marian Lewes," "George Eliot," and "Mrs. John Cross" (not to mention the names of her fictional characters) lay ahead. Certainly, in the 1840s, her name, like the letters in which it appeared, offered another convenient ground for fashioning a self that was fixed and seemingly cut off from lived relationships within the family while also remaining contained within the mediating form that the epistolary correspondence provided.

With their tendency to subvert the notion of a fluid, mediating self, Marian's letters to Maria Lewis were bound to carry their author away from that friendship. In 1841, she moved with her father to Coventry, where she essentially broke off with her Evangelical teacher and entered into a friendship (and accompanying correspondence) with her new free-thinking neighbors, the Brays. From a position of pious acceptance of the mediating process, she moved to a position of apparent opposition to it. But neither could she remain in fixed opposition to her father. Some four months after the break, she was home again. She and her father had arrived at a compromise: she agreed to attend church; he agreed that she might think what she pleased during the service. As a moment's reflection makes clear, this was not an "equal" compromise. It involved no quantifiable change in her father's behavior while it left all the appearance of capitulation to Marian. But it *is* a compromise in the context of the daughter's mediating relationship to the father: Marian was in effect agreeing to mediate between her father (the original site of mediation), and her "created" self (the nonbeliever, superficially born out of her correspondence with the Brays but really having its source in those earliest acts of literary transcription that first made possible a fixed image of herself). The compromise placed her in the same relation to her father that her transcription of *Waverley* from memory had to that text and her letter-writing had to her correspondent. Indeed, her return was both to her father and to her already established, and presumably subversive, friendship with her father's neighbors, the free-thinking Brays.

The compromise was significant in another way. For if it brought father and daughter back together, it also brought Marian back to a position in the family that included her brother Isaac. Isaac had worked the hardest to resolve the conflict, taking Marian into his home and sending his wife to confer with their father and negotiate the compromise. Recently married, he may have feared that the burden of an aging parent might fall on his shoulders alone if Marian did not return. Yet his efforts probably reflected a more profound need to reinstate the original family dynamic in which he continued to play a supporting role. He would make no such effort at conciliation after his father's death, and would, in fact, precipitate a far more definitive rupture than any Marian could have effected in her refusal to attend church.

Gordon Haight has postulated that "the dominating passion of [Marian's] childhood was love for her brother Isaac."[20] He produces as evidence the "Brother and Sister" sonnets written in 1869 and other recollections and allusions to brother-sister love found in the letters and in *The Mill on the Floss*. However, this evidence is convincing only, it seems to me, if we locate Marian's passion for Isaac later rather than sooner—or, rather, if we understand that passion as gaining power when her father had dropped out of the family system. Indeed, I would suggest that the emotion that fueled so much of Marian's fiction-writing was derived from the estrangement. Just as we have seen that Maggie Tulliver's tie to Tom was clearly bound up with her increasing alienation from him (the result of his substitution for her father), Marian's alienation from Isaac must have carried with it the emotional charge of the original, harmonious father-daughter relationship. *The Mill on the Floss*, which so powerfully captures the contradiction between the facts of a relationship and the feeling that it engenders, was embarked upon only a little more than a year after Isaac severed all contact with his sister.

By this reasoning, Marian's relationship with Isaac, like her relationship with her father, was never abandoned. It coexisted alongside and informed all other relationships. Despite her temporary rupture with her father, she had returned to live with him, to perform the mediating role of daughter up until his death while continuing to engage in writing and related friendships off to the side. In the same way, her alienation from Isaac coexisted with the relationships of her later life, reflecting not his absence but his presence in opposition.

It was not, then, that her writing abolished past ties, but rather that it made a life possible alongside them, which both depended upon them for its material and incorporated them into new forms that arranged these materials in new ways.

The process by which these new combinations developed was a slowly evolutionary one. Transcription was her earliest foray into writing (the Scott anecdote finds reinforcement in the many copied poems in her early notebook), followed by letter-writing. Her interest in translation during the 1840s and early 1850s follows a similar pattern. As a translator, Marian was again placed in the position of mediating between another's words and her own interpretation of them, announcing her ownership of the translation while still having the escape of being able to attribute the ideas to another (the "rigid fidelity and the sense of responsibility in interpreting another man's mind" were "the moral qualities" she invoked as proper to the translator[21]). Twice during this period, she also sought translating projects that could be carried on under the cover of a male friend, suggesting an effort to privatize what would otherwise be a public endeavor—to turn translation into something closer to letter-writing (letter-writing had posed its own publicity problem for her, we know, by her requests that letters be returned once her relationship to the correspondent changed). The need for a male cover can also be seen as a complex effort at substitution. It reflects an attempt to return to the original form of mediation (of the father and his male substitutes) while incorporating a textualized self-persona, so to speak, "underneath"—a foreshadowing of her use of a male pseudonym as a fiction-writer. "I beg you to understand that I consider myself *your* translator and the publication as yours, and that my compensation will be any good that may be effected by the work, and the pleasure of being linked to your remembrance" (1:154), she wrote to the Reverend Francis Watts, a friend for whom she had offered to translate Vinet's *Mémoire* in 1842. If the words sound a note of exaggerated self-effacement, they also reflect a desperate desire for the chance to do the work. Although neither the Vinet nor the translation of Spinoza that she had wanted to do for Charles Bray were ultimately offered to her, the opportunity to translate Strauss's *Leben Jesu* finally came, passed on to her by friends who had not had time for it themselves. She would work for two years on Strauss, struggling to interpret with "rigid felicity" a "mind" that grew increasingly unsympathetic to her. The translation appeared anonymously in 1846. Not until 1854, after drafting her translation of Feuerbach's *Das Wesen des Chistenthums,* do we see an acknowledgment in her letters of the interpretive and literary license that must enter into a good translation: "With the ideas of Feuerbach I everywhere agree [she writes to her friend, Sara Hennell], but of course I should, of myself alter the phraseology considerably" (1:153). Her translation of Feuerbach would finally carry her name.

In 1850, on the strength of the Strauss translation, her publisher, John Chapman, had brought her to London, where she served essentially as ghost-editor of his *Westminster Review.* Like so much of her previous work, both her editorship and the book-reviewing she performed anonymously for the *Westminster* were acts of creativity incorporated within the form of mediation. "The woman of large capacity can seldom rise beyond the absorption of ideas [she wrote during this period]. . . . phantasms of great ideas float through her mind, but she has not the spell which will arrest them, and give them fixity."[22] The yoking together of "phantasms of great ideas" with images of floating suggests the interplay of self-personification and mediation that we have analyzed in Marian's writing. The imagery curiously anticipates the final catastrophe in *The Mill on the Floss,* in which Maggie and Tom are swept beneath the flood by just such floating "phantasms" materialized into large pieces of deadly machinery. In one sense, the scene can be said to comment ironically on the earlier remark about women's limitation—the novel, after all, is testimony to the fact that women's ideas could be "fixed" into powerful, coherent narratives. But the irony characteristically strikes both ways. By using the image to kill off her heroine and to effect a profoundly awkward resolution for her novel, the writer also betrays ambivalence toward her own creation—both toward her self-persona, Maggie Tulliver, and toward the novel as a whole.

As has already been noted, the patterns that characterized Marian's relationship to her writing were not confined to writing; they were mirrored in her personal relationships. In her earliest correspondences, we see her cultivating friendships that existed alongside the relationships of her family of origin, and we need only examine the form of these friendships to be struck by a remarkably consistent pattern: in Coventry with the Sibrees, the Wattses, and the Brays; in

Switzerland with the Brabants and the D'Albert Durades; and finally, in London with the Chapmans—each friendship was essentially with the family as a whole but involved an especially close tie with the father/husband. In the case of Dr. Brabant, a scholar with whose family she stayed while visiting Devizes in the 1840s, and John Chapman, the publisher, with whose family she lodged during part of the period she worked on the *Westminster,* the intimacy produced such tension between Marian and the wife in question (and in Chapman's case, the mistress too) that she was forced to vacate the premises. Where such tension did arise, however, she reconciled with family members afterward, continuing on friendly terms with almost all of these people until the ends of their lives. In each case, the male figure, if only superficially and fleetingly, provided that opportunity for mediation that we have analyzed as the formative dynamic in her life. Marian stood in a position of subordination to these men, who were older and more experienced than she, while she also complemented them intellectually, often literally supplementing gaps in their knowledge on a variety of projects that she undertook on their behalf. Her position in relation to them was daughterly (Brabant christened her "Deutera," meaning second daughter, and she referred to Watts as a "father-confessor"), but a sexual element was also present since she was not, after all, their daughter. Yet the amorous boundary seems not to have been crossed, either because the presence of the man's family existed to diffuse the sexual impulse or because the family moved to literally expel her until the heat had died down. This dynamic, which at once encouraged and checked the possibility of an exclusive relationship, was especially useful to Marian's development, I would suggest, in that it allowed her to interact with the male figures in question on new, more symmetrical terms. In other words, her choice of men who were already mediated within families of their own made possible a more equal relationship than would have resulted had she been fully assimilated to the role of either daughter or wife. Her relationships with these men, therefore, while they superficially involved mediation, also reinforced a sense of herself apart from them. As in her writing, where this same double movement is in evidence, her relationships involved new kinds of substitutions within the mediating pattern.

There are two exceptions. One was with the anonymous young man who was rejected by Marian in 1845; the other, with the far from anonymous Herbert Spencer, who rejected *her* proposal in 1852. In the first instance, the rejection is explained in a letter from her friend Cara Bray, who seems to have had access to her reasons: "she made up her mind that she could never love or respect him enough to marry him and that it would involve too great a sacrifice of her mind and pursuits" (1:184). Spencer, however, was another story. He had just the scientifically-based knowledge ("all sorts of theories about plants" [2:40]) to appropriately substitute for that extensive practical knowledge of farming for which Robert Evans had been known across several counties. With the help of his monumental ego, he must have appeared to Marian suitably to complement her own intellectual, imaginative life. "Those who have known me best," she wrote to him in her famous declaration of love, "have always said, that if ever I loved any one thoroughly my whole life must turn upon that feeling" (8: 56–57). In the letter, she asserts her willingness to minister to him entirely: "I want to know if you can assure me that you will not forsake me, that you will always be with me as much as you can and share your thoughts and feelings with me. . . . I would be very good and cheerful and never annoy you." Anyone reading this letter must imagine for a moment what Marian's life might have been (or, more correctly, what might not have been written) had Spencer succumbed to her attractions.

Still, it is significant that her expression of devotion is made in a letter, and that even as she prostrates herself, she retrieves an image of herself as sovereign: "I suppose no woman ever before wrote such a letter as this—but I am not ashamed of it, for I am conscious that in the light of reason and true refinement I am worthy of your respect and tenderness, whatever gross men or vulgar-minded women might think of me." There is something of the fictional drama of Marian's own orchestration in this letter. Although concerned with the mediation of another identity, she creates a self-persona that makes her mediation less all-consuming. "Unlike other women," who would have acted out their devotion, making it their occupation, Marian wrote it down and continued to do other work.

In this context, the rebuff by Spencer and the ensuing meeting with George Henry Lewes are fortuitous events whose outcome allowed Marian to negotiate her way through (without ever entirely abandoning) the debilitating patterns of interaction that had formed her identity as a daughter. With Lewes, she returned to a relationship that was like but unlike the conventional relationships arising out of the nuclear family (although she seems never to have had a friendship with Lewes's wife, Agnes, her fondness and care for Lewes's children, even after his death, recall the pattern of family friendships discussed earlier). The two united off to the side of conventional family ties, creating a life together that mimicked, but was not, respectable marriage. Lewes had long been involved in a domestic triangle in which his wife "mediated" between her husband and his friend Thornton Hunt to the point of bearing both their children. In her positioning within this triangle, Agnes (whose subjective life has been strangely ignored by critics who seem to have displaced onto her the moral outrage that had originally been directed at Marian) deserves comparison with Maggie Tulliver, caught between Philip Wakem and Stephen Guest. Read in this way, the Lewes household becomes an illustration of the difficulty the daughter experiences in carrying on a satisfying substitute relationship in adult life. (It might also suggest that the one creative alternative for a woman of this period who had no talent for writing was to engineer a ménage à trois.)

Whatever Agnes's story, George Lewes's legal tie to her gave his relationship to Marian the appearance of a sidebar—a space of free, nonpatterned exchange. Later, when Lewes and Marian had established themselves as a more conventional couple, Marian's success became another source of freedom. For as soon as she began to make money off her stories and their financial worries disappeared, Lewes took over the role of "silent collaborator" that had once been hers. It was he who now helped do research for her novels.[23]

Writing fiction offered Marian other advantages as well. If letter-writing, translation, reviewing, and editorship are all forms of mediation in which the writer mediates another persona and a self-persona, fiction-writing is mediation of various self-personas. Marian's particularly complicated relation to her pseudonym reflects this. She had assumed the private name of Mrs. Marian Lewes at the time she began writing fiction. Partially because of the dubious nature of that name, partially because of the commercial reality that favored male writers, and partially no doubt because of the familiar pattern that made her need to assume the male cover, she chose the pseudonym of George Eliot for her work. We can see how this name served her especially well in *The Mill on the Floss,* where she can be said to be mediating two self-personas: one, her childhood self, Mary Anne

Evans; the other, the detached professional, mock-male self, George Eliot. Inside the novel, the childhood self is substituted for by the fictional character, Maggie Tulliver, while the male pseudonym is substituted for in the detached, quasi-male narrative voice. In short, Marian had evolved to a point where different self-personas could be substituted for those that would conventionally have been occupied by "real" others. While her earlier writing had made possible a detachment from the self that allowed her a limited opportunity to exist independently of defining others, her fiction-writing extended this opportunity and freed her from a literal dependence upon another text. At the same time, this was still a matter of substitutions on the original configuration of father-daughter interaction in the family.

Indeed, it would be wrong to see her entry into fiction-writing as a moment of transformation in the life of Marian. It seems rather to have been a more comprehensive and successful life to the side, another of those peripheral existences that she had been cultivating since her relationship with the Brays. We see this demonstrated if we shift our sights for a moment to other aspects of Lewes and Marian's life together. Although the relationship of George and Marian appears as an antidote to the familial tangle of Lewes's legal marriage, aspects of Marian's original family dynamic extrapolated from our discussion of *The Mill on the Floss* did, in fact, continue to structure much of their life together. These seem to have contributed at once to her creative drive and to the debilitating headaches and depressions she suffered during her most productive years. One of Marian's early self-appointed tasks in relation to Lewes (a task that continued long after she ceased to "silently collaborate" on his articles) was to translate *him* to her friends—to explain the moral and emotional quality of the man whom others seemed to find vulgar and shabby. In this sense, she was very much his public mediator. By the same token, he had a protective role toward her. The couple cultivated the mythology that she was being scapegoated by the world, and he stood in the unique position (akin to Mr. Tulliver's in relation to Maggie) to shield and protect her. It is well-known that Lewes only let her see the reviews of her work that he knew would please her and that he scribbled messages at the bottom of her letters to friends instructing them on how to respond. Clearly, this kind of protection is double-edged: while it shields, it also publicizes the need for protection; it reinforces the sense of scapegoating and the value of the protector.

It seems to me that Marian's relationship to Lewes made it possible for her to write fiction not because he freed her in some absolute way from the destructive patterns of her early life, but because the relationship allowed her to use those patterns, which might well have been suffocating in other contexts, to work for rather than against her. This had less to do with his support than with her now sophisticated ability to create self-personas and substitute them within familiar mediating patterns. Once again, her literary pseudonym reflects this process. "Mrs. Marian Lewes," the name she assumed in private life during the period of her fiction-writing, explicitly eschews the more conventional "Mrs. George Lewes" (owing ostensibly to the confusion that might have occurred with Agnes), while the pseudonym adopts Lewes's first name, absent in her personal "married" name. "Evans" gets transmuted into "Eliot." The result is a pen name containing fragments of male relationships (father, brother, husband), cut and arranged to fit the objectified self that Marian's writing had helped to make possible.

Ultimately, of course, Mrs. Marian Lewes was substituted for as well. When Marian legally married John Cross in 1880, two years after Lewes's death, she assumed the conventional married name of "Mrs. John Cross." The man twenty years her junior whom she had first made a fictional nephew was now transformed into a real husband. She also reconciled with her brother at this time, and returned to signing her first name as Mary Ann, the pre-1850 (but post-1837) spelling. It may seem strange that she should assume a conventional married name and a familial spelling for her first name, both of which suggest a female self submerged in the mediation of male identity, when she was over sixty and had achieved so much. Yet this return to convention by means of a highly unconventional marriage and a highly contrived reconciliation with her brother indicates to me that she never really severed the patterns and emotional loyalties to which she was conditioned in her family of origin. Instead, she devised so many substituting personas for that original cast of characters that no single set of relations could now entrap her. In the end, she could assume the status of wife and sister because, by then, she had available to her flourishing alternative identities—as the notorious Mrs. Marian Lewes, as the literary lioness and social icon George

Eliot, and as the multiple fictional characters she had created—all self-personas conditioned by and resonant with the past, yet different by virtue of the changes effected by multiple substitutions on the original mediating relationship. In these, she could now take refuge even as she finally assumed the conventional names that she had avoided or that had been denied her for so long.

CHAPTER 6

The Awkward Age: Revision

Historians Nancy Cott, Ann Douglas, and Carl Degler have all discussed how the cult of domesticity produced a new kind of recognition for women in American culture during the nineteenth century that served the needs of an expanding capitalism while it implicitly challenged the rights and values of patriarchy. Nancy Armstrong, concentrating on British culture during the same period, has described a related tendency, fueled by the domestic novel, to support and shape the concept of the modern individual by valorizing qualities associated with the female position. In this book, I also have identified a potential for female empowerment emerging in nineteenth-century culture, explaining this potential in systems terms as the by-product of an ideology of closure. As I have argued in earlier chapters, the daughter/heroine's place in the family and in the novel was as a complement to her father, a positioning destined to privilege her complementary qualities of imagination and emotion in relation to her male peers of brother and husband. In the course of the century, "feminine qualities" became an increasing threat to the form of the family and of the novel even as they were produced by and through those forms. Given the increasing strain involved in accommodating these qualities within a closed form, it seems inevitable that we should finally arrive at a self-conscious perspective on form itself, as we do in the work of Henry James. James is the last novelist in this study and the first, in my opinion, to take the form of the novel and the form of the family as subjects in their own right. In doing so, he is able to postulate their revision.

* * *

Following a visit to America in 1904, the last he was destined to make, Henry James wrote a series of reflective essays on the life of his native country. Among these was included his assessment of the respective roles of men and women in contemporary American society. "American life," he wrote, "... fall[s] upon the earnest view as a society of women 'located' in a world of men ... ; the men supplying, as it were, all the canvas, and the women all the embroidery."[1] In surveying James's canon, these lines become more than a whimsical commentary on the sexual landscape of American life. They summarize a more general awareness, which had been gradually emerging in his fiction, of a reversal of the relative priority of male and female roles in Western culture—a reversal that carried with it a dissolving of the traditional hierarchical, boundaried distinctions associated with patriarchy (as the metaphors of "canvas" and "embroidery" reflect). The valorization of the female position and the effect of this valorization on the shape of experience are connected, I believe, with James's grasp of a new ideological configuration that was emerging toward the end of the nineteenth century to replace the ideology of the nuclear family. James's attitude toward this new ideology was initially uneasy and yet, I will argue, increasingly resigned, and, ultimately, sympathetic.

The shadowy place beyond the domestic sphere associated with the "real" lives of men had retained for English novelists up until James an unassailable authority. Women, despite the increasing complexity that came to characterize their emotional and imaginative lives, were still represented as waiting in their drawing rooms for some male visitor who, as Nina Auerbach has observed of the Austen hero, could "alone bring substance: by inheriting the estate, he will ensure the family the solidity and continuity of income and land."[2] Even where the estate had disappeared and the income been reduced, the prize of the male name—the acquisition of the title of "Mrs."—remained, up until James, the conventional goal of the heroine's story.

At the same time, I have argued, this conventional drive to marry is progressively undermined in the fiction. The patterns of interaction that support the ideology of the nuclear family become increasingly elaborate, to the point where they militate against the genealogical imperative marriage would seem to support. One could say that a conflict begins to exist between the conventions of plot (which remain loyal to an earlier ideology of succession), and the structure and dynamics of the novels that support an ideology of closure. I have already examined the ways in which selected novelists before

James handled this conflict: Austen froze the novel before the daughter could be seen practicing the roles of wife and mother; Richardson, Eliot, and Brontë either killed the daughter off so as to maintain her as the regulating focus of family interaction or engineered a transition that was at odds with the logic of family relations assumed in the novel up until that point.

Even in his earliest novels and stories, James had moved beyond the possibility for such conclusions. Previous novelists had maintained the ineffable power of the male world of business by keeping that world outside the sphere of the novel's plot and, hence, out of sight of the heroine who was its center (Sir Thomas's unseen transactions in the West Indies, for example, carry an undisputed authority in *Mansfield Park,* which an examination of the slave trade during this period would have severely curtailed). Although in James's fiction too, the sites of commercial activity are hidden, there is now the suggestion that they *need* to be hidden—that there is something vulgar, if not vicious, about them. They are sites of a grossly material and routinized existence and of a correspondingly routinized exploitativeness. Even good men like Christopher Newman in *The American,* Casper Goodwood in *The Portrait of a Lady,* and Adam Verver in *The Golden Bowl* are tainted by having at some point been associated with this commercial world. "I'm not stupid; but I don't know anything about money," declares Isabel Archer[3]—and far from making her seem stupid, Isabel's ignorance of financial matters helps to mark her as a superior being in James's world. To be sure, the men in his fiction continue to supply the subsistence—the "canvas"—upon which middle-class female "embroidery" is stitched (and not the least of the factors that links James to the female position is that his own "embroidery"—his novelistic vocation—was made possible through the commercial fortune amassed by his immigrant grandfather); but the imaginative and moral leverage of the provider over those for whom he provides, his ability to lend coherence and meaning to the experience he financially supports, has shrunk in James's world to the point that this monetary backing becomes increasingly anonymous and "corporate."[4] That the issue is essentially one of gender rather than economics, however, is demonstrated by the fact that James's critique of the male role extends beyond a critique of the modern businessman. The noncommercial man—well-born, usually European—fares no better in his fiction than the commercial one.

If the commercial man is the automaton, the well-bred European is simply hollow form. Lord Warburton in *The Portrait of a Lady* is described as a "specimen English gentleman" who "has ceased to believe in himself and doesn't know what to believe in"; Prince Amerigo in *The Golden Bowl* explains what it means to be the end of a rare and noble line of descendants by comparing himself to "a chicken, at best, chopped up and smothered in sauce; cooked down as a *crème de volaille,* with half the parts left out."[5]

Unsurprisingly, many of James's women can be understood as the unfortunate complements of these inadequate men. The self-destructive spontaneity of Daisy Miller, the blind inspiration of Verena Tarrant in *The Bostonians,* and the pathological visions of the nameless governess in *The Turn of the Screw* seem to be an implicit critique of some failure on the part of men to provide suitable moral support for women. Madame Merle in *The Portrait of a Lady* seems intended as a graphic example of how this abandonment of women by men both renders women pathetic and encourages in them a dangerous furtiveness. As she explains to Isabel: "a woman, it seems to me, has no natural place anywhere; wherever she finds herself she has to remain on the surface and more or less crawl."[6]

Of course, women in James's fiction are never only the symptoms of male insufficiency. They are also driven to fill in for that insufficiency and stand as the repositories of value, even if that value is misdirected to sometimes disastrous ends. Left, quite literally, with nothing to do—with no function in relation to their absent men—they are uniquely open to new experience and creative expression. In this respect, the benefits that James's women derive from their inactivity resemble those of sickly Ralph Touchett in *Portrait,* whose "health," we are told, "had seemed not a limitation, but a kind of intellectual advantage; it absolved him from all professional emotions and left him the luxury of being simply personal."[7] Ralph, it must be noted, is an aberration. His illness sets him apart from other men in leaving him, as he puts it, "the luxury" of cultivating personal emotions and values. Women, on the other hand, are "personal" by virtue of the conditions of their sex.

The costs and the benefits of the female position as they revealed themselves to James help account for a double perspective in his novels: on the one hand, he depicts women as desperate regulators of failing systems; on the other, as creative facilitators of new forms of relationship. In some cases, the two perspectives are hard to distinguish—the pathological adjustment merges into the free-ranging creativity. Almost all of James's heroines have been accused of being phobic, obsessive, or generally neurotic (Isabel Archer, for example, has been called a "fleshless robot, a contemptuous prig," and verdicts on later heroines such as Fleda Vetch and Maggie Verver have been even more damning), while women who seem to be structurally placed as villains in his novels have found their partisans (Mrs. Brook and Charlotte Stant, most notably).[8] In systems terms, this blurring is comprehensible. As a system runs down it is often difficult to say whether the old system is being maintained at a very low and disorganized level or whether a new system is in the process of formulation. Yet James's creation of increasingly interesting and weighty female "central intelligences" seems to me evidence of where his loyalties ultimately fall. As the late novels also tend to connect their heroines' destinies with new relational configurations, it becomes clear that James's interest in women is bound up with his interest in the shape of the future.

Although James would not until the 1890s give his heroines his fullest confidence, *The Portrait of a Lady* is an important structural landmark in his canon. In this novel, he introduces a complex female consciousness, then "cuts the cable" of domestic prejudices and confinements that might drag on her freedom (to adapt the language James applies more generally to the making of romance in his preface to *The American*). His interest focuses entirely on "this single small corner-stone, the conception of a certain young woman affronting her destiny . . . the young woman . . . in perfect isolation."[9] What will such a "young woman in perfect isolation" do? Significantly, James's criticism of George Eliot comes down to this point: that she did not give to her female characters the priority that she might have. Even in *Daniel Deronda,* which some critics have hailed as a modern, open-ended novel,[10] we see that Gwendolen Harleth, though physically left "*en l'air*," as James would put it, is nonetheless made to subserve the higher authority of Deronda. His absence from her at the end of the novel only makes him seem a more mythic (and more contrived) version of those Austen men whose authority is linked to their absences in town (with Jerusalem merely replacing London as the male authoritative "outside"). Anne French Dalke has argued that James associated Eliot's formal failure with her personal situation—with the confinement with Lewes that limited her access to a wider society. Had her personal limitation been less, James speculates, "Would her development have been less systematic, more irresponsible, more personal?"[11] The comment is especially ironic given Eliot's flaunting of social convention. It is as though the very unconventionality of her relationship with Lewes made her life correspond to that of the cloistered, circumscribed female stereotype that was already on the way to being superseded by the vaguely liberated "girl of the period," a type that by James's day had evolved into the more formidable end-of-century "new woman."

This is not to say that James's own relationship to what was occurring in England and America during the latter part of the nineteenth century was unproblematic, or that he ever took a simple stance in favor of the women's movement.[12] The Preface to *Portrait* suggests that he is extrapolating upon something he sees germinating around him but which he keeps purposely vague: "the wonder being . . . ," he writes, "how inordinately, the Isabel Archers, and even much smaller female fry, insist on mattering."[13] While this would imply that his insight into a new ideology for the family is reinforced by current events and social trends—by what George Gissing referred to as the "sexual anarchy" of the period[14]—it must also be noted that he tended, almost reflexively, to position himself against popular trends and movements. Thus, in the same portion of the Preface to *Portrait* in which he suggests that Isabel is one of a legion of modern young women who now "insist on mattering," he also cancels that claim, calling attention to his own "due ingenuity" in making Isabel Archer "serve." The implication here is that he, through his artistry, has given the female character a weight and importance that she would not otherwise possess. In final analysis, I think it would be foolish to make too much of either side: James was not untouched by the events of his age but neither was he a propagandist for social reform. Indeed, as I shall argue later in this chapter, if we need to find one powerful influence on James's work, that influence seems more likely to reside not in the public but in the domestic sphere, in the person of his sister Alice. That said, however, it is still necessary to bear in mind that many influences in combination, including a tendency common to the James family to resist ideas and interpretations that their contemporaries found most persuasive, shaped his perspective. His historical positioning, his temperament, his rhetorical skills, the nature of his own family, and his particular role within it—all these, and other factors not available to the historian or the literary critic—made him uniquely suited to grasp and articulate a "new idea" emerging to replace the ideology of closure associated with the nineteenth-century family and novel form.

This new idea gets articulated most forcefully in *The Awkward Age*, often considered the novel to inaugurate James's late style. It is his most profound family novel, and it outlines a vision of family life that both anticipates and carries us beyond modernism. Superficially, it appears to be uncharacteristic of James in that it lacks a "central intelligence" and depends almost entirely on dialogue over explanatory narration. What might at first look like an idiosyncratic experiment, however, seems less so when we examine the context in which *The Awkward Age* was written. It follows upon James's foray into drama in the early part of the decade, which helps account for its formal innovation ("the approximation of the respective division of my form to the successive acts of a Play").[15] It also comes on the heels of one of his most subtle and important novels of female consciousness, *The Spoils of Poynton*, and of his most broadly drawn novel of family relations, *What Maisie Knew*. In *The Awkward Age*, then, a heightened consciousness of certain formalistic issues and a highly developed thematic concern for family and female consciousness come together. This synthesis makes the novel an apotheosis of James's art of fiction and, by extension (since his art of fiction was inextricably linked to what he called "felt life"—reality as experienced), the novel most richly reflective of James's view of reality as shaped through that most personal of institutions: the family.

To better comprehend James's achievement in *The Awkward Age* it is helpful to compare this novel with *What Maisie Knew*, its immediate predecessor. The earlier novel is told from the point of view of a child who ages in its course from six to about twelve. The novel thus culminates with what James in his preface terms "the death of [the heroine's] childhood," and this serves to set off the "special scale" of vision that is the child's and that cannot be sustained by an adult mind. To emphasize the difference between the child's perception and the adult's, the novel encourages us to correct for Maisie's generous construction of what she sees and to register the selfish and exploitative behavior of the adults that make up her world. However, in *The*

Awkward Age James shifts his method. Because he no longer gives us a point of view, we have no corrective, no "outside," for the relations that we see. Nanda appears to be the heroine because the events revolve around her "case," and other characters express admiration and sympathy for her. But ultimately, the whole notion of what it means to be a heroine becomes blurred and uncertain in this novel. Unlike Maisie, who is genuinely different from the other characters—her knowledge is of a different quality—Nanda has no "special scale" of vision; she knows what the others know only too well ("hasn't it come out all round now that I know everything?"[16] she announces at one point). She is "the product of our hard London facts, and of her inevitable consciousness of them" (230), the participant as well as the observer of those around her; she cannot be separated from them. This connectedness of the heroine to the relations that make up her world corresponds to the kind of claims James makes for the novel on the level of form. In the Preface, he expresses his satisfaction with the result:

> [I]t helps us ever so happily to see the grave distinction between substance and form in a really wrought work of art signally break down. I hold it impossible to say, before "The Awkward Age," where one of these elements ends and the other begins: I have been unable at least myself, on re-examination, to mark any such joint or seam, to see the two *discharged* offices as separate. . . . you can't resolve the elements of my whole into different responsible agents or find your way at all (for your own fell purpose).[17]

In these remarks, the author in his position outside the finished whole of the novel emphasizes the connectedness of relations in the novel, to the point that both the author and the reader are excluded from any critical privilege in relation to the finished product ("I find it impossible to say . . ."; "you can't resolve the elements . . ."). In the achievement of a form in which all elements have been broken down, dissolved, fused, James can be said to operate creatively on another logical level of experience—to approach meaning not on the level of individual consciousness but on a level that encompasses and thereby redefines consciousness as part of a larger and ever-shifting design. Thus, while the perspective outside, above, beyond the action and the characters implied by the lack of a central intelligence might appear to resemble the authorial position in the classical novel, from which James's art of fiction had long been at pains to depart, this perspective is in fact very different both from traditional authorial omniscience and from the restricted reportorial perspective of much naturalistic fiction.[18] Rather, to choose an analogy to which I will return, it is more like that of the psychotherapist whose presence is felt behind and within the discourse of a patient, marking it as produced by and for interpretation but reducible only provisionally and incompletely to any single interpretive formula.

The family that we encounter in *The Awkward Age* bears a curious relationship to the families encountered in novels before James. The Brookenham family can be characterized only insofar as it deviates from conventional notions of family. Like James's art of fiction, which begins with "a virus of suggestion" passed to him by others and is then extrapolated into something startlingly different from that original "germ," the Brookenham family is the ostensible core or starting point for the relations that make up the novel, but only to be extrapolated upon in such a way as to parody, subvert, and ultimately radically revise the family idea to which it appears to refer.

This extrapolation occurs in a literal sense as the Brookenham family is "extended"—or appended—through the friends that gather at the family's Buckingham Crescent home. The group that frequents "the Brooks," as the family is called by its friends, describes itself by borrowing the vocabulary of solidarity and closure that we associate with the nuclear family. Thus, Vanderbank (known familiarly as Van), one of the group's most important members, talks of their "collective impression—something in which our trifling varieties are merged" (48); and Mitchett (known as Mitchy), another of the Brooks's "regulars," calls the group "a collection of natural affinities" (107) and explains: "We see ourselves reflected—we're conscious of the charming whole" (223). Even Mr. Longdon, an old man lately arrived in London and new to the group, is soon able to characterize it as "a little sort of a set that hang very much together" (106). Such characterizations, moreover, presume the distinction between inside and outside that is basic to the ideology of the nuclear family. What lies outside the Brook circle, Van explains, is London—"a huge 'squash,' . . . —an elbowing, pushing, perspiring, chattering mob" (39).

But even if the group appropriates the language of the nuclear family, it does so with a difference. The terms used to describe the group as cited above—"collection," "whole," "set"—in what they suggest of stability and closure are also offset by qualifiers: "collective *impression*," "*natural* affinities," "*sort of a* set" (my emphasis). What this does is to call attention to the conventional nature of the terminology as an attempt to locate what exists elsewhere or perhaps nowhere. It is language that defines the family only to place it, as Jacques Derrida would say, "under erasure." We see this gap between language and the physical and emotional coordinates it invokes when we look at how the group actually manifests itself in the novel. For one thing, there is no group in the sense of a physical gathering. The members are perennially scattered or hidden (only once in the novel do we see everyone gathered in one place and this is at a moment of trauma when the whole thing has presumably "gone to pieces"). This physical disconnectedness is accompanied by an affective diffusion. The characters indulge in an extraordinary inflation of language so that everything carries an exclamation point or contains a pregnant pause—but this is purely rhetorical. There is no emotional intensity, no depth of feeling. There is instead a kind of egalitarian circulation of the relational idea: everyone is "involved" with everyone else, but no one feels strongly about anything or anyone in particular (with the possible exception of Nanda, to whom I will return later). "None of the inner circle at Buckingham Crescent was ever angry" (219), we are told; and Mrs. Brook concludes philosophically that they "haven't had the excuse of passion" (230) in their dealings with each other. What replaces passion is "liking" in what it suggests of nonthreatening affection and intellectual compatibility: "people who don't like us . . . don't matter" (223), declares Mitchy. Given the emotional shallowness of the group, a solidarity based on intellectual habits, we can see how it poses a threat to conventional ideas about family devotion and protection. For its very existence as the site of "good talk," that is to say, of speculation about the relationships of others, runs counter to the ideology of the nuclear family as the place where the innocent are screened off from just such speculative knowledge of what lies outside a tidy and well-defined space. This contradiction is exemplified in the case of Mrs. Brook's daughter, Nanda, who, as an unmarried girl (the "awkward age" of the title), is pronounced threatened—in danger of corruption—from exposure to the group's "good talk."

Finally, any comparison of the Brook circle with a conventional model of the nuclear family must note that the group is founded upon a reversal in the priority of male and female (a reversal that I have already noted to be a hallmark of James's later work). Instead of male authority, female imagination and ingenuity organize the experience of the group that visits at Buckingham Crescent. Mrs. Brook, at least initially, performs this organizing role single-handedly. As Mitchy puts it, she "governs" the group in its "mysterious ebbs and flows, very much as the tides are governed by the moon" (107); or as the Duchess explains in a more striking use of metaphor: "Fernanda . . . has set up, for the convenience of her friends, a little office for consultations. She listens to the case, she strokes her chin and prescribes" (95). The description suggests that Mrs. Brook has feminized the traditional male occupation of physician and, in doing so, extended into the social sphere that science of the mind that was only just being pioneered in Europe by Freud and in America by James's brother William. The relevance of this new psychological science and of Mrs. Brook's practice of it to James's art of fiction will be addressed later in this chapter.

At this point, let me digress from the novel and review the systems perspective on family development within which the extrapolated family idea—the antifamily of this novel—needs to be positioned. I began this book with Lévi-Strauss's ideas concerning primitive kinship structure. Lévi-Strauss posits that the incest taboo that stipulates that women not be kept by fathers and brothers but be given up for exchange by them for other women is the organizing principle on which civilization is built. He argues that women originally served as barter—the objects of exchange necessary for moving from nature to culture. Over time, he maintains, primitive structures based on this elementary exchange become complex structures through development and combination, but these complex structures are self-correcting; although the "cycle" of exchange may be longer and more circuitous, the system is always driven to return to an equilibrium based on the exchange of women.

What Lévi-Strauss neglects in this analysis, as I have already noted in my discussion of *Wuthering Heights,* is how the development of complex structures would tend to create a female subject such that equilibrium would be established not on the level of the exchange of

women but on another level of organization. This occurs in the complex structure of the nuclear family, which, according to Lawrence
Stone, began to emerge in the sixteenth and seventeenth centuries
in Western Europe as a bulwark for a more primitive patrilineal
family model but which ultimately superseded that model as the
closed, domesticated nuclear family in the eighteenth and nineteenth
centuries. What supported this new family structure was a "state of
mind," an ideology that understood family life in terms of separation
and closure, and that defined a domestic space in contrast with an
outer world. In the context of this new family ideal, women ceased
to serve as objects of exchange and became instead mediating subjects: "consciousnesses." Specifically, it fell to the daughter in the
nuclear family to invest herself in her father so as to stabilize the
necessary split required of him between outside and inside—between
his functions as breadwinner on the one hand and domestic patriarch
on the other. Thus, the nuclear family, having been built, as it were,
on the father-daughter dynamic, superimposed upon the first-order
change that Lévi-Strauss described as the product of the incest taboo
a second order of complexity. The daughter's role was now that of
an emotionally invested subject who could never be returned to the
status of exchange object.

In *The Awkward Age* we have moved to yet another level of organization issuing out of what I have described above. In this novel, James
depicts a transitional moment in which the nuclear family is being
superimposed upon in turn—producing a third-order change.[19] For
as the closed family system fails to sustain its equilibrium over time
(and I have argued elsewhere that disequilibrium is the necessary
long-term result of the dynamic by which the nuclear family stabilized
itself over the course of the nineteenth century), a new order of
relationship emerges in which the female, formed as a mediating
subject, is no longer under the sway of paternal authority and, hence,
is given free play. Such a female is able to function as a perpetual
daughter by being cut loose from a particular father: she is freed to
mediate relationships without the drag of looking backward that investment in a father within a closed family system had entailed.

The new means of cultural organization that emerges out of the
breakdown of the nuclear family—when the family, in other words,
no longer controls and confines its daughters—consists of interpretive discourse: of talk. Mrs. Brook's circle runs on talk. As the over-

seer of talk, she sets in motion possibilities of relationship, suggesting the appearance of new arrangements and combinations in the lives of herself, her family, and her friends.

Edward Said has noted a fundamental paradox in the drive toward "affiliation"—the engendering of community through discourse—as it relates to "filiation"—the engendering of human beings through procreation. Affiliation, he asserts, involves "a philosophical drive to trace origins with an inapplicability of these explanations in light of evidence of dispersion, divergence, diversification."[20] However, Said's analysis does not take the affiliative drive to its limits. In *The Awkward Age* we see that any certainty about origins has become positively dangerous, and hence the drive to trace origins is counteracted at every point by a drive to evade them. One could say that where the filial model demands knowledge of paternity and where the affiliative model in its earlier manifestation seeks knowledge of paternity, the affilial model in its extreme manifestation demands that paternity be brought into question to serve as the focus for speculation. Thus, we are told that the occupants of Mrs. Brook's circle, "almost more concerned for each other's vibrations than for anything else, were apt rather more to exchange sharp and silent searchings than to fix their eyes on the object itself" (96). The fact of whether someone is having an affair with someone else is not of interest to the group; what interests them is that the speculation continue, that it not be reducible. It is "the excitement, every day, of plucking the daisy over" (141), declares Mrs. Brook regarding the uncertainty attached to her friend Lady Fanny's liaison; were Lady Fanny to "bolt," leave her husband for her hypothetical lover, "what would become of us?" But Lady Fanny would be of no use to the group either were she to become either simply pure like the angelic Little Aggie prior to her marriage, or terribly obvious in her promiscuity like Carrie Donner (who in the naiveté of her aesthetic and moral lapses seems, we are told, to carry the label "Fresh paint"). These women are opposites who serve similar functions in the novel as sites where discourse is stopped.

In this affiliative world, the only apparent threat to Mrs. Brook and her friends is the threat that they stop talking. This is the threat, we are led to assume, that Nanda represents to the group. As the Duchess puts it: "She [Mrs. Brook] is in a prodigious fix—she must sacrifice either her daughter or what she once called to me her

intellectual habits" (192). Early on, indeed, Mrs. Brook presents a
poignant picture of herself as the incipient victim of usurpation—
destined to be silenced by her daughter's appearance "on the stage":
"'I sit here now face to face with things as they are. They come in
their turn, I assure you—and they find me,' Mrs. Brook sighed,
'ready.' Nanda has stepped on the stage and I give her up the house"
(133). But the exaggeratedly dramatic tone of this speech reveals it
as just that—a speech that no one, least of all Mrs. Brook, sees as
more than a temporary dramatic pose. It is significant that she will
follow this speech with the observation that Nanda, far from being
the traditional child successor to her aging mother, is "quite maternal. . . . That's the modern daughter"; and only a few pages later,
Mrs. Brook will cast Nanda in yet another role, that of her peer:
"From the moment she is down, the only thing for us is to live as
friends" (140). Such remarks indicate—and their ever-shifting content as much as anything else—that Mrs. Brook's relationship to her
daughter holds not at all to a linear model of succession but to a much
more protean model; it is not a relationship that will silence talk but
one that will continually be defined and redefined by it and, in this
sense, will continually fuel it.

For one thing, the gender of the participants already separates the
relationship from a traditional, genealogical one. We are not dealing
here with a father and son but with a mother and daughter. Daughters in novels before James either didn't have mothers or had mothers who were discredited by male authority and hence rendered already open to daughterly replacement.[21] Mrs. Bennet in *Pride and
Prejudice,* for example, bears a resemblance to Mrs. Brook with the
difference that, from the outset, Austen's character is put in her place
through an implied authority existing outside her family and, by
extension, outside the novel itself, which directs its female author.
At the same time that Mrs. Bennet is discredited in Jane Austen's
novel, moreover, the content of her silliness—her desire to marry her
daughters—is, in fact, upheld as a socially desirable content: it serves
the patrilineal goal of succession fostered by the society that the novel
professes to represent. Thus, Mrs. Bennet's power as an individual
is doubly erased: both in the form of her expression, which is made
to seem trivial and foolish, and in the content of the desire that drives
that expression, since its realization will render her totally expendable
(the implication at the novel's conclusion is that the center of the

family will now shift to Pemberley and that Mrs. Bennet is not welcome there).

Like Mrs. Bennet, Mrs. Brook is often described as silly, as a lover of gossip, and as a woman intent on marrying off her daughter. And yet the context of these traits and desires is quite different. She is no longer contained by an outer authority that directs and closes off her mediating function, anchoring it in the home and soldering it to familial concerns. When such anchorage is gone, concepts concerning both female intelligence and female foolishness lose their measure—indeed, Mrs. Brook is referred to as both sublimely silly and sublimely intelligent. By the same token, notions of family loyalty and exclusiveness no longer operate either. For Mrs. Brook, the difference between being a mother, a wife, and a friend is not really discernible—all these relations are subject to her interpretive intervention and invention. She employs the same nurturant but nonparticularized language in addressing both her family and her friends. Her scheme to marry off her daughter is pursued, but so are other schemes and interests; Nanda's future is simply one part of the extension and elaboration of a more complex design involving all the relations within which Mrs. Brook is implicated. When her daughter's attempt to marry threatens the fabric of these relations, threatens to unravel her own carefully woven place within it, she thwarts that marriage and scavenges for an alterative that will at once settle her daughter "with a man of her own" and leave her own position intact.

In short, Mrs. Brook gains, sustains, and amasses power throughout the novel. She is never used up—or to continue the more Jamesian metaphor, her "embroidery" never stops, although there may be temporary unravelings and she may succumb, as Mitchy puts it, "to temporary despair" concerning the elaboration of a particular design. Still, the key word is "temporary." In a world in which patriarchal authority has disappeared, there is no one to make her give up her mediating function and stop talking—and hence the possibility for the recuperation of relations always exists for her despite her failures. As Mitchy explains to Nanda, Mrs. Brook is destined to continue undimmed by the passage of time: "the generations will come and go, and the *personnel,* as the newspapers say, of the saloon will shift and change.... *We* shan't last, but your mother will ... "(367–68); Van voices a similar sentiment when he refers to Mrs. Brook as "youth"—impossible to "give up"—comparing her in her perpetuity to "the moon or the Marble Arch" (357). Mrs. Brook is forty-one but appears a "mere baby" owing to her apparently limitless ability to make meaning free from the controls and judgments of any authority that would seek to edit, judge, or silence her. Although the danger that her talk poses for her own daughter is made the subject of the novel, it remains throughout a purely theoretical or, rather, a rhetorical danger—merely an excuse for more talk.

Of course, there is Mr. Longdon, "an old boy who remembers the mothers" (33). The product of an earlier age of apparent stability and closure for the family, he seems to occupy a patriarchal role in the novel. He finds Mrs. Brook's talk distasteful, even frightening, and wants to take Nanda away from her mother's house. It is significant, however, that Longdon is the rejected suitor of Mrs. Brook's mother. In other words, he not only failed to get Lady Julia as a wife, he also failed to get Mrs. Brook as a daughter: "he might have been my *own* father" (146), exclaims Mrs. Brook, a remark that is as significant in asserting what is not the case as it is in asserting what is. By virtue of this mock-paternal positioning, Longdon serves not to censor Mrs. Brook but to empower her—to mark her as a daughter and yet to leave her free from emotional investment in a real father. Emily Brontë introduced a similar combination at the end of *Wuthering Heights,* placing Cathy Jr. in a mock-daughterly relationship to Heathcliff and thereby enabling her to escape a debilitating role in a family triangle. But James takes the liberating combination that Brontë engineers for the end of her novel and makes it the starting point for his.

In the process, James raises a new question: if the daughter is placed opposite a father figure in whom she is not invested and hence who does not control and limit her mediating role, where then can her own daughter go? Again, the question turns out to be a rhetorical one. The problem of the daughter's place exists only when one continues to think of the family as a closed system with a limited number of roles—a family in which the daughter structurally complements the father, improving upon the romantic complementarity that her mother had originally provided to her father. The Brookenham family is a family that no longer holds to this closure, and the question of where Nanda is to go given her mother's unwillingness to give up her intellectual habits is posed purely by virtue of Longdon's presence on the scene. Longdon, the representative of an earlier age, sees

Nanda as the very image of her grandmother. His idea of her thus activates both Mrs. Brook and Nanda herself in their roles as mediating daughters: they are spurred, that is, to help give shape to his traditional family idea. Mrs. Brook's contribution to this creative process is to throw Longdon and Nanda together and to "work" Longdon by displaying the group in such a way as to make him want to remove Nanda and settle something on her. Nanda's contribution to Longdon's idea is through the cultivation of a passion for Van. Without the passion Nanda provides, Longdon's marriage plot (his "idea" that Van and Nanda should marry) would be unviable in the terms of that old-fashioned idea that Nanda and Mrs. Brook are helping him to sustain. What I am arguing is that Nanda's passion is more for Longdon's *idea* than it is for Van himself—and, as we shall see, passion for an idea occurs on another logical level than passion for a person.

If Mrs. Brook is "not the ancient mother," as she puts it, but the modern one, the mother who is no longer anchored to a family of origin and yet will not relinquish her daughterly role, Nanda is, as Mrs. Brook also reminds us, the "modern daughter," the daughter who is her mother's peer, even, at times, her mother's mother. She is a daughter for whom the hierarchical and opposing categories of innocence and experience, daughter and mother, self and other are provisional positionings—for whom all meaning is a matter of temporary spatial design, of what for the moment "groups together." Nanda and her mother are not complicitous as some critics have argued[22]; they are simply cut out of the same cloth as mediating daughters operating free of the anchorage of a nuclear family and a patrilineal succession. The issue of whether Mrs. Brook will stop talking is clearly not an issue for Nanda, who has been exposed from infancy to her mother's way of life. "Everything, literally everything, in London, in the world she lives in, is in the air she breathes—so that the longer she's in it, the more she'll know" (273), explains Van to Mitchy in a graphic description of the way barriers between outside and inside have dissolved for the Jamesian heroine. "I must take things in at my pores" (248), explains Nanda. The daughter's "exposure" is her access to an outside that had been so completely curtained off before. If it involves a loss of old, formal distinctions it also represents the availability of new material—infinite material—upon which female mediation can act and make meaning.

Further, Nanda's difference from her grandmother, as she ex-

plains to Longdon, rests on her knowledge not only in its quantity
but also in its quality. Comparing herself to her grandmother at one
point, she explains, "when I say things she wouldn't then I put before
you too much . . . what I know and see and feel. If we're both partly
the result of other people, *her* other people were so different" (176).
What this says is more than that Nanda knows about sex and death
and betrayal in ways that her grandmother didn't; it means that she
knows about her own implication in all these things. This is the knowledge of a self aware of its own psychology—aware of itself as multi-
layered and in process. It is what I shall refer to as the *psychologized
self*. For such a self the illusion of innocence and of separateness is
no longer possible. Longdon grasps the nature of such a self when
he compares Nanda at one point with little Aggie. Both are lambs,
he says, but while Aggie is one "fed by the hand," Nanda has "struggled with instincts and forebodings, with the suspicion of its doom
and the far-borne scent, in the flowery fields, of blood" (181). Aggie
resembles Freud's hysterics, young women who could think that they
were "innocents"—unconscious of sex and death—"fed by the hand"
of a society that created an unconscious in its daughters by its imposi-
tion of limits, boundaries, repressions to knowledge. The result was
that these daughters unconsciously knew about that to which they had
been bred to be innocent. Nanda, however, is at another stage of
consciousness that assimilates knowledge of the unconscious to itself—which is as acutely aware of what it doesn't know and can't know
as of what it does. Thus, Nanda consciously knows that she knows
things unknown to most girls her age, but she also knows that knowledge "depends on other people" (175) and, in this dependency, is
never complete or static, is only a matter of "instincts," "forebodings,"
"suspicions." All meaning is, therefore, for her, provisional and subject to violation, disruption, and revision. James mimics Nanda's
knowledge in the form of his novel. In his refusal to privilege a
"central intelligence," he in effect admits that his characters are not
knowable as individuals but only as continually shifting and infinitely
interpretable relations. They cannot be separated from the whole,
and are mutually dependent and reinforcing in even their seemingly
most private and self-interested acts.

The climax of the novel occurs in Nanda's final meeting with
Van, in which the possibility of a marriage between them is laid to

rest. Why does Van fail to take Nanda as his wife despite powerful incentives to do so? It has been suggested that he doesn't "love" Nanda or that his reverence for traditional sanctities prevents him from marrying a girl too much exposed to her mother's scandalous talk.[23] Yet such explanations seem out of touch with the larger concerns of the novel, and Van's failure must be understood in a wider context. If he were to embrace the idea of a marriage (as Longdon's fairy-godmother beneficence and Nanda's long-suffering passion define it), he would be entering a closed plot and, as it were, burying himself alive. For the static values of loyalty and love attached to the traditional marriage plot, like anything that professes to the originating, the absolute, or the transcendent in this novel, define the limits of discourse and hence of the elusive, surface self that discourse brings into being. Van's old-style loyalties refer to a set of ideas that now must be supported by talk, that cannot be lived in the old-fashioned sense that Longdon lived—secluded and silent—his love for Lady Julia. Van's personal power, that "sacred terror" Mitchy ascribes to him, which has been interpreted too simply as sexual attractiveness, is his ability to arouse the desire not for sex but for interpretation—to tease into being the suggestion of relationship (which is precisely what he does so successfully for the reader as regards Mrs. Brook). Mrs. Brook is Van's partner ("my youth and my old age," as he puts it to Nanda), because she mediates him—she "works" him for just those complexities of motive and those relational possibilities that he preserves in maintaining an undefined relationship with Nanda.

If we accept the radically free nature of Mrs. Brook's and Nanda's mediation, then we see that critics who have quibbled over whether Mrs. Brook's talk is really witty and intellectual enough to warrant all the fuss that is made about it have missed the point.[24] It is precisely the absence of any measure for what is "good talk" that is the issue in this novel. What once might have been called trivial domestic gossip is, with the discreditation of the authority of the public sphere, no longer in thrall to some larger, public discourse. It becomes as "good," that is, as those who participate in it as characters and as readers are willing to acknowledge it to be. This now free-ranging female-mediated talk is necessarily emotionally shallow, or at least must tend not to attach itself in any powerful way to any one relationship or relational configuration. This seems to be the conclusion reached between Mrs. Brook and Van in a conversation toward the end of the novel:

> "And yet to think that after all it has been mere *talk*!"
> ... "Mere, mere, mere. But perhaps it's exactly the 'mere' that has made us range so wide."
> ... "You mean that we haven't had the excuse of passion?" (230)

The absence of passion, which has served as the anchor for the domestic novel since Richardson, is precisely what separates this novel and, in some degree, all James's work from that tradition. It is the absence of such passion that caused the critic Edmund Wilson to refer to a "morbid element" in James's novels and in *The Awkward Age* in particular. Jamesian women, Wilson writes, are "innocent, conventional and rather cold," subject to "Freudian complexes or a kind of arrested development." He accounts for this by appealing to some frustration, "something incomplete and unexplained about James's emotional life."[25] James refers several times in *The Awkward Age* to a phenomenon that he terms "morbid modernity." To associate morbidity with modernity is to give that which from Wilson's more traditional perspective reflects a personal neurosis a larger social reading. It suggests further that there must always be a morbid aspect to the modern, existing as it does on the body of what came before. Modernity is the superseding of one configuration by another, that at once denounces its predecessor and springs from it. Van's failure to embrace Longdon's idea and marry Nanda is symbolic of the general superseding of a desire anchored in place through its creation within a closed family system (what, in another vocabulary, could be termed "Oedipalized desire") by a desire that can be changed and redirected through discourse—"mere talk"—produced through the opening up of and the imagining around a closed idea of the family.

Nanda fails to give Longdon the marriage that his original old-fashioned idea had proposed, but she can immediately enter into another idea that has been emerging in him through her influence: the idea that he has been converted and modernized by her—that he can take the place of Van as her companion ("I'm really what you may call adopting him. I mean I'm little by little changing him" [238]). Similarly, although Nanda has been said to feel passion for Van, it is significant that her passion is a workable one, different from the passion we are accustomed to see in earlier novels that either gets satisfied in the end through a happy marriage or drags the heroine to a horrible fate. Instead, Nanda's passion seems only another interpretive stance, a temporary positioning within a shifting design. Her motive for seeing Van at their final meeting, originally formulated as the desire to declare her passion, can transform itself without hypocrisy into another, even opposing, motive: her desire that he not desert her mother. What may seem like a loss for Nanda is thus recouped and recirculated in a new form. If Van's failure impoverishes Nanda as an old-fashioned girl (the part she has been playing for Longdon), it enriches her as a member of a modern group. By throwing Van back she essentially makes him available to others as well as herself in new combinations.

An analogous situation occurs with Mitchy: she engineers a marriage for him with Aggie that backs one idea, but when that idea proves unworkable, she then reclaims it as the designated motive for a new relationship between them. This new relationship will continually need to be reclaimed through interpretation. Indeed, it is her interpretive implication in Mitchy's marriage that belies the seeming separation of Nanda from her mother, whom she has made Mitchy promise not to desert just as she has done with Van. By being attached to Mitchy, who will remain attached to her mother, she also remains attached to her mother. In her relation to Mitchy, moreover, we see an explicit reformulation of the family cut free from blood ties and conventional roles of any kind and, as such, made both more durable and more elastic. As Mitchy describes it, hers is "the certainty of finding herself saddled for all time to come with a gentleman whom she can never get rid of on the specious plea that he's only her husband or her lover or her father or her son or her brother or her uncle or her cousin. There, as none of these characters, he just stands" (363). Mitchy's declaration of an unfamilial relation to Nanda reverses Lovelace's declaration in *Clarissa* that he will be all family to the heroine: "a father, uncle, brother, and . . . husband . . . all in one" (1:480). In the opposing ways they invoke blood and kinship, these men define the respective limits of a transformation in family ideology.

In the end, Mrs. Brook has not assimilated her daughter into her scheme any more than Nanda has assimilated her mother into hers. Instead, we must see the two women not hierarchically but laterally, as two competing and mutually reinforcing mediating daughters who achieve a kind of equilibrium in the coordination of their two orbits. We see this spatialization of their roles near the end as Mrs. Brook entertains her visitors downstairs while Nanda entertains hers in her own room upstairs. In most cases, the visitors are the same but undergo different though related "treatment" from the two women. Taking our cue from this iconography, it would seem that James has in mind not a retreat of the daughter into an old-world patriarchal idyll but a stretching of the family to include Longdon's Suffolk home—to include the daughter, the mother, and the old man (and through him the grandmother) and thus to subsume the past and the future into the present through that interpretive discourse, that "mere talk," that is the novel.[26] One could say that history itself is "worked out" of Longdon in the end, and he is flattened—spatialized—alongside Nanda and her mother. "History" (and James puts the word in quotation marks in his Preface as if aware that it is already an archaism in his world) implies that "principle of growth," of aging and succession and deep psychological structure, that Nanda declares she lacks. What she has is a principle of *design*—the eternal promise of multiple and always newly suggestive combinations—which the novel itself embodies in its infinite suggestiveness, in its "quantity of meaning and number of intentions,"[27] and which is reflected and reduplicated in the rich body of interpretive literature to which it has given rise.

* * *

The constantly allusive, open-ended, assimilating discursiveness of *The Awkward Age* can be compared to Freud's "talking cure"—that continually bringing to the surface of repressed material in analysis. However, there is a salient difference between the talk of James's characters and the talk of Freud's patients. Psychoanalysis was born as an activity of opposition—as a counter to tendencies to keep silent and unaware in certain aspects of life.[28] But in a world in which this kind of talk goes on continually, where it goes unchecked and unresisted, there is no longer an "outside" to it; that is, it can no longer be understood as existing in opposition to something else. Talk now becomes less the antidote for repression than the replacement of it: the maker and unmaker of meaning cut free from unconscious desire. Leo Bersani has referred to James's writing as "desublimated," noting that in James "it is as though human relations implied what we call human feelings into existence, but they are so to speak, the elaborations of surfaces—they have no depth."[29] I have tried to argue that James arrives at his particular perspective by traveling through conventional notions of family and self to where there is no longer an anchorage in a set of stable relationships, and where desire, in what it suggests of fixity and intensity, is replaced by criticism and interpretation of oneself and others. This fully psychologized universe carries with it the erasure of a unified, boundaried self. For where one is continually in search of one's own and others' motives, knowing full well that they cannot be wholly known, one's relationship to reality becomes provisional and plastic. Thus, each individual is known through relationship, and each relationship suggests some other relationship in its place. This produces a sense of indeterminacy that "good talk" constantly attempts both to suggest and to do away with. Such talk resembles that proliferating sexual discourse that Michel Foucault has associated with modern society since the seventeenth century. Yet in its self-consciousness, and in its awareness of the essential irrelevance of its own content, it is more like Foucault's own metasexual discourse than it is like the sexual discourse he writes about. In ideological terms we can say that where repression and its counterpoint, psychoanalysis, assured the stability of the nuclear family, the free-ranging talk of Mrs. Brook's circle assures the stability of the new, open-ended (anti-)family, a stability that is a matter not of closure but of a mobile connectedness made possible through the continual potential for a new or extended interpretation.

How did this perspective on culture, this formulation of a new order of relationship that redefines the whole idea of family and of self on the level of discourse, become available to James? The answer lies, I believe, in the unique circumstances of his life, which overlapped with a particular historical moment when the ideology of the nuclear family was beginning to exhaust itself. It is significant that James came from a family that was intensely nucleated in its loyalties but unorthodox and unlocalized in its teachings and behavior. The Jameses were, by their own account, exceptionally devoted to a family ideal: they held their family up as a site of extraordinary intellectual and creative nurturance. This devotion can be largely attributed to the efforts of Henry James, Sr., who made his family his occupation, continually shuttling back and forth between Europe and America in search of the ideal education and cultural climate for his children. But the father's teachings were in some sense at odds with the devotion that prompted them. James Sr. preached against competition and professionalism and expressed scorn for conventional hierarchies and distinctions.[30] Since family closure is a function of drawing a boundary and maintaining a hierarchy of roles and concerns, this means that the teachings of the father were implicitly in conflict with the idea of the family—the very thing that inspired these teachings. It seems significant that in his early letters, Henry James expressed a wish that he could feel "homesick." While this may literally refer to the fact that his family's peripatetic existence during his childhood made it impossible for him to have that longing for a particular place that other children experienced, the remark might also be said to reflect a sense that his family was so nonconformist in its attitudes that it could include any amount of physical distancing or rebellious action. What Henry James may have wanted and couldn't have was to feel himself outside the family. Even his seemingly classic act of separation from the family—his decision to settle in Europe—was never articulated either by himself or by his family as an act of separation.[31]

How, then, did the Jameses, a family that seemed intent upon avoiding all manner of conventional roles and attitudes, define itself and allow its members to define themselves? The answer, I would suggest, resides in the role that Alice James, youngest child and only daughter, played in the family.[32]

Alice appears to have been an extreme case of a regulating daughter within a family in which forces of dispersion and fragmentation operated with more vigor and self-consciousness than in most families of the period. Indeed, one could say that, in their very attempt to be different, the Jameses simply exaggerated tendencies that were less explicit in other families. All of the Jameses (with the notable exception of the mother[33]) suffered psychosomatic illnesses. These illnesses seem to have served them as at least a temporary means of evading a commitment to work or settling down. However, Alice's assumption of the invalid role eclipsed that of the others in its severity and was the most prolonged, extending from her first "crisis" at the age of fourteen to her death at the age of forty-two. The last fifteen years of her life were spent almost entirely in bed in her parents' house until their death, after which she moved to London to be near Henry.

The special role in the family assigned to Alice is expressed in a letter from Henry James, Sr., when his son Robertson was suffering from depression and alcoholism: "Any other care upon our hands, while this absorbing state of things [i.e., Alice's illness] endures, would be intolerable, especially to me whose own nerves would bear no stouter tension than they now have."[34] The message couldn't be clearer: James Sr. assigns Alice the invalid role and orders Robertson not to be sick unless he wants to destroy his father's health as well. In keeping with this policy that the daughter's illness supersede and, in so doing, mitigate the ill health of other family members, Alice's health seems to have been worst at the point of her brothers' separation from the family and to have flared during times of special stress for other family members.

How unconscious was this use to which Alice was put? We know that the Jameses openly espoused a "bank account" concept of family health, believing that one member paid through sickness for the other's well being. This concept was referred to in letters between Henry James and his brother William, who alternately suffered from back ailments and nervous depression during their early careers. Yet the more comprehensive use to which Alice seems to have been put in the family was never directly alluded to by the brothers (although Alice in her journal makes some suggestive remarks about Henry's attendance at her sickbed).[35] If Alice's role as family regulator went unremarked by her brothers it may be that they sensed in it something stereotypical rather than original—that in using Alice to keep the family whole they were acting more like other families of the period than they would have liked to admit. Indeed, it could be said that Alice's chronic illness dynamically counteracted James Sr.'s unorthodox, permissive philosophy toward his sons. By existing in her invalidism as the exaggeration of certain conventional female traits, she defined the family for her brothers so that, despite their aging, their wandering, and their unstereotypical choices, they never lost their anchorage in a childhood idea of home.

I believe that Henry James did finally achieve some insight into his sister's case after his parents' death, when she moved to London to be near him. Both her presence nearby after so many years of physical separation and her death not long afterward must have helped James to articulate to himself what had been implicit in his life and his work from the beginning—that his act of separation and indeed all the binary oppositions in his work were assimilable to a family idea of tolerance in some sense paid for by his sister.

We do know, moreover, that James made a concrete discovery following his sister's death: he found her diary. He had never known her to write, and the journal is, as he readily admitted to his brother William, an extraordinary document. It is personal and yet without any particular intensity of emotion. It skims over topics as diverse as Irish politics, marriage, pregnancy and virginity, digestion, and the events and personalities of the neighborhood. It has wit and great intelligence, but it has no plot, no pretense at closure. One of the most telling entries describes a reaction she used to have to her father:

> I used to sit immovable reading in the library with waves of violent inclination suddenly invading my muscles taking some one of their myriad forms such as throwing myself out of the window, or knocking off the head of the benignant pater as he sat with his silver locks, writing at his table. . . .[36]

Although written in the bland fashion typical of the journal, the lines suggest that there existed a complex emotional bond between Alice and James Sr., and that her illness on the one hand and her journal writing on the other were opposing modes of coping with that bond.

How did the diary affect Henry James? His recorded response is ambivalent.[37] He acknowledged its literary value but wished to suppress it, fearing that some of Alice's remarks might embarrass the family. In his modesty, he continued to cling to an idea of family closure that his novels had already begun to critique. Even so, I believe that Alice's diary played an important role in accelerating and deepening that critique by making present to him the other side of her debilitating illness or what might have helped it—namely, a more protracted and ongoing analysis carried on by her not in the family exclusively but in a wider society that included the family. With a greater access to social surfaces over familial depths, with more of a freedom to talk rather than feel, with a dispersal of investment in a particular father, Alice might not have been sick.

If James understood, as I believe he must have, that his freedom was in some sense paid for by Alice's sickness, the diary also must have suggested to him that his sister could have played a different but equally facilitating role in his life and the lives of others that would not have involved her debilitation. His later work indicates that he found such a female role imaginatively compelling even as he found the literal fact of his sister's diary to be a personal embarrassment. The manifestations of family dispersal occurring around him he had treated broadly in *What Maisie Knew*. To view that dispersal from a new angle as he did in *The Awkward Age* was to posit the existence of a nonnucleated, truly dispersed family of relations in which female mediation might operate freely. It is significant that James would depend on the society of fashionable women to lend interest to his life and to "germinate" his stories—to offer that shallow network of interpretive relations from which both his life and his art can be said to have taken shape. These women's talk was probably not so different from Mrs. Brook's (one thinks, for example, of the way in which he was woven into the fabric of Edith Wharton's intrigues[38]). As for Alice, she seems to me to shimmer behind his greatest heroines. The Alice broken free of family closure—the Alice of the diary—speaks like Nanda Brookenham.

Conclusion

Henry James is an appropriate end point for this book because he is a domestic novelist who sees around the domestic plot. As we move through his canon, he increasingly relays the conviction that conventional family relationships are constraints upon the self-actualization and knowledge of individuals. In *The Portrait of a Lady*, Isabel Archer, whom circumstance had liberated from the weight of family at the beginning of the novel, is maneuvered through the pressures of society and the machinations of friends to burden herself with a husband and stepdaughter. James leaves her struggling with the consequences. In his novels of the 1890s, the protagonists form connections that derive from, but are unlike, conventional family relationships. Fleda Vetch is paired off with the mother of her former lover; Maisie, with her governess; Nanda, with an octogenerian who could have been, but is not, her grandfather. In the novels of James's "major phase," the institutions of marriage and family are more directly critiqued, although they remain the controlling context for the action. In *The Ambassadors,* Lambert Strether is sent to Europe to retrieve a philandering young man for his family only to suspect, even as he succeeds in his mission, that the higher value might lie with the young man's disregard for family loyalty. In *The Wings of the Dove*, Merton Densher is confronted with a moral dilemma that makes a longed-for marriage impossible to him. In *The Golden Bowl,* Maggie Verver recaptures her husband at the expense of her father, and in such a way as to make her triumph seem bizarre and morally dubious.

In his representation of the restrictiveness of family relations, James anticipates literary modernism but cannot be categorized as part of that movement. In the proto-modernist and modernist fiction of such writers as Conrad, Lawrence, Joyce, Hemingway, and Faulkner the central character is generally defined through his complete alienation from family ties, or through an intense and encompassing subjectivity that obscures or radically distorts these ties. James's protagonists are never so totally isolated or self-involved. Literary modernism is also a movement that focuses predominantly on male rites of passage and identity struggle,[1] while James's interest centers on the young woman, as he put it, "affronting her destiny." And yet the modernist tradition must also be understood in connection to the family ideology that it appears to disregard. We are led to recall one family theorist's observation that emotional cutoff from one's family is as much a reflection of emotional dependence on that family as never leaving home.[2]

If James's continued interest in external relationships and his preference for the heroine over the hero appear to separate him from the modernist tradition he anticipates, where precisely does James "fit" in the history of culture? James loads his mostly female protagonists with those forms of domestic life—the ritualized talk, the routine visits and occasions, the furniture and bric-a-brac—that do not encumber the modernist hero; but I would argue that in locating these forms within a context that brings the domestic frame into question, he projects himself beyond the alienation and identity struggles of modernism into the realm of postmodernism. In James, the validity of identity is itself called into question and the patterns of social intercourse—the arrangement of things, people, and talk—become the subject of creative manipulation and speculation.

James, then, can be said to anticipate more than the birth of a turn-of-the-century literary movement and the decline of a nineteenth-century literary tradition of domestic realism. He anticipates a new ideology for the century as a whole; he glimpses a new organizing principle to serve in the wake of the dispersal of relations arising out of the breakdown of the nuclear family. Just as Samuel Richardson had grasped an ideology that organized experience in terms of closure that would dominate the nineteenth century, James grasped an ideology that would organize experience in terms of interpretive discourse—an ideology that has increasingly dominated the twentieth century. If Freud gave a scientific form to what Richardson had described, laying the groundwork for the next order of perception, Gregory Bateson, the great communication theorist of our age, gave a scientific form to what James described. Bateson writes:

In this world . . . "I" as a material object have no relevance and, in this sense, no reality. "I," however, exist in the communicational world as an essential element in the syntax of my experience and in the experience of others, and the communications of others may damage my identity, even to the point of breaking up the organization of my experience.[3]

In this communicational world, we are dealing not simply with a new arrangement emerging out of an old pattern but with a new perspective on form itself—with another logical level or degree of abstraction in relation to the idea of closure as it pertains to both human relationships and literary form.

In all the novelists preceding James, the effort was to work within an ideology of closure through various sleights and manipulations. The novel's task, like that of the nuclear family, was to repress meaning in order to make meaning. This process was expressed inside the novel through the role of the mediating daughter contained within a closed family system—a role mythologized in the death of Clarissa. The effort to institute and then increasingly to save a family ideology of closure and stability and a theory of representation that corresponded to it (in which plot lines were drawn together and sealed) was also an effort to retain a belief in empirical reality, in the unitary nature of truth. James's heroines also try to save meaning—especially as it regards the identities of the male characters—but such saving always occurs within a self-conscious frame where it is exposed as a temporary solution based, not on some absolute truth, but on the critical power and generous vision of the female mediator. Thus, Nanda saves Van the pain of one meaning in which his identity would be destroyed, and proceeds to the creation of a new meaning in which his identity is bolstered. Her act is not a falsification of Van or of herself, but a deconstructing of the notion that there is one essential, true interpretation of motive and relationship.

James demonstrates in his work that once closed form is seen around (once, that is, that one can imagine positioning oneself outside it), it is open to revision. It now becomes possible to see that any given interpretation of life involves the repressing of that which can return and become part of a new interpretation. I have called Nelly Dean an example of this kind of mobile mediation of meaning in *Wuthering Heights,* but she stands on the boundary of the action, and the story that she helps to bring about is not hers. In James, the Nelly Deans become "central intelligences" and their creative efforts are presented as precious sites of meaning and value.

The ideological transformation that James glimpsed in his novels has, to some extent, been realized in the varied shapes families are now acknowledged to take in our society. Yet I would argue that one of the crucial and transformative leaps undergone by the family in this century, one that James's *The Awkward Age* points toward, is the introduction of the figure of the mother into our cultural mythology toward the beginning of this century (Mother's Day became a holiday in 1907; Freud did his work on the pre-Oedipal mother in the 1920s). In light of the perspective of this study, the modern "discovery" of the pre-Oedipal phase by psychoanalysis and a related surge of interest in the mother's role in culture more generally represent an effort to integrate the female into the family system at a later stage in her development, that is, to integrate the daughter into the family of the next generation. This effort appears both as a response to strains in the core dynamic of father and daughter that required further bolstering and as a substitute for that relationship: a new orientation for the daughter (toward motherhood) and a new center for the family as embodied by the maxim: "mother will be there for you." James's Mrs. Brook anticipates and, in anticipation, satirizes, the mother as a newly conceptualized pivot for familial relations. Virginia Woolf's Mrs. Ramsay embodies the concept of the intuitive, ministering, controlling mother as it had begun to hold sway in the culture.

Barbara Ehrenreich and Deirdre English have argued that the rise of "domestic science" in the beginning of this century was a means by which society kept women in their place by manufacturing work for them to do.[4] I would simply widen the lens and say that such work, by conventionalizing and publicly promoting the maternal role, gave the family a new anchorage that would continue to serve until the 1960s and 1970s when, with a newly invigorated feminist movement, maternity became imbued with the language of liberation. Thus, Marianne Hirsch has described how feminist writers like Adrienne Rich looked to the image of the mother to help in the creation of a "new feminist subject."[5] Certainly, a central feminist concern (and a more general postmodern project) of the past two decades seems to have been the recovery, or at least postulation about, our early experiences with our mothers in an effort to escape the constraints of patriarchal institutions, values, and language itself. But the ground also continues to shift beneath us. Hirsch, for example, in "excavating" the mother-daughter plot in novels takes pains to explain that although women have begun to explore their relationship to the maternal they must also explore what it means to speak from the position of the maternal. In other words, having acknowledged the mother from her position as a daughter, the female critic must now discover the mother in herself. But it seems to me that no such call to discovery is necessary. We are simply riding an ideological wave that is transferring women inevitably from the daughter's to the mother's position. In other words, both our "discovery" of the mother and our shift in perspective on her from iconic and controlling to *"jouissante"* and self-identifying reflect the cresting of an ideology of the family within which we are struggling to keep our footing before the wave crashes. When that happens, "the maternal" may become so diffused or so radically transformed as to cease to be a meaningful idea.

But let me explain the transformation I see occurring from a slightly different angle. The anthropologist Mary Douglas, in attempting to describe the direction in which the modern family is tending, has postulated the emergence of what she calls "the fully personal family"—a home situation in which "no meals [would be] taken in common and no hierarchy recognised, but in which the mother would attempt to meet the unique needs of each child by creating an entirely individual environment and time-table and services around each of her brood."[6] A family that operates this way is perhaps as personal as one can get while still retaining the semblance of a nuclear family, but it is certainly not a *fully* personal arrangement. Although it caters to the unique needs of the children and, presumably, the father, it still defines the role of the mother in a nonpersonalized, other-directed way, reinforcing my earlier point that the maternal role, emerging relatively late in the ideological history of the family, now stands at its center and functions as the last bulwark for the institution. Douglas's description sounds very close to the operation of many contemporary families, which, by virtue of the mother's role, still cling to some remnant of an idea of closure. But because other family members do not occupy conventionalized roles, this family model is highly precarious, operating at the edge of its own dissolution. Christopher Lasch seems to be referring to a related situation when he describes the "pseudo-mutuality" of the modern family, in which the mother is intent on maintaining a sense of unity that is purely formal and that involves no profound communication or emotional contact among members.[7] Again, in such a family situation, the nuclear family idea still prevails in the imagination but is drained of the affective charge that made it a durable idea—an ideology—in the nineteenth century. If the mothers in these families are functioning by rote, they may not formally differ from the stereotypical or dead mothers of nineteenth-century fiction. Yet the ministrations of the postmodern mother seem to me more akin to the "little office of convenience" set up by Mrs. Brook. To mediate everyone's experience is, as I have tried to argue, finally to cease to be invested in anyone's, to be free to create and elaborate relationships at will. In this context, the mother that Mary Douglas describes emerges as the extreme case or upper limit of the mediating daughter, the route through which possibilities of role and relationship that were closed to women in the nineteenth century are being opened and transformed.

The mother as she stereotypically operates in our present culture also points to other transformations. The greater distancing of the father from the family system as indicated by statistics on divorce (with mothers still retaining custody of children in the majority of cases) makes the daughter's mediation of the father less intense and sustained. As a result, the daughter's mediating role becomes more generalized, less linked to a particular father. New family arrangements such as single parent homes, new kinds of extended families created through divorce and remarriage, shared parental responsibilities, and greater reliance on day-care centers may seem contradictory in some of their effects, but they would all seem to discourage an intensive emotional investment in a family of origin. With the loss of this investment comes the possibility of still more flexible and varied relational and child-care arrangements. To postulate along these lines is to consider how even the generalized mediating capabilities bequeathed to women as the last legacy of an ideology of closure might eventually become accessible to everyone, as individuals are made to create and interpret their own relational arrangements. In other words, it is not toward Douglas's "fully personal family" that we are logically tending but toward what I would term a "fully maternal relational system." Such diffusion of maternal behavior would, of course, render the particular role obsolete.[8]

Postmodern literature seems to reflect a corresponding movement toward reconfiguration. The current emphasis on feminist critical theory and, in fiction, on the female interpretation of experience indicates that gender difference is still a defining issue in literature. However, there also appears to be a growing number of male critics who call themselves feminists as well as an increasing interest in themes dealing with role reversal, sexual transvestism, and alternative forms of relationship. These trends suggest that what constitutes gender difference in the realm of literary discourse is becoming problematic to say the least, and that we are moving, in one critic's words, "from an oppositional to a differential logic."[9] Indeed, I believe we are about to enter a new literary moment in which the distinctions that have been drawn between male and female writing will become blurred (one is reminded of Virginia Woolf's reflections on a future "androgynous" literature), in which emphasis will be placed more on ecological structure and design—on "differences" and "contexts"— than on gender opposition.[10]

* * *

It may appear ironic that the revolutionary vision of family and of novel form that would involve a shift in emphasis from male authority to a new kind of female interpretive power occurred in the work of Henry James and (albeit less profoundly) in the work of other male novelists such as Thomas Hardy, George Meredith, and George Gissing, and not in the work of female novelists who were their contemporaries.[11] Yet if we admit the conception of women as mediators (formed first as the elements of trade organizing families in primitive kinship, and then as the mediating consciousnesses for stable male identity within the nuclear family), it is perhaps less surprising that a male writer would achieve the metaperspective necessary to document fully a new role for women as the interpreters of a world of meaning in flux. We could say that the female writer, as a woman conditioned to regulate and mediate already represented systems, could not be the one to imagine for herself a new creative role in culture.[12]

Of course, this raises a question about the essential nature of the feminist movement and of apparent female empowerment in novels such as James's. Does the patriarchal basis of culture as we understand it continue to cast its shadow over all future forms of organization, making them at core patriarchal and exploitative of women? It would seem to me that the answer is no. The evolution of a system can produce such extraordinary variations as to make the supposed point of origin too oblique to be relevant. If women seem to be regulating male systems still, we must also recognize that where such systems cease to be privileged, then the distinction between creation and mediation—between content and form—may cease to be meaningful. In other words, we may no longer be able to punctuate the relationship between men and women in culture in terms of power. Bateson makes the point that power ceases to be an appropriate mode of comprehending experience in the ecological paradigm (the more comprehensive, third-order perspective that he associates with the world of communication).[13] James also renders this idea in the kinds of demands his writing makes on his readers.

To demonstrate how James's work supports this perspective, let me return to the last scene between Nanda and Van in *The Awkward Age*. In this scene, Van must inform Nanda that he does not intend to marry her. Not wanting to look cruel or foolish in this act of rejection, he scrambles to place her in relation to the heroines of literature in a way that would elevate her unattached position. The result is embarrassing to read; one feels his desperation:

> Isn't there a girl in some story—it isn't Scott; what is it?—who has domestic difficulties and a cage in her window and whom one associates with chickweed and virtue? It isn't Esmeralda—Esmeralda had a poodle, hadn't she—or have I got my heroines mixed? You're up here yourself like a heroine; you're perched in your tower or what do you call it?—your bower. You quite hang over the place, you know—the great wicked city, the wonderful London sky and the monuments looming all through: or am I again only muddling up my Zola? (349)

Van is a creature of talk, a man of poses and rhetorical flourishes, who enjoys nothing more than teasing new meaning out of seemingly innocuous appearances. It is therefore appropriate that, in trying to let Nanda down, he take his descriptors from literature. But for all his facility in conversation, Van has no independent creative power. He has neither a unified place in a closed system, like Mr. Longdon, nor the ability to mediate freely in open space, like Mrs. Brook or Nanda. His references are thus a literary word salad, and he looks like he is suffering a kind of narrative nervous breakdown. Before things get out of hand, however, Nanda comes to the rescue—gives reason to his embarrassment, covers over his failure, and "props him up." She situates herself as a heroine if only by saving him face. Here, I think, James is not so much ridiculing the ineptitude of Van as he is showing the man (or male writer) to be dependent in an entirely new way on the woman (or female reader). Van's need to be "saved" by a generous Nanda is an analogue for the novel's own need to be saved by a generous reader, and James emerges in this context as a male author dependent on the interpretive aid of a female critic (the role, incidentally, that I am performing for him here).

However, the metaphorical context in which this dependency is cast ends up erasing the dependency on a literal level. The third-order change that is critical discourse not only obliterates the opposition between domestic space and outer world and between self and other but also the opposition between male and female, writer and critic. In James's preparation of the New York Edition of his work (which included both the writing of the Prefaces and the comprehensive revision of the novels), he engages in an extraordinary effort at cross-dressing—at being both the male "canvas" and the female "embroidery" in relation to himself. Thus, in his Preface to *The Awkward Age,* James proudly refers to a healthy self-sufficiency as the most gratifying thing about his novel. What makes this self-sufficiency different from the self-sufficiency of a closed system is that it is not exclusionary. If he has assimilated the critical faculty to himself, he has also extended the creative faculty to the reader. In late James, the reader gets assigned the role of authorial surrogate: James's extension into future time. In the Preface to *The Golden Bowl,* for example, he refers to the possibility that the reader may rescue some of his novels from their flaws: "I could but dream the whole thing over ... and ... hope that, some still newer and shrewder critic's intelligence operating, I shouldn't have breathed upon the old catastrophes and accidents ... wholly in vain."[14] The comment reflects James's view of the way in which the creative and the critical perspective may eventually become indistinguishable: author and reader may come to share the same infinitely elaborated "dream" and merge into what Bateson would call "an ecology of mind."

Leo Bersani, in his writing on James, has argued that critical discourse occurs at the point of the erasure of style.[15] This seems to me to be the point to which James's late work tends. Nanda, we can recall, is characterized as being without style and *The Awkward Age* itself, in its avoidance of a central intelligence, seems to want to purge itself of the moral and emotional directives that tend to accompany style. Style, after all, is a derivative of individualism: of consciousness anchored in place as the result of an emotional investment in a family of origin. Where that anchorage is removed, the resonance produced by depths of guilt and desire disappears; the fixed distinctiveness of style is transformed into the turns and twists of improvisational design. In *The Golden Bowl,* James enacts this transformation for his heroine. He has her achieve success by repudiating the style that had defined her, and she finally unites with her husband through what Quentin Anderson has termed the "androgynization" of them both.[16]

Yet this styleless, "open" perspective must be understood as a tendency rather than an achieved stance (indeed, to achieve it would be to contradict its premises), and James often seems to hark back to an earlier relationship to form, even in his later work. In the Preface to his novel *Roderick Hudson,* for example, he seems to want to justify the novel's more traditional loyalties even as he sees around them. "Really, universally, relations stop nowhere," he explains, "and the exquisite problem of the artist is eternally but to draw, by a geometry of his own, the circle within which they shall happily *appear* to do so."[17] What the statement does is locate James at a crossroads of ideology where one can still choose to assert an opposition between "inside" and "outside"—to draw the novel frame, to cling to a stable knowledge of self and other and produce an illusion of continuity and style. In writing about his early novel, James seems to support this traditional option, but the late work and the overall effect of the Prefaces (within which this statement appears) belie his words. They are efforts to ride the flux. They do not attempt to render an illusion of design through closure but to open the novel itself into experience, to merge art and life, author and critic, male and female, self and other. For to see the choice between closed and open form, if one is devoted as James was to "seeing" as much as possible, must lead one ultimately, it seems to me, to choose the position that seems the more all-encompassing, that carries the logic of the future. Those who denigrate James for his late style (in my terms, an evolution into stylelessness) fail to appreciate the logic that drove his development as a novelist.

* * *

In the end, this book turns back to question itself. To what extent is this a personal exploration, to what extent is it the product of ideo-logical constraints? If I am acting as a "female mediator," improvising meaning, to what extent does my argument have explanatory value?

To attempt to answer these questions, it is helpful to place this book within the context of an evolution in feminist criticism. Feminist criticism over the past twenty years seems to me to have involved two principal stages of development.[18] First, it has encouraged a more expanded examination of female characters and female authors and of the conditions that went into their making. Following on this, it has encouraged the examination of these as well as other subjects from a female point of view (a point of view that is both derivative of and different from the once-dominant male point of view). This point of view must be broadly defined as the point of view now being applied by all good critics, male and female, and made possible less by a surge of sympathy for women than by the ideological shift that James anticipated, which has begun to blur the boundaries of male and female, author and critic, self and other. It is a perspective that allows us as critics to exist in our interpretation of a text in two guises: both as the shaper of the interpretation (the role that the critic would always have played) and as part of the subject, its residue or substitute in the systems terms of this book. By mediating Marian (George Eliot), I am both her interpreter (i.e., the voice through which she speaks) and her substitute—I see myself in her conflicts and choices, in the mediating patterns of her life, as these have evolved in my own. The critical perspective, then, is not just a provisional theoretical stance, it is a process of self-formation. It is theory made indistin-guishable from practice. It has provided me with an arena in which to make meaning, allowed me to move in time and across the bound-aries of fiction and "real life" (what biographies were once thought to reflect). In short, in writing this book, I could detach myself from the cramped position of a mediator within a closed family system and engage in more wide-ranging mediation. This kind of interpretive detachment and reengagement—which I see as the form of postmodern experience—offers solace as well as illumination. It makes the patterns within which we live and which define us feel less oppressive and seem more capable of being shaped in multiple, alternative directions.

Of course, postmodern feminist criticism could only emerge once the ideology of the family had begun to suffer radical breakdown and the idea of a self had become sufficiently distanced from an ideology of family closure and stability. Feminist criticism has as its most generalized ideological agenda the deconstruction of a once-accepted idea of the self. Yet its operation depends upon its historical positioning beyond the point at which that idea of the self held sway. In other words, feminist criticism (and this book as an example of it) is able to deconstruct the self associated with an earlier age precisely because it is of a later one. I have said that George Eliot could intellectually understand that her relationship to experience grew out of gender-based role patterns in her family of origin, but she nonetheless portrayed this relationship as emotionally and morally compelling because she could not ultimately sever the roots of her own identity. Likewise, deconstruction, for all its skepticism about meaning, is still an act of meaning-construction within a deconstructive ideology: it grows out of who we are; it affirms our relationship to experience. Henry James reminded us through the character of Mr. Longdon that "we're in society and that's our horizon." At present, this simply means that our horizon is to imagine the horizon gone.

In systems terms, the deconstructive point of view is both a vantage point on the old and a new place of its own. If it provides us with a critical perspective on mediating and mediated selves, it also derives from such mediation and offers a substitute for the emotional glue of an earlier age. Criticism and mobile relationship are the legacy of an ideology of closure, replacing fiction and family as our temporary site of meaning.

Notes

Introduction

1. There has been a veritable library of books written over the past twenty years about anorexia nervosa. The best clinical discussions of the illness can be found in Hilde Bruch's two classic studies, *Eating Disorders: Obesity, Anorexia Nervosa and the Person Within* (New York: Basic Books, 1973) and *The Golden Cage: The Enigma of Anorexia Nervosa* (Cambridge, Mass.: Harvard University Press, 1978); Salvador Minuchin, Bernice L. Rosman, and Lester Baker's *Psychosomatic Families: Anorexia Nervosa in Context* (Cambridge, Mass.: Harvard University Press, 1978); and M. Selvini Palazzoli's *Self-Starvation* (New York: Jason Aronson, 1978). Bruch's methodology is eclectic; Minuchin et al. and Selvini take a systems approach. All contain clinical case studies of typical patients as well as theoretical explanations of the nature of the illness and the treatments they employ. For a history of the illness, see Joan Jacobs Brumberg's *Fasting Girls: The Emergence of Anorexia Nervosa as a Modern Disease* (Cambridge, Mass.: Harvard University Press, 1988). The book provides comprehensive notes and bibliography. Among the many "literary" treatments of the subject, a sample includes Kim Chernin's highly expressive, confessional *The Obsession: Reflections on the Tyranny of Slenderness* (New York: Harper Colophon Books, 1981), Steven Levenkron's tear-jerker of a novel (since made into a television movie), *The Best Little Girl in the World* (New York: Warner Books, 1978), and Minuchin's dramatization of the case of a nineteenth-century anorectic daughter, "The Triumph of Ellen West" in *Family Kaleidoscope: Images of Violence and Healing* (Cambridge, Mass.: Harvard University Press, 1984). The classic literary-critical treatment of the illness is Sandra M. Gilbert and Susan Gubar's, in *The Madwoman in the Attic: The Woman Writer and the Nineteenth-Century Literary Imagination* (New Haven: Yale University Press, 1979), pt. 1 especially. Gilbert and Gubar take the standard feminist line that anorexia is the physical manifestation of female repression, but they extend the sexual sense in which repression is generally understood to include imaginative repression. They concentrate on the link between psychosomatic symptoms like anorexia and the obstacles to creativity in the lives of nineteenth-century female British writers.

2. John Kucich's thesis in *Repression in Victorian Fiction: Charlotte Brontë, George Eliot, and Charles Dickens* (Berkeley: University of California Press,

191

1987) supports my own argument that repression served as a form of self-definition in Victorian society, and that the characters, especially the female characters, in the literature are shown to achieve their subjective identities through strategies of self-denial and self-effacement.

3. "Form" as I use it here refers to the system of representation that supports a prevailing cultural ideology while also making possible its transformation. Throughout the book, I sometimes use "pattern" or "structure" interchangeably for this idea, but I also sometimes differentiate "structure," as inert, from "interactive pattern" or "dynamics," which involve feedback and hence assure that the structure of a system will eventually change.

4. Surprisingly, the connection between the history of the family and the history of the novel has been made only obliquely by historians and literary critics. Ian Watt suggests it in passing in his chapters on Samuel Richardson in *The Rise of the Novel* (Berkeley: University of California Press, 1957). More recently, feminist critics have treated aspects of the subject. Nancy Armstrong's *Desire and Domestic Fiction: A Political History of the Novel* (New York: Oxford University Press, 1987) examines the relationship of the novel to the definition of sex roles in society, but without linking these specifically to the structure and dynamics of the nuclear family. Christine van Boheemen in *The Novel as Family Romance: Language, Gender, and Authority from Fielding and Joyce* (Ithaca, N.Y.: Cornell University Press, 1987) traces a connection between the "rise" of the novel and the emergence of what she calls "transcendent subjectivity," noting as well that the "supposed 'death' [of the novel] may relate to a changing notion of that subject" (4); again, however, an analogous relationship between novel form and family form (where the subject is engendered) is not drawn. Stephen Mintz, *A Prison of Expectations: The Family in Victorian Culture* (New York: New York University Press, 1983), illuminates nineteenth-century family patterns by looking at five noted Victorian authors, but the literature produced by these authors, while it provides evidence, is not of formal importance in the study. Other social and literary critics such as Georg Lukacs, T. B. Tomlinson, and Michel Foucault have also dealt with related issues without making an explicit or detailed formal connection between the nineteenth-century family and the nineteenth-century novel. I tend to think that the failure on the part of these critics to draw such a connection relates to the absence of an appropriate methodology by which to bring corresponding patterns into relief. Family systems theory provides such a methodology.

5. The classic discussion of the novel's shift from a picaresque genre to a psychological one is Watt's. For discussion of the evolution of the genre into modernism, see Alan Friedman, *The Turn of the Novel* (New York: Oxford University Press, 1966). On privatization and related affective changes in the family, see the discussion of these topics in chap. 1 of this book. On the evolution of the bourgeois nuclear family into the twentieth century, see Mark Poster, *Critical Theory of the Family* (New York: Seabury Press, 1978), chap. 7.

6. Two good general introductions to the epistemology of family systems

theory are Bradford P. Keeney's *Aesthetics of Change* (New York: Guilford Press, 1983) and Keeney and Jeffrey M. Ross's more recent and complex *Mind in Therapy: Constructing Systemic Family Therapies* (New York: Basic Books, 1985). For a more accessible and readable introduction to the family systems approach, which follows a single family through a therapeutic experience and explains general trends in the field along the way, see Augustus Y. Napier and Carl A. Whitaker's *The Family Crucible* (New York: Bantam Books, 1978). For an excellent textbook-like overview that also introduces some of the more innovative trends facing the field, see Lynn Hoffman's *Foundations of Family Therapy: A Conceptual Framework for Systems Change* (New York: Basic Books, 1981).

7. The concept of a strategic interaction that mimics a destructive, covert interaction but reveals it for what it is by reframing or exaggerating it has appeared in family therapy literature since Gregory Bateson. Keeney employs the term "transform" (elaborating on a more indefinite use of the term by Bateson) in *The Aesthetics of Change* to refer to such strategies. Other therapists have used phrases like "prescribing the symptom" or "paradoxical intention." See Richard Rabkin's *Strategic Psychotherapy* (New York: Basic Books, 1977) for a comprehensive discussion of the concept.

8. Terry Eagleton, *Criticism and Ideology: A Study in Marxist Literary Theory* (London: Verso, 1978), 69.

9. Ian Gregor, Introduction, *The Brontës: A Collection of Critical Essays*, ed. Gregor (Englewood Cliffs, N.J.: Prentice-Hall, 1970), 3.

Chapter 1

1. This view, in fact, goes back to the nineteenth century. Nineteenth-century historians Frederic Le Play and Wilhelm Heinrich Riehl saw the "modern" family as resulting from the breakup of the extended family through the impact of industrialization. Both criticized the nuclear family by invoking a past ideal (see Peter Gay's discussion of Le Play and Riehl in *The Bourgeois Experience: Victoria to Freud,* vol. 1: *The Education of the Senses* [New York: Oxford University Press, 1984], 423–27). In mid-twentieth-century studies of the family, the same general association of the nuclear family with the middle class and industrialization was made but was viewed in positive, proevolutionary terms. This is most notably the position of Talcott Parsons and Robert F. Bales in their influential *Family, Socialization and Interactional Process* (Boston: Houghton Mifflin, 1955).

2. Philippe Ariès, *Centuries of Childhood: A Social History of Family Life* (New York: Random House, 1962), 413.

3. Lawrence Stone, *The Family, Sex and Marriage in England, 1500–1800* (London: Weidenfeld and Nicolson, 1977), and Randolph Trumbach, *The Rise of the Egalitarian Family: Aristocratic Kinship and Domestic Relations in Eighteenth-Century England* (New York: Academic Press, 1978). See also Robert Goldthwaite, *The Building of Renaissance Florence: An Economic and Social History* (Baltimore: Johns Hopkins University Press, 1980), who associates the

new family type with an "aristocratic mentality" but situates the change in fourteenth-century Florence, linking it to the rise of cultural patronage. Let me note that my overview of the various positions held by historians on the "rise" of the nuclear family is undeniably simplified and incomplete. It is difficult to give a full account of the controversy that has surrounded this topic in recent years and the degree to which some historians have challenged Stone's views, in particular, on the various developmental stages of the nuclear family and its relationship to English social and economic development. Yet as Stone's work appears most helpful in a discussion of the novels and as its assumptions are largely born out by "evidence" from the novels (although admittedly, I risk circularity here), I feel comfortable relying upon him for background on most points.

4. Edward Shorter, *The Making of the Modern Family* (New York: Basic Books, 1975), 21.

5. This raises the question of the relationship between family structure and family ideology. The whole thrust of this study supports the idea that they mutually inform each other. If some Victorian families appeared to be crawling with relatives, this does not mean that the affective dynamic did not center on the nuclear group of parents and children. By the same token, this argument can be used to rebut claims for an earlier nuclear family put forward by the Cambridge demographers and by Alan Macfarlane, *The Origins of English Individualism: The Family, Property and Social Transition* (Oxford: Basil Blackwell, 1978), who have argued that English families took a nuclear form as early as the thirteenth century. A small household does not in itself reflect a nuclear family. Indeed, Macfarlane's assertion that preindustrial families often tended to hire out or apprentice their children (149–50) suggests that even if families were small during an earlier period, they did not possess the family dynamic that creates emotional investment and a sense of solidarity in its members.

6. Again, the traditional assumption that England was the original site of development of the nuclear family has come under fire recently, notably by historians who, like Goldthwaite, have argued for its origins in Renaissance Italy. Still, Stone, 179, has maintained that though factors supporting the development of the nuclear family appeared throughout Europe, in England they achieved "highest development" owing to the legacy of Puritanism, the traditional intermingling of upper bourgeoisie and gentry, the absence of censorship, and the high level of literary production; Macfarlane, *Marriage and Love in England: Modes of Reproduction, 1300–1840* (London: Basil Blackwell, 1985), has more recently argued along similar lines.

7. Jeffrey Weeks, *Sex, Politics and Society: The Regulation of Sexuality since 1800* (New York: Longman, 1981), 25.

8. G. M. Young's *Portrait of an Age* (London: Oxford University Press, 1936) and Walter E. Houghton's *The Victorian Frame of Mind* (New Haven: Yale University Press, 1957) are two of the more well-known and influential invocations of this idyllic view of Victorian family relations, although they also suggest a darker side to the idyll. Indeed, there have been many studies,

past and present, that attempt, through various perspectives, to expose that family ideal. These range from the work of nineteenth-century family historians Riehl and Le Play, to that of the late Victorian novelist Samuel Butler, to the scornful diatribes of the Bloomsbury Group, and more recently to such contemporary scholarly unveilings as those of Steven Marcus, Peter Cominos, Sandra M. Gilbert and Susan Gubar, Elaine Showalter, and many other feminist critics. Yet these attacks, I would argue, though helpful in adding to our knowledge of the period, seem ultimately to fall into the same trap as those which see the nineteenth-century family as an idyll to be nostalgically invoked. Abuses, inconsistencies, and hypocrisies associated with that family ideal must be understood in the context of the larger stabilizing effects of the ideology of the nuclear family during the nineteenth century. Peter Gay's weighty *The Bourgeois Experience*, vols. 1 and 2: *The Tender Passion* (1986), is a helpful corrective in this regard. His study is an attempt, as he puts it, "to encompass historical experience in all its dimensions" and "to complicate and correct" misconceptions (1:6). Gay, however, is an orthodox Freudian and while he does not reduce the Victorians to a thesis, he does assume the universal validity of the psychoanalytic perspective.

9. Christopher Lasch, *Haven in a Heartless World: The Family Besieged* (New York: Basic Books, 1977).

10. Ludwig von Bertalanffy, *Organismic Psychology and Systems Theory* (Barre, Mass.: Clark University Press, 1968).

11. Minuchin et al., *Psychosomatic Families*, 83.

12. The original pioneers in ego psychology were Heinz Hartmann, Ernst Kris, and Rudolf Loewenstein, Freudians who stressed social adaptation over instinctive drives and who found support in Talcott Parsons's work in sociology. Erikson built on this foundation, but by coding individual life crises as proper to life cycle changes his work effected a kind of reversal on theirs. Instead of trying to adjust individuals to social norms, he sought to make individuals accept the stresses and strains of growing up in the family as a normal part of the life-cycle process. Thus, while Erikson's philosophy supported the institution of the nuclear family, it also reflected the more elaborate compromises and justifications that the institution now required of its members. See his *Childhood and Society* (New York: W. W. Norton, 1950) and *Identity: Youth and Crisis* (New York: W. W. Norton, 1968).

13. See the excellent biography by David Lipset, *Gregory Bateson: The Legacy of a Scientist* (Boston: Beacon Press, 1982). Mary Katharine Bateson, herself an anthropologist, offers additional insight into her father's character and work in *With A Daughter's Eye: A Memoir of Margaret Mead and Gregory Bateson* (New York: William Morrow, 1984) .

14. Bateson, Don D. Jackson, Jay Haley, and John H. Weakland, "Toward a Theory of Schizophrenia," in Bateson's *Steps to an Ecology of Mind* (New York: Ballantine Books, 1972).

15. The tendency to blame the mother is evident in the work of Margaret Mead and Erikson and in the early work of R. D. Laing.

16. Family systems epistemology as it is now interpreted by the more

advanced theorists essentially discredits the notion of "blame" by making the designated problem a contextual issue, a matter of dynamic interaction to which everyone contributes. This has currently become a focus for debate, however, as feminists seek to distinguish instances of oppression such as rape and childhood incest, in which the notion of the victim's participation becomes akin to reactionary notions regarding female sexuality and seductiveness. See Paul F. Dell, "In Defense of Lineal Causality," and the subsequent "Discussions" papers in *Family Process* 25 (1986): 513–29, and Rachel T. Hare-Mustin, "The Problem of Gender in Family Therapy Theory" and the subsequent "Discussions" papers in *Family Process* 26 (1987): 15–33. I agree with Dell that we must distinguish between the particular case and how we treat it and the larger context in which that case can be understood. The victim of a rape can hardly be said to participate in it, but the dynamics of the rapist's family certainly have bearing on his behavior as does the society that supports a family ideology in which gender roles and dynamics that are no longer appropriate are being sustained.

17. The antipsychiatry movement directs its hostility against the mental health industry but indirectly against the family that the industry bolsters and which serves the society as a dumping ground for those members who do not conform. The movement is largely associated with Thomas Szasz and R. D. Laing. The most radical expression of these ideas that focuses exclusively on the family is from Laing's associate, David Cooper, in *The Death of the Family* (New York: Pantheon, 1960). Utopian movements of the late nineteenth century and early twentieth century like that of Charles Fourier were also critical of the nuclear family, but their ideas tended to be elaborations of philosophical systems that centered on other issues. For a critique of these movements with respect to feminist issues, see Barbara Taylor's *Eve and the New Jerusalem: Socialism and Feminism in the Nineteenth Century* (New York: Pantheon, 1983).

18. Bateson's influence is reflected in the frequent reverential invocations of his name and ideas in the most important theoretical work emerging from the family systems field. Both Keeney, *The Aesthetics of Change*, and Froma Walsh, ed., *Normal Family Processes* (New York: Guilford Press, 1982), dedicate their books to Bateson.

19. The question of the therapist's position in relation to the family continues to be debated. So-called "strategic" therapists like Selvini and her Milan group emphasize neutrality and the ability to keep aloof from family entanglements. By contrast, Minuchin's so-called "structural" approach emphasizes the involvement of the therapist in the family system to alter established relational configurations.

20. John Ruskin, "Of Queens' Gardens," *Sesame and Lilies* (New York: E. P. Dutton, 1960), 59.

21. See Michael Brooks, "Love and Possession in a Victorian Household: The Example of the Ruskins," in *The Victorian Family: Structure and Stresses,* ed. Anthony S. Wohl (New York: St. Martin's Press, 1978), 82–100.

22. Nathan W. Ackerman, *The Psychodynamics of Family Life: Diagnosis and*

Treatment of Family Relationships (New York: Basic Books, 1958), 112. Virginia Goldner, in her feminist critique of the family systems field, "Generation and Gender: Normative and Covert Hierarchies," *Family Process* 27 (1988): 24, refers to the persistence of this ideological notion of the family as a safe haven among theorists from Bateson through Minuchin: "there is always an idealization of the family as constituting some kind of poetic, transcendent unity. This vision of ultimate interdependency is covertly ideological because its power comes from an implied comparison with the outside world, a place where individuals are set against each other in the marketplace of daily life."

23. Don D. Jackson, "The Study of the Family," *Family Process* 4 (1965): 6, 12.

24. Alan S. Gurman and David P. Kniskern, eds., *Handbook of Family Therapy* (New York: Brunner/Mazel, 1981), 248.

25. See Murray Bowen, *Family Therapy in Clinical Practice* (Northvale, N.J.: Jason Aronson, 1978), 382.

26. Ivan Boszormenyi-Nagy and Geraldine M. Spark, *Invisible Loyalties: Reciprocity in Intergenerational Family Therapy* (New York: Harper and Row, 1973), 97.

27. See Hoffman, *Foundations of Family Therapy*, 50–52.

28. Indeed, theorists such as Hoffman and Keeney who have gone over to the side of the epistemology by embracing advanced theories of constructivism and esthetics have had their work criticized by their peers in the field as clinically unviable. See, for example, the critique by Paul Robert Falzer, "The Cybernetic Metaphor: A Critical Examination of Ecosystemic Epistemology as a Foundation of Family Therapy," *Family Process* 25 (1986): 353–64.

29. Bowen, *Family Therapy*, 373.

30. Shorter, *Making of the Modern Family*, 7.

31. Lasch, *Haven*, 22–25, sees the welfare state as an insidious substitution for family ties in which the individual is placed at the mercy of seemingly absolute and incomprehensible social forces, of a presumed "reality," rather than of a legitimate authority. Yet he does not question the legitimacy of family authority or the fact that, in its heyday, the nuclear family appeared seamless, as much an unconquerable reality as social institutions appear now.

32. Bowen, *Family Therapy*, 249. Also see Foucault, *Madness and Civilization: A History of Insanity* (New York: Mentor Books, 1965), for a different though related perspective in his discussion of the "creation" of mental illness through a process of demarcation and categorization that coincided with the rise of the nuclear family.

33. See *The Family Letters of Samuel Butler*, ed. Arnold Silver (Stanford, Calif.: Stanford University Press, 1962) and the comments on Butler's life and work throughout Steven Mintz's *A Prison of Expectations*.

34. Fred Weinstein and Gerald M. Platt, *The Wish to Be Free: Society, Psyche, and Value Change* (Berkeley: University of California Press, 1969), especially chap. 3. Joseph Boone's argument—that the American novelist William Dean Howells treated innovative themes without challenging traditional formal

conventions so that his work ended up supporting a traditional ideology—could also be fitted to this thesis ("Wedlock as Deadlock and Beyond: Closure and the Victorian Marriage Ideal," *Mosaic* 17, 1 [1984]: 65– 81).

35. Ruskin, "Of Queens' Gardens," 23.

36. William Blackstone, *Commentaries on the Laws of England,* 4 vols. (Chicago: University of Chicago Press, 1979), 1:430.

37. Claude Lévi-Strauss, *The Elementary Structures of Kinship,* trans. J. H. Bell, J. R. von Sturmer, and R. Needham (Boston: Beacon Press, 1969),115, is explicit on the point of asymmetry between men and women: "They have neither the same place nor rank in human society. To be unmindful of this would be to overlook the basic fact that it is men who exchange women, and not vice versa." Goldner, "Generation and Gender," 22, also argues that even in contemporary family systems theory sexual asymmetry is ignored because "we simply cannot tolerate the idea that arrangements of inequality between men and women may be structurally essential to family relations." For a provocative critique of how this inequality has evolved into pathological, suffocating configurations for men and women (a critique that dovetails with my own in many places but takes a strongly polemical stance I have tried to avoid), see Eve Kosofsky Sedgwick, *Between Men: English Literature and Male Homosocial Desire* (New York: Columbia University Press, 1985).

38. See Bateson, "Cultural Contact and Schismogenesis" in *Steps.*

39. For a brilliant feminist psychoanalytic treatment of male-female complementarity and its relation to sadomasochism in *The Story of O,* see Jessica Benjamin's "The Bonds of Love: Rational Violence and Erotic Domination," in *The Future of Difference,* ed. Hester Eisenstein and Alice Jardine (New Brunswick, N.J.: Rutgers University Press, 1985), 41–70.

40. Deborah Gorham, *The Victorian Girl and the Feminine Ideal* (Bloomington: Indiana University Press, 1982), 7.

41. Many family systems theorists identify cross-generational alliances as major contributing factors in family dysfunction (see, for example, Jay Haley's theory of "perverse triangles" in "Toward a Theory of Pathological Systems," in *The Interactional View,* ed. P. Watzlawick and J. Weakland [New York: W. W. Norton, 1977]). But while these theorists see cross-generational alliances as creating confusion and disorder in the family role system, they fail to acknowledge how such alliances may have been historically helpful in solidifying family structure. Also see Lynda E. Boose and Betty S. Flowers, eds., *Daughters and Fathers* (Baltimore: Johns Hopkins University Press, 1989), for a wide-ranging feminist discussion of related issues.

42. For a discussion of the absent mother in nineteenth-century novels, see Marianne Hirsch, *The Mother/Daughter Plot: Narrative, Psychoanalysis, Feminism* (Bloomington: Indiana University Press, 1989), chap. 1. Although relating the mother's absence to the ideology of the family, Hirsch differs from me in conceiving of the absence as a repression.

43. I find Elisabeth Badinter's *Mother Love: Myth and Reality* (New York: Macmillan, 1981) particularly provocative in this context. I would argue that the excavation of the mother-child "plot," first by Freud with his concept of

the pre-Oedipal phase and, more recently, by feminist critics in their work on the so-called "body" or "semiotic" in language, is connected with the dismantling of an ideology of closure. It is, in short, a particular ideological position that makes this plot available to interpretation. The cultural anthropologist Clifford Geertz, *The Interpretation of Cultures: Selected Essays* (New York: Basic Books, 1973), 452, has written that "the culture of a people is an ensemble of texts." One cannot speak of the pre-Oedipal phase "really" existing before, if the cultural text was not available to be read.

44. Historians and social critics have described a trend toward female empowerment at a variety of historical junctures and from a variety of perspectives. The German historian Riehl was already documenting a decline in patriarchal authority and a "dangerous" rise in female power by the mid–nineteenth century. Mead and Erikson in mid-twentieth-century America both lamented an emasculating tendency in culture that they attributed to "Momism"—the influence of a narcissistic, devouring mother. Among contemporary critics, Lasch has connected the decline of the nuclear family since the end of the nineteenth century with the rise of feminism; Ann Douglas has attributed the vulgar, sentimental strain in late nineteenth-century culture to a "feminization" of culture. In counterpoint to these theories are those that associate "the feminine" with essential values that have been repressed. See, for example, feminist anthropologist Riane Eisler's *The Chalice and the Blade: Our History, Our Future* (San Francisco: Harper and Row, 1987).

45. Freud treats the issue of the daughter's separation in "The Dissolution of the Oedipus Complex" and "Female Sexuality," *The Standard Edition of the Complete Psychological Works of Sigmund Freud*, ed. and trans. James Strachey (London: Hogarth Press, 1964), vols. 19 and 21. For the now classic contemporary feminist interpretation of the issue see Nancy Chodorow's *The Reproduction of Mothering: Psychoanalysis and the Sociology of Gender* (Berkeley: University of California Press, 1978) and Juliet Mitchell's *Psychoanalysis and Feminism: Freud, Reich, Laing and Women* (New York: Vintage Books, 1974); both attempt to contextualize Freud socially, but both lack an evolutionary perspective in relation to their subject. Chodorow's critique calls for a utopian redistribution of family responsibility, while Mitchell essentially anatomizes a nineteenth-century ideology that has ceased to be wholly applicable to contemporary culture.

46. Minuchin et al., *Psychosomatic Families*, 61.

47. See Selvini and Maurizio Viaro, "The Anorectic Process in the Family: A Six-Stage Model as a Guide for Individual Therapy," *Family Process* 27 (1988): 129–48. They identify the father-daughter alliance as a stereotypical interactional formation in anorectic families. (Significantly, the other common alliance identified by Selvini and Viaro is that of the daughter with the mother, only here the daughter is not so much a favorite as a confidante. This creates a feeling of superiority in the daughter that can be said to allow her to usurp her mother's position through another channel.)

48. "Illness it seems was a natural corollary of the frail and sickly constitution—both physical and mental—which all refined women were said to pos-

sess," explains Lorna Duffin in "The Conspicuous Consumptive: Woman as Invalid," in *The Nineteenth-Century Woman: Her Cultural and Physical World,* ed. Sara Delamont and Lorna Duffin (New York: Barnes and Noble, 1978), 30. For further discussion of the nineteenth-century association of femininity with illness, see Barbara Ehrenreich and Deirdre English, *For Her Own Good: 150 Years of the Experts' Advice to Women* (New York: Anchor Press, 1979), chap. 4; Showalter, *The Female Malady: Women, Madness and English Culture, 1830–1890* (New York: Pantheon, 1985) and "Victorian Women and Insanity" in *Madhouses, Mad-doctors, and Madmen: The Social History of Psychiatry in the Victorian Era,* ed. Andrew Scull (Philadelphia: University of Pennsylvania Press, 1981); and Carroll Smith-Rosenberg, *Visions of Gender in Victorian America* (New York: Alfred A. Knopf, 1988).

49. Smith-Rosenberg and Ehrenreich and English note this functional aspect of nineteenth-century female illnesses, and Duffin observes that female illnesses "filled the gap of inactivity," 30. It must be pointed out, however, that this was a diffuse functionality; the tendency to "break down" was not concentrated in a particular time of life or even social class. Although Showalter, *The Female Malady,* chap. 6, refers to hysteria as "the daughter's disease," her examples refer to women of different ages and familial situations. Similarly, Rudolph Bell, *Holy Anorexia* (Chicago: University of Chicago Press, 1985), traces the illness back to female saints of the Middle Ages but acknowledges that, unlike modern anorexia, the earlier version of the illness was not restricted to any age group.

50. Boone, *Tradition Counter Tradition: Love and the Form of Fiction* (Chicago: University of Chicago Press, 1987), 81.

51. Jean E. Kennard, *Victims of Convention* (Hamden, Conn.: Archon, 1978).

52. Patricia Dreshel Tobin, *Time and the Novel: The Genealogical Imperative* (Princeton: Princeton University Press, 1978).

53. Foucault, *The History of Sexuality,* trans. Robert Hurley (New York: Vintage Books, 1980), 107–9.

54. Peter K. Garrett, *The Victorian Multiplot Novel: Studies in Dialogical Form* (New Haven: Yale University Press, 1980).

55. Peter Brooks, "Freud's Masterplot: Questions of Narrative," *Yale French Studies* 55/56 (1977): 280–300.

56. See Frank Kermode, *The Sense of an Ending: Studies in the Theory of Fiction* (New York: Oxford University Press, 1966), for some related points. Kermode, like Brooks, doesn't address the question of how much a given text relies for its meaning on the ideology in which it was written versus the ideology in which it is read. I believe that, for purposes of historical insight, one can try to understand a text in relation to the ideology in which it was written by looking at past critical opinion, authorial intention, and related developments in the culture at the time (as I try to do in my analysis of *Clarissa* in the next chapter), although such an attempt will always be colored by one's position in contemporary ideology. See Gerald Graff, "Narrative and the Unofficial Interpretive Culture," in *Reading Narrative: Form, Ethics, Ideology,*

ed. James Phelan (Columbus: Ohio State University Press, 1989), for some helpful ideas on this subject.

57. See Bateson's discussion of the controversy as it relates specifically to Samuel Butler's ideas in *Mind and Nature: A Necessary Unity* (New York: Bantam Books, 1980), 20. What distinguishes Butler from Lamarck is that he is not arguing for the inheritance of particularized "learned" habits but for the inheritance of a more abstract ability to be adaptive—another logical level of knowledge. Bateson discusses this distinction in "The Role of Somatic Change in Evolution" in *Steps*.

58. Contemporary African-American women's fiction seems to me to represent a special case. This literature, derived as it is not only from the Anglo-American domestic novel but also from oral history and slave narrative, results in a different kind of narrative content and structure. If the white, middle-class daughter has been contained within her family system, the African-American woman has had a history of being cut off from her family and made to serve other families. Unsurprisingly, therefore, while the idea of a conventional nuclear family may be undermined in black women's fiction, the fiction nonetheless tends to exhibit a drive for an alternative form of refuge—for some kind of communal reconstitution and closure.

Chapter 2

1. Samuel Richardson, *Clarissa, or the History of a Young Lady*, 4 vols. (New York: Everyman's Library, 1962), 1:21. All future citations from the novel will be given in the text.

2. Stone, *Family, Sex and Marriage*, 71.

3. Lévi-Strauss, *Elementary Structures*, 115–16.

4. It is significant that Freud in "Totem and Taboo," *Standard Edition*, vol. 19, in attempting to extrapolate an origin for civilization based on his Oedipal model of the psyche, should see the murder of the primal father and the guilt resulting from that murder as the point of origin. Freud's primal myth seems to blend Lévi-Strauss's concept of the incest taboo to a patrilineal concept of the family: killing the father would symbolically reflect the patrilineal succession, while guilt concerning the murder would make what had been acquired through it—namely the mother—the focus of the taboo.

5. See Stone, *Family, Sex and Marriage*, pt. 3,123–220.

6. Historians and sociologists of the family have employed a variety of terms to describe the emotional binding that occurs in the nuclear family. Talcott Parsons referred to the "expressive function" proper to the family. More recently, Shorter refers to the "surge of sentiment" as the distinguishing characteristic of modern nuclear family life. Perhaps most in circulation is Stone's phrase, "affective individualism," to describe the kind of self-defining and self-linking feeling arising out of the nuclear family. I should also include here Foucault's concept of the "deployment of sexuality," whose intensification (though not its origin) he connects with the nuclear family. See Janice Haney-Peritz's treatment of this idea as it relates to the family

depicted in *Clarissa* ("Engendering the Exemplary Daughter: The Deployment of Sexuality in Richardson's *Clarissa*," in Boose and Flowers, *Daughters and Fathers*). Haney-Peritz's discussion of the novel parallels mine in places.

7. See Hoffman, *Foundations of Family Therapy*, 89, on morphogenesis: the way in which systems change their structure.

8. Lévi-Strauss, *Elementary Structures*, 7.

9. See Riane Eisler, *Chalice and Blade*, who argues for a female-centered origin for civilization. Although her ideas can be reconciled with mine in places, we differ in that she sees the "feminization" of culture as the return of a true origin while I see it as evolving out of patriarchal culture and the nuclear family in particular.

10. Joseph Wood Krutch, *Five Masters: A Study in the Mutations of the Novel* (Bloomington: Indiana University Press, 1961), 112.

11. Biographical background on Richardson comes from T. C. Duncan Eaves and Ben D. Kimpel, *Samuel Richardson: A Biography* (Oxford: Clarendon Press, 1971).

12. Stone, *Family, Sex and Marriage*, 107.

13. Quoted in Eaves and Kimpel, *Samuel Richardson*, 50.

14. S. H. Steinberg, *Five Hundred Years of Printing* (New York: Penguin, 1966), 215.

15. Terry Eagleton, *The Rape of Clarissa: Writing, Sexuality and Class Struggle in Samuel Richardson* (Minneapolis: University of Minnesota Press, 1982), makes a similar observation about Richardson's relationships with his female readers, noting as I do that they seemed to correspond to a father-daughter model. Linda S. Kaufman, *Discourses of Desire: Gender, Genre, and Epistolary Fictions* (Ithaca, N.Y.: Cornell University Press, 1986),126–27, also makes the point that in Richardson's correspondence with Lady Bradshaigh there occurs a kind of role reversal, with Richardson expressing diffidence and Bradshaigh often sounding dictatorial—an observation that fits my view of how the father-daughter dynamic operates.

16. Watt, Stone, and Eagleton have all suggested that a conflict between the right of parental authority and the right of the individual was inherent in the transitional nature of the times. See Watt, *Rise of the Novel*, 140–41, on the debate between Filmer and Locke.

17. See Jay Fliegelman, *Prodigals and Pilgrims: The American Revolution against Patriarchal Authority, 1750–1800* (New York: Cambridge University Press, 1982), for a discussion of Locke's advocation of control through conditioning. Locke's concern, explains Fliegelman, was in "rendering [parental authority] more effective by making it noncoercive" (13).

18. Shorter, *Making of the Modern Family*, 5.

19. See Keith Stewart, "Towards Defining an Aesthetic for the Familiar Letter in Eighteenth-Century England," *Prose Studies* 5 (1982): 179–92. For an informative overview of the evolution of the letter form and its relationship to the female narrative voice as specifically regards Jane Austen's use of the genre, see Julia L. Epstein, "Jane Austen's Juvenilia and the Female Epistolary Tradition," *Papers in Language and Literature* 21 (Fall 1985): 399–416.

20. Watt, *Rise of the Novel,* 188.

21. Quoted in Eaves and Kimpel, *Samuel Richardson,* 93.

22. Margaret A. Doody, "Saying 'No,' Saying 'Yes': The Novels of Samuel Richardson," in *The First English Novelists: Essays in Understanding,* ed. J. M. Armistead (Knoxville: University of Tennessee Press, 1985), 68. Eagleton, 54, also writes that "the letter in *Clarissa* . . . lies on the frontier between private and public worlds, symbol at once of the self and of its violent appropriation."

23. Stewart, "Towards Defining an Aesthetic," 184.

24. My reading opposes the argument of John Allen Stevenson's "The Courtship of the Family: Clarissa and the Harlowes Once More," *ELH* 48 (1981): 757–77, that the incest theme in *Clarissa* is the expression of an underlying primitivism in the novel.

25. Dorothy Van Ghent, *The English Novel: Form and Function* (New York: Rinehart, 1953), 47. Even among contemporary critics, the tendency is to read Clarissa as an integrated subjectivity trapped within the structure of her family's bourgeois ideology from the beginning. Both Eagleton and Terry Castle, *Clarissa's Cyphers: Meaning and Disruption in Richardson's* Clarissa (Ithaca, N.Y.: Cornell University Press, 1982), for example, argue that Clarissa has been "raped" by critics trying to fix and interpret her. Yet by so protecting her, Eagleton and Castle give Clarissa a value that is not so different from that of their predecessors—they simply ascribe her a "reality" unavailable to interpretation but which they nonetheless interpret by affixing their own polemical symbolism. Unlike Eagleton and Castle, William Beatty Warner, *Reading* Clarissa*: The Struggles of Interpretation* (New Haven: Yale University Press, 1979), offers a consistently deconstructionist reading of the novel. Warner argues that Clarissa and Lovelace engage in what he calls a "struggle of interpretation" in which each encodes the other in the creation of her/himself. My objection to this is that in making the struggle an equal and never-ending one Warner misses the sense in which Richardson's novel is about the production not of arbitrary and shifting meaning but of a particular meaning located in Clarissa. Clarissa, that is, is a family-generated product at the center of the novel, and Lovelace serves as a helpful agent in and by-product of the process. The novel is about the making of meaning and of self, but it locates meaning and self in a more definite place than Warner would have it. Haney-Peritz's Foucauldian reading of the novel seems to support my position here.

26. *Selected Letters of Samuel Richardson,* ed. John Carroll (Oxford: Clarendon, 1964), 72.

27. This is notwithstanding Dr. Johnson's well-known comment concerning Clarissa that "there is always something which she prefers to truth" (quoted in John Carroll's Introduction to *Samuel Richardson: A Collection of Critical Essays,* ed. Carroll [Englewood Cliffs, N.J.: Prentice-Hall, 1969], 6).

28. The metaphor of dance is commonly used by family systems theorists to describe the seemingly choreographed nature of family interaction. Significantly, dance as an important social ritual and as a motif in the novel

is prominent in the eighteenth century but no longer popular in the nineteenth, where the details of personal life and individual psychology began to eclipse the broader outlines of social life and ritual. By reactivating the social metaphor of dance and applying it to familial interaction, family systems theorists are perhaps signaling their position within a new ideology in which the social and the personal are being reconnected and redefined.

29. See Leo Braudy, "Penetration and Impenetrability in *Clarissa*," *New Approaches to Eighteenth-Century Literature: Selected Papers from the English Institute*, ed. Phillip Harth (New York: Columbia University Press, 1976),177–206, for a discussion of the dynamic of Clarissa's self-definition that is compatible with my argument. Braudy compares Clarissa to a schizophrenic daughter in one of R. D. Laing's case histories.

30. The relationship between ambivalence and the unconscious is a matter of some confusion in Freud's work. Clearly, ambivalence as it is discussed in his case histories is meant to be the expression of unconscious desires, but this is an ambivalence that overlays an already established "psychological" self. In "Totem and Taboo," 13:143, he hypothesizes the origin of the psychological self, and in this myth, it is the ambivalence of the sons toward the father in the primal horde that seems to be the catalyzing factor: "They hated their father, who presented such a formidable obstacle to their craving for power and their sexual desires; but they loved and admired him too. After they got rid of him, had satisfied their hatred and had put into effect their wish to identify themselves with him, the affection which had all this time been pushed under was bound to make itself felt. It did so in the form of remorse. A sense of guilt made its appearance, which in this instance coincided with the remorse felt by the whole group. The dead father became stronger than the living one had been." This passage seems to imply that "pure" ambivalence when left unchecked results in a violent act that paves the way for repression and the creation of the id as well as the super-ego. At the same time, by referring to the act of violence as an act of hatred in which affection "had all this time been pushed under" Freud seems to imply that repression already existed, even before the mechanism that would bring it into being had been created.

31. My argument here that Lovelace serves Clarissa's needs corresponds, in some sense, with Warner's view. The more common view, with which I also concur, is that Lovelace is the tool of her family ("a kind of moral employee of the father" [Van Ghent, *English Novel*, 60]), helping them achieve their goal of excluding and punishing her. Indeed, according to my argument, Clarissa and her family are, in some sense, complicitous, and Lovelace serves them both.

32. Stevenson, "Courtship of the Family," 770, makes a similar point in another context when he observes that Clarissa's family's efforts to control her are "ultimately an effort at self-definition."

33. Bateson, *Steps*, 68, might be glossing the predicament of the Harlowes when he describes behavior he terms "complementarity differentiation" or *schismogenesis* and notes that "this differentiation may become progressive. If,

for example, the series, O, P, Q includes patterns culturally regarded as assertive, while U, V, W includes cultural submissiveness, it is likely that submissiveness will promote further assertiveness which in turn will promote further submissiveness. This schismogenesis, unless it is restrained, leads to a progressive unilateral distortion of the personalities of the members of both groups, which results in mutual hostility between them and must end in the breakdown of the system." Keeney, *Aesthetics of Change*, 123, also discusses the destructive effects of this phenomenon, which he calls "escalating runaway," noting, however, that when the original system breaks down a higher level of equilibrium is consequently achieved. This is precisely what I suggest happens in *Clarissa* as the family system is shattered only to form a new unity in guilt.

34. See Claudia Brodsky, "Narrative Representation and Criticism: 'Crossing the Rubicon' in *Clarissa*," in *Reading Narrative*, for a discussion of how the heroine's rape and subsequent death destroy the possibility of her representation "as another's immediate source of revelation" (217). Haney-Peritz maintains that it is "the methodical expulsion of Clarissa's *body* that guarantees the inclusion of her sexuality in the realm of signification" (201). Both of these critics connect Clarissa to a new kind of subjectivity. Armstrong and Van Boheemen make more general related points when they connect the "rise" of the novel to the birth of a new kind of subjectivity connected to the female role. On the other hand, Joel Fineman, *Shakespeare's Perjured Eye: The Invention of Poetic Subjectivity in Shakespeare's Sonnets* (Berkeley: University of California Press, 1986), has argued that the "invention" of a "psychologistic" subject occurred in Shakespeare's sonnets. I would argue in response that the assertiveness with which the heroic couplet produces closure in the Shakespearean sonnet may account for its anticipating the effects of a nineteenth-century ideology of closure, but that the sonnet form as Shakespeare defines it is singular to him in a way that the closure of nineteenth-century novels weren't to their authors. Fineman's formalistic approach would seem to support this view.

35. Family systems theorists try to get around the paradox that scapegoating within limits is necessary to the maintenance of the family by arguing that healthy families have shifting scapegoats so that no one individual is always providing the regulating focus (Walsh, *Normal Family Processes*, 23). This seems a dubious solution, however, since shifting roles would tend to erode the family's conventionalized identity: the means by which it defines itself in opposition to what lies outside of it. This paradox has already been alluded to in chapter 1 and will be further discussed in chapter 4.

36. James B. Twitchell, *Forbidden Partners: The Incest Taboo in Modern Culture* (New York: Columbia University Press, 1987), 251, has noted that Freud, in recounting his story of the origin of the psychological self in "Totem and Taboo," "did not really believe that the primal horde 'scenario' had to take place; it did not have to, for we act as if it did." Like Richardson's *Clarissa*, it is a myth of origin.

Chapter 3

1. Jane Austen, *Mansfield Park,* ed. Tony Tanner (New York: Penguin, 1966), 234. All future citations from the novel will be given in the text.

2. Lionel Trilling, "Mansfield Park," in *The Opposing Self* (New York: Viking, 1955).

3. See Stone, *Family, Sex and Marriage,* 135–38, and Gorham, *Victorian Girl,* 4.

4. Ariès, *Centuries of Childhood,* 412.

5. Boszormenyi-Nagy and Spark, *Invisible Loyalties,* 72, 89. Jean H. Hagstrum, *Sex and Sensibility: Ideal and Erotic Love from Milton to Mozart* (Chicago: University of Chicago Press, 1980), 195–99, defines "sensibility" in *Clarissa* in much the same terms.

6. I am using the term *replacement* here much as Jacques Derrida, *Of Grammatology,* trans. G. C. Spivak (Baltimore: Johns Hopkins University Press, 1976), 145, uses the term *supplement:* "It adds only to replace. It intervenes or insinuates itself in-the-place-of; if it fills, it is as if one fills a void." Also see Jonathan Culler's discussion of Derrida's concept of the traces of absent signs in the present sign in *Structuralism and Since: From Lévi-Strauss to Derrida,* ed. John Sturrock (New York: Oxford University Press, 1979), 154–80.

7. Tony Tanner, *Adultery in the Novel* (Baltimore: Johns Hopkins University Press, 1979), 14.

8. John Halperin, *The Life of Jane Austen* (Baltimore: Johns Hopkins University Press, 1984), 155.

9. I am excluding Austen's mentally handicapped brother, George, who lived away from home.

10. The question of what constitutes an incestuous relationship by law and why the prohibition of incest operates in certain instances and not in others is relevant here. Trumbach has contributed some useful observations on the specific meaning of variations in the taboo in relation to the English aristocracy. He notes that by the eighteenth century aristocratic first-cousin marriages were being sanctioned, where they had previously been prohibited, to assure that the inheritance remained within the family (hence bolstering the patriarchal law of primogeniture). Yet, ironically, as this chapter shows, sanctioning first-cousin marriage also encourages the conception of the family as a closed system, conducive of personal as opposed to social/historical relations; in this sense, the aristocratic defense would prove antagonistic to traditional patriarchal law. This may also help support and further explain Stone's argument that the nuclear family developed as early as the seventeenth century among the aristocracy but not until the nineteenth century among the working class. (In addition, as argued in this chapter, the increased leisure of the upper classes would have encouraged the earlier development of affective ties characteristic of the nuclear family.) The Bertrams present us with an interesting case as regards the taboo on marriage between cousins as Trumbach discusses it. Not members of the aristocracy as such, they are

nonetheless landed gentry and thus partake of what Tony Tanner has termed the "aristocratic attachment to the land" (Introduction to *Mansfield Park*, 11), which would tend to align them with the aristocracy on the subject of marriage between cousins (i.e., they would sanction it). At the same time, a marriage between cousins would only make patriarchal sense if it occurred between the children of male relations and not, as in the Price-Bertram case, between a son and his mother's sister's daughter, since here neither party is preserving anything through the marriage (see further discussion of this in note 27 below). Moreover, to the extent that the Bertrams' values oppose the values of Mary Crawford's London, they would tend to be more attached to traditional biblical views on the subject of incest. Trumbach further notes that even among the aristocracy, marriage between cousins, though sanctioned, was discouraged, and that middle-class authors still generally assumed that it fell within the taboo. Thus, given that Austen was a middle-class clergyman's daughter, that the Bertrams are also of the middle class (and hence likely to be sensitive to the taboo to at least some extent, as Mrs. Norris's early reaction indicates), and that Fanny comes to live with the Bertrams at the age of ten and is placed on the footing of a daughter and sister, the issue of what constitutes incest and how it should be viewed must definitely be considered central to this novel.

11. Lévi-Strauss, *Elementary Structures*, 24–25.

12. Quoted in Tanner, *Adultery*, 11.

13. Thorstein Veblen, *The Theory of the Leisure Class: An Economic Study in the Evolution of Institutions* (New York: Macmillan, 1899).

14. Shorter, *Making of the Modern Family*, 5.

15. Playacting in *Mansfield Park* functions like the reading of gothic novels in *Northanger Abbey;* both provide the characters with structures that are both like and unlike the "proper" structure of experience. In both novels, Austen seems to be using these structures as a means to arrive at a new place where they can then be discredited and discarded. In this sense, the play and the gothic novels function like therapeutic "transforms," interventions used by family therapists to exaggerate and thereby expose unhealthy patterns of behavior while also supplying the random "noise" necessary for the fashioning of new patterns (see Keeney, *Aesthetics of Change*, 169). Thus, for the family system at Mansfield Park, the play must be passed through in order to arrive at a new, improved structure for family experience. (Of course, Fanny Price, unlike Catherine Morland, never enters the "improper" structure, she only observes it. However, her remaining outside the play while being inside the family functions as a marker of her position as an outsider-insider in the Bertram family system, a position that will be discussed later in this chapter).

16. Note that Fanny's critique of life at the Prices' versus life at the Bertrams', with its emphasis on placement and pacing, sounds like a critique of bad versus good stage direction; as noted above, Fanny, while she never participates in the play, is its most attentive audience.

17. Weinstein and Platt, *Wish to Be Free*, 15.

18. Ruth Bernard Yeazell, "The Boundaries of Mansfield Park," *Representations* 7 (Summer 1984): 133–52.

19. Nina Auerbach, *Woman and the Demon: The Life of a Victorian Myth* (Cambridge, Mass.: Harvard University Press, 1982). Also see Jane Gallop, *The Daughter's Seduction: Feminism and Psychoanalysis* (Ithaca, N.Y.: Cornell University Press, 1982), for a witty discussion of a postmodern reinscription of this dynamic in the father-daughter relationship of psychoanalysis and feminism.

20. Bowen, *Family Therapy*, 382.

21. In line with this interpretation I should like to note the observation of Gilles Deleuze and Felix Guattari in their critique of the Oedipus complex, *Anti-Oedipus: Capitalism and Schizophrenia*, trans. Robert Hurley, Mark Seem, and Helen R. Lane (Minneapolis: University of Minnesota Press, 1983), 55, that the form crippled desire takes is precisely that of a theater, by which they mean Freud's Oedipal drama: "The unconscious ceases to be what it is—a factory, a workshop—to become a theater, a scene and its staging." In like fashion, we can say that Maria's adulterous passion is structured like the play earlier in the novel. Both serve the family as a staged unconscious in opposition to which, or by repression of which, acceptable, "conscious" relations can be carried on.

22. Tanner, *Adultery*, 13.

23. The trinity of roles may suggest that Fanny is by herself the Trinity of the family, but this would be an oversimplification of her saving function in the novel. The true Trinity of the Bertram household, as this chapter attempts to demonstrate, involves the father, the daughter, and the father-daughter synthesis (achieved here by way of the son). In their critique of the Oedipus complex, Deleuze and Guattari write: "It will hardly come as a surprise to learn that Oedipus as a structure is the Christian Trinity whereas Oedipus as a crisis is a familial trinity insufficiently structured by faith . . . " (82). In the reformulated Trinity of *Mansfield Park*, the "crisis" is by-passed as the family comes to rest in the "structure" when the daughter remains within the family—tied to the father through marriage to the son. This static configuration is very different from the unstable triangular interaction depicted in *Wuthering Heights*, discussed in the next chapter.

24. Foucault, *History of Sexuality*, 109.

25. Max Weber, *Basic Concepts of Sociology*, trans. H. P. Secher (Secaucus, N.J.: Citadel Press, 1980), 52.

26. Gayle Rubin, "The Traffic in Women," in *Toward an Anthropology of Women*, ed. Rayna R. Reiter (New York: Monthly Review Press, 1975).

27. Parsons, in *Social Structure and Personality* (New York: Free Press, 1964), 65, provides a pertinent observation when he notes the tendency anthropologists have discerned in primitive societies for "the asymmetrical type of cross-cousin marriage which rests primarily on marriage with the mother's brother's daughter" because "if the masculine role is more instrumental than the feminine in the sense I have discussed, then men should have more direct and important anchorages in the extended kinship groupings than the

women." Trumbach makes a similar point in his discussion of the incest taboo among the eighteenth-century aristocracy, noting that the rarest cousin marriage was that between a woman and the son of her mother's sister, since this was least likely to have meaning in terms of preserving family name or property. Austen's novel corrects this patriarchal asymmetry by having Fanny, the mother's sister's daughter, enter the family and ultimately marry the son. This is indicative of a shift away from the more primitive, extended male anchorage of the open-lineage family to the nuclear family, where the female takes on an internal stabilizing role.

28. It does not seem especially relevant to me whether Freud did, in fact, espouse biological determinism as many feminist critics maintain, or whether, as Juliet Mitchell has argued, his work is really an analysis of a culture in which female anatomy is a signifier of biological inferiority. Read either way, Freud's work can be understood to reflect a desire on the part of culture to cancel and reverse the potential for female domination (for patriarchy could only conceive of female power as a simple reversal of its own laws) implicit in the structure of the nuclear family.

29. Trilling, Introduction to *Emma* (New York: Riverside, 1957).

30. Cited in *Steps*, 239.

31. Bowen, *Family Therapy*, 373–74.

Chapter 4

1. F. R. Leavis's remarks on *Wuthering Heights* in *The Great Tradition* (1948; rpt. New York University Press, 1964), 27, contain elements characteristic of critical opinion since. Referring to the novel as "a kind of sport," he continues: "she broke completely . . . both with the Scott tradition that imposed on the novelist a romantic resolution of his themes, and with the tradition coming down from the eighteenth century that demanded a plain mirror reflection of the surface of 'real' life." The presumption of deviance both from an established literary tradition and from a social reality is picked up but elevated as a mark of the novel's unique greatness by such critics as David Cecil, Dorothy Van Ghent, and Arnold Kettle, and more recently by feminist critics such as Gilbert and Gubar.

2. Tobin, *Time and the Novel*, 40.

3. Bowen, *Family Therapy*, 307.

4. In my use of the concept of triangulation as a dysfunctional pattern I am relying upon a standard family systems idea. It should be noted, however, that Minuchin et al., *Psychosomatic Families*, 33, define triangulation as a particular case of family dysfunction ("the child is put in such a position that she cannot express herself without siding with one parent against the other"), while I use the term more generally to refer to the basic tendency of the nuclear family in its paradigmatic nature to triangle the girl child. Thus, my critique of this pattern is also a critique of the nuclear family itself. This view of triangulation should also be differentiated from the concepts employed by Lévi-Strauss and René Girard. Differences from Lévi-Strauss's view of the

triangle, in which the woman is an object of exchange and never a subject, will be treated throughout this chapter. My concept of triangulation has more obvious affinities with Girard's "triangular desire"; indeed, Girard also criticizes Lévi-Strauss's mechanical model (*Deceit, Desire and the Novel*, trans. Yvonne Freccero [Baltimore: Johns Hopkins University Press, 1965], 2). However, Girard's is a general theory of individual desire that argues for the transcendence of that desire in the hero's (and the novelist's) ability to recognize the self in the Other and to see that the mediator is in an analogous situation to one's self; the thrust is to uncover similarity, not difference. In short, Girard's is essentially a masculine theory of desire, for it ignores the differences in the formation of the male and female subject in the nuclear family and in the analogous structure of the novel.

5. Walsh, "Conceptualizations of Normal Family Functioning," in *Normal Family Processes*, 23.

6. Steven Goetz, "Genealogy and Incest in Wuthering Heights," *Studies in the Novel*, 14 (1982): 359–76, grounds his argument in the laws of elementary kinship structure and, specifically, of dual organization.

7. Emily Brontë, *Wuthering Heights* (New York: Penguin, 1965), 84. All future citations from the novel will be given in the text.

8. Bowen, *Family Therapy*, 307.

9. As already noted, this is not to suggest the repression of the mother, but rather to argue that family ideology had not yet evolved to a point where it needed to conceptualize the mother as a primal influence. Weinstein and Platt, *Wish to Be Free*, 182, have also argued that there is no history of the pre-Oedipal mother prior to the period of full industrialization, but they explain this by way of the incomplete assertion that, before the modern period, both the mother and the father had equally affective roles in the family. Also see Ehrenreich and English, chap. 4, for a discussion of the variety of ailments and complications, including childbirth, of course, that tended to kill or at least incapacitate women at a young age in the nineteenth century.

10. The notion of relatedness and separation as functions of identity formation has become something of a cliché in modern psychology. The most thorough exploration of these concepts has come from a feminist perspective but has tended to ascribe gender difference to a simple opposition: separation is associated with males and relatedness with females (see, for example, Chodorow, *Reproduction of Mothering*, and Carol Gilligan, *In a Different Voice: Psychological Theory and Women's Development* [Cambridge, Mass.: Harvard University Press, 1982]).

11. Bowen, *Family Therapy*, 373.

12. The inconsequence of female subjectivity in Lévi-Strauss's model seems appropriate given the elementary structures with which he is largely concerned. It is my thesis, indeed, that both male and female subjectivity is a product of complex kinship systems (Nancy Armstrong has also dealt with this shift into subjectivity during the same period). However, while Lévi-Strauss, *Elementary Structures*, 475–76, alludes to the evolution of generalized

exchange from the gift of a woman by her family to the gift of the woman by herself, he fails to see this as a shift into female subjectivity or to take into account the radical complications that must ensue.

13. See Keeney's discussion in *The Aesthetics of Change*, 123, of the ways in which systems in "run-away" must eventually either self-destruct or reorganize at another level. He explains that these two alternatives are, in fact, one and the same, since the destruction of a system *is* its reintegration in a broader context. An example of this process can be seen in the case of Hindley and his wife. If Heathcliff and Cathy are a dyadic system moving toward run-away, so too are Hindley and Frances, whose relationship is equally uncontrolled, though in the opposite direction of conjugal devotion and domestic confinement. Frances's death thus reflects the inevitable breakdown of the system insofar as it cannot accommodate a third (the baby Hareton). Following his wife's death, Hindley spirals into alcoholism and gambling until he too is finally destroyed. Left over from the dead couple, the now adult Hareton eventually gets reintegrated into a stable system at the end of the novel.

14. The metaphorical qualities attributed to hysterical behavior in the nineteenth century were varied and contradictory, yet the most common associations seem to have been with an excess of sexual energy, understood as a manifestation of "hyper-femininity," since experts often viewed the hysterical "fit" as a sexually provocative tantrum (see Smith-Rosenberg, *Visions of Gender*, 197–216, and Showalter, *The Female Malady*, chap. 6). The association of anorexia with delicacy and scrupulousness is made consistently by anorectics themselves, whose driving wish is to be ethereal, perfect, never "gross" (see, for example, Bruch's case histories in *The Golden Cage*).

15. If we shift to a Darwinian model, a related point emerges. Gillian Beer, *Darwin's Plots: Evolutionary Narrative in Darwin, George Eliot and Nineteenth-Century Fiction* (Boston: Ark Paperbacks, 1985): 210–35, has pointed out that women, once they cease to be viewed as reproductive vessels, are anti-genealogical if placed within Darwin's theory of evolution. They stand in modern society not for what is strong but for what is beautiful and unique, and hence their function in a system of survival of the fittest is problematic.

16. Parsons, *Role Structure and Personality*, 50.

17. A graphic depiction of the split occurs in Steven Marcus's *The Other Victorians: A Study of Sexuality and Pornography in Mid-Nineteenth Century England* (New York: Basic Books, 1964), in which the Victorian male is portrayed as both the upright *pater familias* and the debauched frequenter of brothels. Nina Auerbach, *Communities of Women: An Idea in Fiction* (Cambridge, Mass.: Harvard University Press, 1978), chap. 2, alludes in less radical terms to the split when she notes that in Jane Austen's novels women wait for men who enter and leave the domestic sphere.

18. Quoted in Bruch's *The Golden Cage*, 75.

19. Gilbert and Gubar, *Madwoman*, 264–67, note Cathy Sr.'s original request for a whip and interpret Heathcliff as the personification of that whip, empowering the young Cathy. They see Cathy's later life as a diminishment,

but fail to recognize the systemic connection between Cathy's sadistic empowerment and her destruction. In referring to Cathy Jr. as wielding a "despot's sceptre" over her father's heart, Brontë seems to be interested in introducing another whiplike image that may both empower and destroy its user.

20. This corresponds to Lévi-Strauss's assertion that generalized exchange, pushed to its limit, eventually engenders regressive solutions: restricted exchange or endogamy. But his logic in postulating these results omits how the emergence of subjectivity in the object of exchange contributes to it. By dealing purely in the structural tendencies of the systems, he ignores the degree to which the daughter in a nuclear family introduces a different element into the kinship model such that the mechanical laws governing exchange can no longer be applied. In contrast to Lévi-Strauss, Freud acknowledged the daughter's unwillingness to leave home, but he attributed this to the psychological implications of female anatomy (see his "Three Essays on Sexuality," "The Dissolution of the Oedipus Complex," and "Femininity," *Standard Edition*, 7:19, 22). It would seem to me that Lévi-Strauss's structuralist social model and Freud's individual psychological model come together when we consider how complex kinship systems engender a certain kind of female subjectivity that inhibits exchange.

21. Lévi-Strauss, *Elementary Structures*, 475. The traditional tendency among critics has been to associate Heathcliff with a primitive incestuous drive: David Cecil maintains that he acts as a "foreclosure of patrilineal succession," and David Daiches connects Heathcliff's avarice with incestuous "hoarding" consistent with Lévi-Strauss's interpretation of incest as a preprimal, nonsocial tendency—a keeping of love inside the family, thus preventing it from being circulated and shared (*Twentieth Century Interpretations of* Wuthering Heights, ed. Thomas A. Vogler [Englewood Cliffs, N.J.: Prentice-Hall, 1968],103, 110). Gilbert and Gubar, *Madwoman*, 293–98, are among the more recent critics to see Heathcliff's behavior as asocial and, specifically, antipatriarchal. Goetz, "Genealogy and Incest," 371, is an exception in associating Heathcliff's plotting with "culture," but he sees the failure of this plot as part of a master-plot of correction and reconciliation.

22. See Susan Koppelman, Introduction, *Old Maids: Short Stories by Nineteenth-Century U.S. Women Writers* (New York: Pandora Press, 1984).

23. Boone, *Tradition Counter Tradition*, 168–72, also notes the "stalled" situation that precedes the novel's conclusion but fails to explain what serves as the catalyst to set things in motion again.

24. See Keeney, *Aesthetics of Change*, 169.

25. It is noteworthy that even radically divergent views of the novel seem to come to the same conclusion about the conventional nature of the ending. Thus, Leavis, *Lectures in America* (London: Chatto and Windus, 1969), sees it as the restitution to Hareton of his rightful patriarchal role in a conventional Victorian family; Thomas Moser, "Whatever is the Matter with Emily Jane? Conflicting Impulses in *Wuthering Heights*," *Nineteenth-Century Fiction* 17 (1962), as an appeal to conventional feminine tastes, and Gilbert and Gubar, *Madwoman*, and Patricia Meyer Spacks, *The Female Imagination* (New York:

Avon, 1972), as a return to conventional constraints and role expectations. Boone, *Tradition Counter Tradition,* 170, is unique in finding the ending unconventional: he interprets the Hareton-Cathy relationship as an expression of "visionary possibility." However, while he notes that this relationship is shadowed by the "unquiet slumbers" of Heathcliff and Cathy Sr., he does not structurally connect the two relationships.

26. Moser, "Whatever is the Matter?" 15.

27. A vast number of articles have been written over the years concerning Nelly Dean's peculiar role in the novel. While an unorthodox reading casts her as a villainous arch-manipulator (J. Hafley, "The Villain in *Wuthering Heights,*" *Nineteenth-Century Fiction* 13 [1958–59]: 199–215), most take her as well-meaning but limited, with a point of view that requires correction by the reader. Carl W. Woodring, "The Narrators of *Wuthering Heights,*" *Nineteenth-Century Fiction* 11 (1957): 298–305, has provided a more systems-oriented reading by arguing that her insider role is complemented by Lockwood's outsider role: together they provide the reader with the necessary coordinates for understanding. Boone, *Tradition Counter Tradition,* 164, sees her as a limited "arranger" but grants her little effective power. Gilbert and Gubar, *Madwoman,* 289–92, take a more negative position on Nelly; they refer to her denigratingly as "patriarchy's housekeeper," the character who keeps men's stories and houses in order. But this ability to arrange stories and houses without getting caught in the plot or under the sheets seems to me to be no small accomplishment.

28. Ellen Moers, *Literary Women: The Great Writers* (Garden City, N.Y.: Anchor Press, 1977), 74–78.

29. See Charlotte Brontë, Preface (1850), *Norton Critical Edition of* Wuthering Heights (New York: W. W. Norton, 1972), and Winifred Guerin, *Charlotte Brontë: The Evolution of Genius* (Oxford: Clarendon, 1968), chap. 20.

30. Principal biographical background on Emily Brontë is drawn from W. Guerin, *Emily Brontë: A Biography* (New York: Oxford, 1971), and Edward Chitham, *A Life of Emily Brontë* (New York: Basil Blackwell, 1987).

31. Vogler, Introduction, *Twentieth-Century Interpretations of* Wuthering Heights, 1.

32. Richard Chase, "A Centennial Observance," in *The Brontës: A Collection of Critical Essays,* 20.

33. Daiches, "Introduction to *Wuthering Heights*" in *Twentieth-Century Interpretations,* 110.

34. Quoted in Guerin, *Emily Brontë,* 5.

35. See Chitham, *Life of Emily Brontë,* 89. He also notes that Emily appears to have denied herself any remedy that had not been available to Branwell in his last illness (238).

36. Biographers have tended to pair Emily with Anne, and Charlotte with Branwell. However, in the context proposed here, these sibling relationships might be best understood as secondary, substitute relationships, with each pair existing as a kind of derivative of the central Patrick Brontë–Emily–Branwell triangle. Moreover, these substituting relationships were fleeting

214 / Notes to Pages 115–20

and incomplete, I would suggest, largely owing to Patrick Brontë's continued presence on the scene (he outlived all his children). By contrast, substitutions for George Eliot's original relationship with her father and brother were highly developed, and will be a focus of discussion in the next chapter.

Chapter 5

1. Elaine Showalter, *A Literature of Their Own: British Women Novelists from Brontë to Lessing* (Princeton: Princeton University Press, 1977), 107.

2. Virginia Woolf, *The Common Reader* (London: Harcourt, Brace and World, 1925), 217.

3. Although Leavis, *The Great Tradition,* 39, was not altogether critical of what he called Eliot's "emotional tone," he clearly felt this tone tended to detract from the more important intellectual strengths that the novels might otherwise have exhibited: "the emotional quality represents something, a need or hunger in George Eliot, that shows itself to be insidious company for her intelligence—apt to supplant it and take command." Leavis's focus on Eliot's less sagelike, more emotional side was anticipated by Gordon Haight, *George Eliot and John Chapman* (New Haven: Yale University Press, 1940), viii, who had taken issue with John Cross's representation of Eliot as the embodiment of the Wise Woman in *George Eliot's Life as Related in Her Letters and Journals,* 3 vols. (1885; rpt. Philadelphia: Richard West, 1973).

4. Phyllis Rose, *Parallel Lives: Five Victorian Marriages* (New York: Vintage Books, 1984), 208.

5. George Eliot, *The Mill on the Floss* (New York: Penguin, 1979), 53. All future citations from the novel will be given in the text.

6. The sense in which Maggie's character originates with her father is also suggested by U. C. Knoepflmacher, *George Eliot's Early Novels: the Limits of Realism* (Berkeley: University of California Press, 1968), who argues that the basic collisions of the story are introduced through Mr. Tulliver and result in "Maggie's consequent self-division" (194).

7. On the subject of feminine "acuteness," it can be noted more generally that female education took different turns over the course of the nineteenth and early twentieth century. The prescribed lady's education of Jane Austen's time thus was not that of George Eliot's. However, I would argue that these changes were less the result of a linear progress toward some utopic goal than they were the reflection of the changing characteristics required for women to continue to serve as complements to men. It is questionable, for example, whether the creation of women's colleges was a simple step forward in the march for equality or whether they provided rather institutionalized and hence more powerful sites for female conditioning in forms of behavior that were being threatened by changing family structure. See Gorham, *Victorian Girl,* chap. 2, on the paradoxes of nineteenth-century educational reform for women, and Ehrenreich and English, *For Her Own Good,* chap. 5, on the insidiousness of the "science" of home economics in the late nineteenth century.

8. For interesting feminist discussions of Maggie's (and Eliot's) relationship to books and language, see Mary Jacobus, "The Question of Language: Men of Maxims and *The Mill on the Floss*," in *Writing and Sexual Difference*, ed. Elizabeth Abel (Chicago: University of Chicago Press, 1982), 37–52, and Elizabeth Weed, "The Liquidation of Maggie Tulliver" in *Modern Critical Views: George Eliot*, ed. Harold Bloom (New York: Chelsea House, 1986), 111–26.

9. Bateson, *Steps*, 211.

10. Curiously, critics have tended to ignore the results of Maggie's irresponsibility about the rabbits and to react as Maggie herself does in thinking Tom wholly unfair in his treatment of her. This rather stunning critical oversight mimics Maggie's oversight; it is, of course, the author's identification with Maggie that so skews the scene on her behalf.

11. See Bateson's "Toward a Theory of Schizophrenia" in *Steps*, the paper that introduced the concept of the "double bind." Also see my article, "The Pattern of Conditioning in *The Mill on the Floss*," *CEA Critic* 48 (Fall 1985), 54–60, for an earlier (and incomplete) analysis of this scene with respect to Bateson's theory.

12. See Girard's discussion of the significance of the son's imitation of his father in *Violence and the Sacred*, trans. Patrick Gregory (Baltimore: Johns Hopkins University Press, 1977), chap. 7.

13. Eliot's earliest mention of the novel is in January of 1859 and refers to research that she and Lewes did on "cases of *inundation*" (quoted in Haight, *George Eliot: A Biography* [New York: Penguin, 1985], 302).

14. The view taken by F. R. Leavis, Barbara Hardy, and U. C. Knoepflmacher is that the ending is highly contrived and reflects Eliot's immaturity as a novelist. There have, of course, been revisionist views that interpret it more positively or find in it important ideological significance. This position has generally been taken by feminist critics, though the interpretations are different: for Gilbert and Gubar, *Madwoman*, the flood is an act of feminist rage and annihilation, 497; for Weed, "Liquidation of Maggie Tulliver," it reflects the "liquidation" of the feminine and "the reproduction of the male . . . within the closed logophallocentric system of representation," 121; and for Laura Comer Emery, *George Eliot's Creative Conflict: The Other Side of Silence* (Berkeley: University of California Press, 1976), 7, it is "a painful confrontation . . . which ultimately gives [Eliot's] creative imagination greater vitality than ever before." Felicia Bonaparte, *Will and Destiny: Morality and Tragedy in George Eliot's Novels* (New York: New York University Press, 1975), has argued that the novel's ending provides Maggie with the widest perspective on her situation, while Margaret Homans, "Eliot, Wordsworth and the Scenes of the Sisters' Instruction," *Critical Inquiry* 8 (Winter 1981), 223–41, sees a sexist ideology getting in the way of a Wordsworthian "visionary" conclusion for the novel.

15. See George Levine, "Intelligence as Deception: *The Mill on the Floss*," in *George Eliot: A Collection of Critical Essays*, ed. George R. Creeger (Englewood Cliffs, N.J.: Prentice-Hall, 1970), 107, for a related argument concern-

ing the scope and limitations of Eliot's vision: "she pushed the boundaries of Victorian experience as far as any of her contemporaries and moved to the brink from which one can observe the modern sensibility, but inevitably she pulled back." Also see Thomas Pinney, "The Authority of the Past in George Eliot's Novels," in the same collection, for a discussion of the importance of early affections for Eliot.

16. Biographical material is drawn from Haight, *George Eliot;* Cross, *George Eliot's Life;* Jennifer Uglow, *George Eliot* (Virago/Pantheon Pioneers, 1987); Ruby Redinger, *George Eliot: The Emergent Self* (New York: Alfred A. Knopf, 1975); and *The George Eliot Letters,* ed. Haight, 9 vols. (New Haven: Yale University Press, 1978). All citations from the letters will be from Haight and will be given in the text.

17. Redinger, *George Eliot,* 33. For a broader view of "the Holy War," see Rosemarie Bodenheimer, "Mary Ann Evans's Holy War: An Essay in Letter Reading," *Nineteenth-Century Literature* 44 (Dec. 1989): 335–63. Bodenheimer sees Eliot's conflict with her father as coding a process of moral reversal that would repeat itself in her fiction. Her argument, that Eliot turned back from the espousal of revolutionary action because of her respect for the "roots" of the past, is compatible with my reading, but it does not examine the more basic family patterns that fueled this movement.

18. Critics of Eliot now tend to make at least some reference to the highly self-conscious persona of Eliot's letters in considering her development as a novelist; however, as Bodenheimer points out, the letters were treated dismissively as recently as the 1950s.

19. Redinger, *George Eliot,* 88–89, makes a similar point.

20. Haight, *George Eliot,* 5.

21. Quoted in Redinger, *George Eliot,* 146.

22. Quoted in Gilbert and Gubar, *Madwoman,* 450.

23. See Rose, *Parallel Lives,* 193–238, on the dynamics of the Eliot-Lewes relationship.

Chapter 6

1. Henry James, *The American Scene* (New York: Scribner's, 1946), 64.

2. Auerbach, *Communities of Women,* 39.

3. Henry James, *The Portrait of a Lady* (New York: Penguin, 1982), 27.

4. For Marxist readings of James that stress the economic background of the novels, see Mimi Kairshner, "The Traces of Capitalist Patriarch in the Silences of *The Golden Bowl,*" *Henry James Review* 5 (Spring 1984): 187–92, and Eagleton, *Criticism and Ideology,* 144ff.

5. *Portrait,* 71. James, *The Golden Bowl* (New York: Penguin, 1979), 32.

6. *Portrait,* 196.

7. *Portrait,* 337.

8. William Bysshe Stein's "The Portrait of a Lady *Vis Inertiae,*" *Western Humanities Review* 13 (Spring 1959): 177. See also, for example, Leavis's condemnation of Maggie in favor of Charlotte in *The Great Tradition,* and

Dorothea Krook's (albeit qualified) championing of Mrs. Brook in *The Ordeal of Consciousness in Henry James* (Cambridge: Cambridge University Press, 1962).

9. Henry James, *The Art of the Novel* (New York: Scribner's, 1962), 48.

10. See Boone, "Wedlock as Deadlock."

11. Quoted in Anne French Dalke, "'So much drawing and so little composition': The Literary Criticism of Henry James and the Novels of George Eliot," *American Transcendental Quarterly* 58 (Dec. 1985): 70.

12. Two noteworthy articles that attempt to place James's work in the context of a feminist movement and a new female role stereotype include Sara deSaussure Davis's "Feminist Sources in *The Bostonians*," *American Literature* 50 (1978–79): 570–87, and Annette Niemtzow's "Marriage and the New Woman in *The Portrait of a Lady*," *American Literature* 47 (1975–76): 377–95. Joseph Boone, "Modernist Maneuverings in the Marriage Plot: Breaking Ideologies of Gender and Genre in James's *The Golden Bowl*," *PMLA* 101 (May 1986): 374–88, is also helpful in situating James in relation to more conventional New Woman novelists.

13. *The Art of the Novel*, 49.

14. Showalter borrows Gissing's phrase for the title of her recent book, *Sexual Anarchy: Gender and Culture at the Fin de Siecle* (New York: Viking, 1990). The book traces parallels between trends in gender representation at the end of the last century and in the present.

15. *The Art of the Novel*, 110. See Walter Isle, *Experiments in Form: Henry James's Novels, 1896–1901* (Cambridge, Mass.: Harvard University Press, 1968).

16. Henry James, *The Awkward Age* (New York: Penguin, 1983), 368. All future citations from the novel will be given in the text.

17. *The Art of the Novel*, 115–16.

18. See William R. Goetz, *Henry James and the Darkest Abyss of Romance* (Baton Rouge: Louisiana State University Press, 1986), on James's avoidance of first-person narration.

19. See Bateson's "The Logical Categories of Learning and Communication" in *Steps*, 279–308. His "Learning III"—what I call the third-order perspective—has since been referred to by family systems theorists as the "cybernetics of cybernetics," "second-order cybernetics," or "ecosystems theory." (See articles debating the concept in *Family Process* 21 [1982].)

20. Edward W. Said, *The World, the Text, and the Critic* (Cambridge, Mass.: Harvard University Press, 1983), chap. 5. Also relevant, though employing a different vocabulary, is Lionel Trilling's provocative essay, "The Fate of Pleasure," in *Beyond Culture: Essays on Literature and Learning* (New York: Viking, 1955), 57–87. Trilling posits a "mutation" in modern culture in which the drive for pleasure is superseded by a drive he associates with Freud's death instinct, which concerns itself exclusively with self-definition.

21. See Martha Banta's "They Shall Have Faces, Minds and (One Day) Flesh: Women in Late Nineteenth-Century and Early Twentieth Century American Literature," in *What Manner of Woman: Essays on English and Ameri-*

can Life and Literature (New York: New York University Press, 1977) and Hirsch, Part 1: Realism and Maternal Silence, for further discussion of the absent mother in the literature of this period.

22. See Gerald Levin, "Why Does Vanderbank Not Propose?" *UKCR* 27 (1960–61): 314–18.

23. See Edward Wagenknecht, *Eve and Henry James* (Norman: University of Oklahoma Press, 1978), 145.

24. Wagenknecht, *Eve and Henry James*, 142, makes this point a subject of debate when he questions critics who maintain that the Brook circle is intellectually sophisticated: "nobody in the Buckingham Crescent group ever says anything that shows any concern with ideas, power to grasp an idea, or any capacity for disinterested or impersonal considerations." The criteria Wagenknecht uses to define good ideas (and "good talk") tie him to an earlier critical tradition still dominated by an ideology of closure.

25. Edmund Wilson, "The Ambiguity of Henry James," in *The Triple Thinkers* (New York: Penguin, 1962),140, 148.

26. Nanda's precise fate at the end of *The Awkward Age* has been a subject of much critical speculation. The usual interpretation sees the heroine as retreating to her protector's Suffolk Arcadia from a corrupt society. Krook makes this argument eloquently, but this assumes the notion of an "outside" to the Brook circle and, by extension, to society, that the novel as a whole, I argue, has consistently denied. Even Longdon admits that "we're *in* society . . . and that's our horizon" (168).

27. *The Art of the Novel*, 116.

28. Foucault, *History of Sexuality*, writes that repression was a means of self-affirmation for those who adopted it. Thus, for example, he notes that "the discourse that oppressed homosexuality also gave it a voice in which to speak on its own behalf" (101); the same, of course, can be said for women in the repression of their sexuality (as Kucich also has noted). Foucault later goes on to explain that eventually psychoanalysis was created by the bourgeiosie as a means of lifting this self-imposed repression in the domain of the imagination: "it allowed individuals to express their incestuous desire in discourse" (129)—yet he seems to ignore the full effect that such discourse, practiced continually, would tend to have on desire. Also see Poster,198, on how the contemporary middle-class has succeeded in lifting its self-imposed repression in experience as well as in imagination.

29. Leo Bersani, *A Future for Astyanax: Character and Desire in Literature* (New York: Columbia University Press, 1984),148.

30. See Howard M. Feinstein, *Becoming William James* (Ithaca, N.Y.: Cornell University Press, 1984), Leon Edel, *Henry James*, vol. 1: *The Untried Years*, 1843–1870 (New York: Avon Books, 1953), and Jean Strouse, *Alice James: A Biography* (Boston: Houghton Mifflin, 1980), for useful insights into the character of Henry James, Sr.

31. See Henry James, "Notes of a Son and Brother" and "A Small Boy and Others" in *Henry James: Autobiography*, ed. F. W. Dupee (New York:

Criterion Books, 1956). Also see Edel's *Henry James,* vol. 1, for a comprehensive discussion of James's peripatetic childhood.

32. For background on Alice James's case, see *The Diary of Alice James,* ed. Leon Edel (New York: Penguin, 1982), *The Death and Letters of Alice James,* ed. Ruth Bernard Yeazell (Berkeley: University of California Press, 1981), and Strouse. Also see my article, "The Shadow of Alice James in Henry James's Family Novels of the Nineties," *American Literary Realism, 1870–1910* 18 (Spring and Autumn 1985): 1–13.

33. If one looks at James's autobiographical writing, one finds few references to his mother, but those there are express a worshipful admiration that approaches platitude. Edel, *Henry James,* 1:41, discusses the tone of these remarks at some length and notes that in general Mary James seems to have been a "phantasmal form" in the family. This fits with the hypothesis that the nuclear family required that the maternal role be removed from the central family dynamic. Indeed, the portrait (or lack thereof) that emerges of James's mother seems to allow for her eclipse by Alice's very insistent and visible invalid presence. It is significant that Alice's most healthy period occurred during the short time following her mother's death and prior to her father's death when she was called upon to care for her father and perform the principal domestic role in the household.

34. Quoted in Yeazell's Introduction, *The Death and Letters,* 15.

35. See Feinstein, *Becoming William James,* chap. 14, for more on the symbiotic theory of health and sickness held by Henry and William. Strouse notes that Alice subscribed to this "bank account" theory in the intellectual domain at least—her having "so little mind" accounted for William's having so much (*Diary,* 115–16). In her diary, Alice also refers to an imaginary exchange of symptoms with Henry: "my nerves are his nerves and my stomach his stomach" (104), and records asking her nurse at one point: "don't you wish you were inside of *me!*" (48). A theory of parasitical relationship in which one's loss is another's gain is also held by the protagonist of James's 1901 novel, *The Sacred Fount.*

36. *Diary,* 149.

37. See Strouse, *Alice James,* 318–22, on James's reaction to Alice's diary.

38. See Wharton's letters to James in *The Collected Letters of Edith Wharton,* ed. R. W. B. Lewis (New York: Scribner's, 1988).

Conclusion

1. The popular view of modernism as a male cultural movement has not in itself been seriously challenged, although interesting theories as to the defensive nature of the movement have been given by recent feminist critics, most notably Gilbert and Gubar in *No Man's Land: The Place of the Woman Writer in the Twentieth Century,* vol. 1: *The War of the Words* (New Haven: Yale University Press, 1988).

2. Bowen, *Family Therapy,* 382.

3. Bateson, *Steps*, 251.

4. Ehrenreich and English, *For Her Own Good*, chap. 5.

5. Hirsch, *Mother/Daughter Plot*, chap. 4.

6. Mary Douglas, *Natural Symbols: Explorations in Cosmology* (New York: Pantheon, 1970), 27. Douglas attributes the original use of the concept of the "fully personal family" to Basil Bernstein.

7. Lasch, *Haven*, 153.

8. For statistical data on changes in family configuration with specific reference to a new female role in culture, see Esther Wattenberg and Hazel Reinhardt, "Female-Headed Families: Trends and Implications," in *Women and Mental Health*, ed. Elizabeth Howell and Marjorie Bayes (New York: Basic Books, 1981). Also see Poster, *Critical Theory of the Family*, 198ff., on new family configurations in contemporary culture, and Shorter, *Making of the Modern Family*, chap. 8, on the effects on the individual and the family of the disappearance of a sense of family history.

9. Van Boheemen, *Novel as Family Romance*, 10. Also see the critical anthology, *Men in Feminism*, ed. Alice Jardine and Paul Smith (New York: Methuen, 1987). I should note that the tendency to universalize "the feminine" has to some extent been realized by French critics such as Jacques Derrida and Julia Kristeva, for whom the concept has become a metaphor for reading and is not linked specifically to women.

10. Virginia Woolf's well-known argument in *A Room of One's Own* (New York: Harcourt Brace Jovanovich, 1929), 102–3, that a "fully developed mind" is "androgynous" and "does not think specially or separately of sex" is actually a self-admitted appropriation (mediation?) of an idea first proposed by Samuel Coleridge.

A striking example of the tendency I see to be emerging in contemporary fiction is evident in Doris Lessing's work. Her fiction describes an evolution from feminist political concerns to ecological (or perhaps one should say cosmological) ones. Her novel *The Fifth Child* (New York: Alfred A. Knopf, 1988) focuses on the disruption of a family ecology.

11. Showalter, *Literature of Their Own*, made claims for an innovative turn-of-the-century literature by women in her chapter on feminist novelists. However, it must be argued that the innovativeness of these novelists was undercut by their tendency to incorporate thematically the position of the Social Purity Movement that tended to reinforce traditional notions of female innocence, asexuality, delicacy, etc.

12. The fact of female mediation of male texts in the realm of literary theory in particular seems to be either ignored by feminist critics or justified as involving a specifically "female" transformation and revision on the male tradition. I have not yet seen a treatment of feminist criticism that views the theory's tendency to derive itself from male models from the evolutionary perspective I am suggesting here. Admittedly, Alice A. Jardine, *Gynesis: Configurations of Woman and Modernity* (Ithaca, N.Y.: Cornell University Press, 1985), seems aware of the issue in her treatment of French feminism. Her theoretical orientation, however, although ultimately compatible with

many of my own conclusions, involves little practical historical analysis of the postmodernist trends she discusses.

13. In a 1969 paper, "Pathologies of Epistemology," in *Steps*, 483, Bateson elaborates upon the incompatibility of his ecological perspective with what he terms the *"idea of power"*: "in mid-nineteenth-century England, Darwin proposed a theory of natural selection in which the unit of survival was either the family line or the species or subspecies or something of the sort. But today it is quite obvious . . . that the unit of survival is the *organism* plus *environment*. We are learning by bitter experience that the organism that destroys its environment destroys itself."

14. *The Art of the Novel*, 344–45.

15. Bersani, *Future for Astyanax*, 145.

16. Quentin Anderson, *The Imperial Self* (New York: Alfred A. Knopf, 1971). See Boone, *Tradition Counter Tradition*, 187–201, for an interpretation of Maggie's character as "closed" rather than "open" and androgynous, although Boone understands the novel as a whole to be open-ended.

17. *The Art of the Novel*, 5.

18. My discussion of the two stages of development of feminist criticism is a variation of sorts on Showalter's distinction between "feminist critique" and "gynocritics" ("Feminist Criticism in the Wilderness," in Abel, *Writing and Sexual Difference*).

Index